D1451843

The Meiningen Court Theatre, 1866–1890

The
Meiningen Court Theatre
1866–1890

John Osborne

Professor of German, University of Warwick

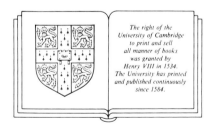

The right of the
University of Cambridge
to print and sell
all manner of books
was granted by
Henry VIII in 1534.
The University has printed
and published continuously
since 1584.

Cambridge University Press

Cambridge
New York   New Rochelle   Melbourne   Sydney

Published by the Press Syndicate of the University of Cambridge
The Pitt Building, Trumpington Street, Cambridge CB2 IRP
32 East 57th Street, New York, NY 10022, USA
10 Stamford Road, Oakleigh, Melbourne 3166, Australia

First published 1988

Printed in Great Britain at
the University Press, Cambridge

British Library cataloguing in publication data
Osborne, John
The Meiningen court theatre, 1866–1890.
1. Meininger Hoftheater – History
I. Title
792'.0943   PN2656.M5

Library of Congress cataloguing in publication data
Osborne, John, 1929–
The Meiningen Court Theatre, 1866–1890.
Bibliography.
Includes index.
1. Meininger Hoftheater.   2. Theater – Germany –
History – 19th century.   3. Georg II, Duke of Saxe-
Meiningen, 1826–1914.   I. Title.
PN2656.M52H66   1988   792'.0943'22   87–23889

ISBN 0 521 30394 X

FP

For Elisabeth Genton

Contents

Illustrations

Preface

I am deeply grateful for the help received from colleagues, friends, and institutions in the writing of this book.

Parts of chapter 6 are based on the introduction to *Die Meininger: Texte zur Rezeption* (Tübingen, 1980); I thank the publishers, Max Niemeyer, for permission to re-use the material.

My thanks are due to the University of Warwick for the generous provision of study leave; to the Alexander von Humboldt Foundation, the Leverhulme Trust, the British Academy, and the Academy of Sciences of the German Democratic Republic for research and travel grants.

For their assistance in helping me to obtain and to exploit otherwise inaccessible material I am particularly indebted to the University Library, Warwick and its photographic services, the Niedersächsische Staats- und Universitätsbibliothek, Göttingen, the Theatre Museum of the University of Cologne (Sammlung Niessen), the Deutsches Theatermuseum, Munich, the Theaterwissenschaftliches Seminar of the Free University, Berlin, the Literaturwissenschaftliches Seminar of the University of Hamburg, the Kunstsammlungen der Veste Coburg, the Deutsche Staatsbibliothek, Berlin, DDR, the Staatsarchiv Meiningen, the Staatliche Museen Meiningen, the Goethe–Schiller Archiv Weimar, and the staff of all these institutions.

For their practical support, the interest they have shown, and the encouragement they have given me, I am especially grateful to: Colin Bearne, Gustav Erdmann, Roswitha Flatz, Helmuth Grosse, Dieter Hoffmeier, Rolf Hübner, Peter Larkin, Laci Löb, Edward McInnes, Minni Maedebach, Marie Mahr, Jean Moes, Lydia Mohr, Helen Osborne, Richard Parker, Volker Reißland, Renate Schipke, Albrecht Schöne, Peter Stern, Irmgard Strahl, Ronald Taylor, Gotthart Wunberg, Ann O'Quigley, Sarah Stanton, and, as always, Janet Osborne.

A very special debt is acknowledged in the dedication.

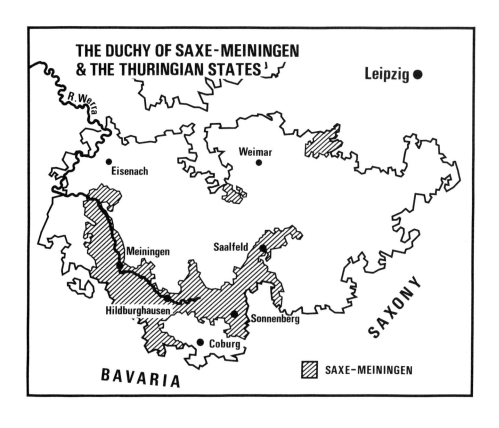

THE DUCHY OF SAXE-MEININGEN
& THE THURINGIAN STATES

Leipzig ●

R.Werra

Weimar ●

● Eisenach

Meiningen   Saalfeld ●

Hildburghausen
                    Sonnenberg ●

● Coburg

BAVARIA

SAXONY

▨ SAXE-MEININGEN

Culture and politics: the Duchy of
Saxe-Meiningen in the nineteenth century

*It is a fact not altogether without significance that the reign of the present Duke
began in the year 1866, which for ever put an end to the political importance of the
minor German princes. A more dignified and useful occupation of the leisure thus
granted to him could not well be imagined than the fostering of that refined spirit of
art which is too frequently lost in the bustle and noise of the great centres of modern
life.*

    The Times, 27 May 1881

D URING THE COURSE of its history the development of the town of
Meiningen has been decisively influenced by fire. On 5 March 1908
the old theatre, which had been built by Duke Bernhard in 1831, was
burnt out and destroyed.[1] The effect of this local disaster was to produce a
wave of national sympathy for the little Duchy whose theatre had once
captured the imagination of the whole country, given a word to its language,
and had been the focus of attention in the theatre capitals of Europe, but of
which little had been heard for two decades. As has happened so often at
important moments in the history of the German theatre, thoughts turned
once again to the idea of a national theatre, to be built in Meiningen, and to be
financed by public subscription.[2] The proposal was not carried out because
the Duke of Meiningen did not wish it. Instead he rebuilt the theatre very
quickly from his own resources and with a local architect, *Hofbaumeister*
Behlert. It is a fine building, and it is still in use today as the *Landestheater*, so
that Meiningen possesses a theatre far superior to anything the uninformed
visitor would expect to find in this small provincial town at the end of the
main railway line.

    The decision not to do in Meiningen what was later to be done at Stratford-
upon-Avon did not stem from any failure of ambition on the part of the Duke
whose energies, as a younger man, had taken his theatre company so far. Nor
did it reflect any self-centred wish that the triumphs of the Meiningen
Theatre should be exclusively associated with his reign and his name. It
stems rather from a real understanding of the nature of his achievement, and
the very special combination of historical, political, cultural, and personal
circumstances which made it possible. The 'Meininger' are a phenomenon of
the Germany of Kaiser Wilhelm I, the *Gründerzeit*, rather than of the later

Wilhelminian epoch, ruled over by his grandson, Wilhelm II; their once-for-all success could not have been repeated, and the attempt to revive their past glories in the age of Reinhardt, whose work represents the renewal and further development of their tradition, could only have tarnished their reputation.

At the time of its greatest successes the Meiningen Court Theatre had acquired the standing of a national institution. In its journeys beyond the frontiers of the *Reich* it had assumed a representative status for German national culture, and at home it had frequently been held up as a model by advocates of reform in the German theatre.[3] In its preservation of its base in Thuringia, its status as a court theatre, and its practice of descending upon the capital in the theatrical close season, it remained a consciously provincial enterprise, and the tension which this provoked is a recurrent theme in the critical reception of the Meininger. Particularly evident in the discussion of the company in those cities such as Berlin, Vienna, London, Moscow, and Paris, which could lay claim to a certain reputation as major cultural centres and theatre capitals, the theme was subject to a full range of variations, from patronising irony, by way of amazement, to near outrage that the court theatre of a minor German duchy should presume to compete with the leading theatres of Europe on their home territory. That the ruling Duke himself – a dilettante! – should have played a leading part in the venture only made matters worse.

The happy combination of exactly the right individual talents – the Duke himself, his third (morganatic) wife, the former actress, Ellen Franz, and his stage-director, a Jewish actor from the middle ranks of the company, Ludwig Chronegk – was a major factor in the successes of the theatre and its tours; but this cannot be seen as the isolated success of a few gifted, but untypical or alienated individuals. From Albert, the Prince Consort, younger brother of Ernst II, Duke of Saxe-Coburg-Gotha and a cousin of Duke Georg II of Saxe-Meiningen, by way of the Dukes of Hessen-Darmstadt and Weimar, to King Ludwig II of Bavaria, the princes from the lesser German courts were enormously active and versatile in the contributions they made to the culture of industrial, bourgeois, late-nineteenth-century Europe. Moreover, standing somewhat above, though not entirely outside, the cultural institutions of the day, they often showed an astute insight and an unprejudiced eye when it came to the choice of collaborators, as is wonderfully clear from the example of Prince Albert and Joseph Paxton, the designer of the Crystal Palace.[4] So striking are the contributions they made to this culture, in what we now recognise as its most characteristic form, that any investigation of an individual manifestation must begin by asking whether such contributions were not perhaps possible because of, rather than despite, the modesty of the amateur sources from which they sprang.

★   ★   ★

The history of the Duchy of Saxe-Meiningen as an independent state goes back only to 1680, when the territories of Duke Ernst of Gotha were divided among his seven sons, the third of whom became Duke Bernhard I of Saxe-Meiningen. The Duchy survived the Napoleonic Wars under the regency of Duchess Marie, widowed on the death of Georg I in 1803; and in 1815 it took its place alongside other, mostly larger, sovereign states in the German Confederation (*Deutscher Bund*). At his coming-of-age in 1821 Duke Bernhard II Erich Freund began a reign of forty-five years; even this was, however, to be exceeded by that of his son, who ruled as Georg II from 1866 to 1914. In 1826 the Duchy experienced the only significant territorial expansion in its history; together with the neighbouring duchies of Saxe-Coburg and Altenburg it acquired a share of the Duchy of Gotha, which had been left without an heir on the death of Duke Friedrich IV. The Duchy of Saxe-Meiningen continued to exist within these new boundaries, but with progressively diminishing sovereignty, until 1920, when it was incorporated into the Weimar Republic as part of the province of Thuringia. Today, of course, the former Duchy lies within the German Democratic Republic, separated from what was neighbouring Saxe-Coburg-Gotha by the border with the Federal Republic.

Saxe-Meiningen was a small state covering some 2,500 km² but, from the point of view of communications, it was disadvantageously stretched out along the valley of the river Werra from Salzungen, in the north, to Eisfeld, in the south, with enclaves at Cambach and Kranichsfeld. It was not a prosperous area, being heavily wooded (over 40 per cent of the surface-area in the 1880s) and with a less-than-average amount of agricultural land in comparison with the *Reich* as a whole.[5] In 1846 the population of the Duchy numbered 160,515, three-quarters of whom lived in rural areas, working mostly in forestry and agriculture; here feudal practices still prevailed widely, inhibiting the development of the already poor state.[6] The other principal sources of employment were in ceramics (Henneberg porcelain), woodworking, and toymaking, but the Duchy did not have the resources to sustain a strong entrepreneurial bourgeoisie, nor to prevent significant emigration during the first half of the century.

Saxe-Meiningen therefore shared the weaknesses which afflicted most of the smaller German states at this time: isolation, poor internal and external communications, and the consequent absence of any significant commercial and political activity. The 1830s saw some first steps in the direction of economic modernisation and some improvement in trade and communications as the Duchy entered the Customs Union in 1834. This marked the beginning of an orientation towards Prussia, rather than the economically weaker and more feudal Austria, but such moves towards centralisation and, ultimately, unification were viewed with suspicion by the rulers of the smaller states within the German Confederation, for they saw them (rightly) as a threat to their independence and power. Liberal ideas began slowly to penetrate the Duchy, but, typically for this period, the centre of liberal activity was a cultural rather than a directly political organisation, the *Bibliographisches Institut*, which Carl Joseph Meyer transferred from Gotha to Hildburghausen in 1828. From here, and in collaboration with Friedrich Hofmann, later to be an editor of the middlebrow journal, *Die Gartenlaube*, Meyer began to publish an illustrated cultural journal, *Meyers Universum oder Abbildung und Beschreibung des Sehenswertesten und Merkwürdigsten der Natur und Kunst auf der ganzen Erde* (10 vols., 1833–43). Subsequently he was to become very well known for his great encyclopaedia, *Meyers Konversations-Lexikon*. He also became involved in the early industrial developments, which began with the exploitation of the coal and iron resources at Neuhaus. Meyer's political activities culminated in a 'Reform Address' directed to the Duke during the political unrest of 1848, but this did not achieve any lasting results.[7]

The reign of Duke Bernhard II saw the introduction of the railway to Saxe-Meiningen: a line was opened to serve the valley of the Werra in 1858; but it was not until 1870 that rail connections with the rest of Germany began to be developed. In 1874, the year of the first visit by the Meiningen Theatre to Berlin (and the tours would have been unthinkable without rail transport), a line was opened to Schweinfurth; ten years later a link was made with Erfurt, via Suhl, which brought Berlin considerably closer.[8] The rapid industrialisation which took place in Germany during the two decades after 1850 brought other changes to the Duchy. By 1880 the population had risen to around 200,000, of whom just over 11,000 lived in the ducal capital, the *Residenzstadt* Meiningen itself, and the greater part of the working population was now divided almost equally between agriculture and forestry, on the one hand, and industry and mining, on the other. Commercial and industrial activity continued to be fairly limited in scale, and the years of world-wide recession, the late 1870s and the 1880s, saw no economic expansion within the Duchy.[9]

In the period between the end of the Napoleonic Wars and the Austro–Prussian War of 1866 the citizens of Saxe-Meiningen led a politically passive existence, without much contact with the events of the world outside the boundaries of the Duchy. The revolutionary climate of 1848 produced a brief flurry of political activity, but the reforms agreed by Duke Bernhard either did not materialise, or, as in Prussia, were progressively withdrawn in the period of reaction in the early 1850s.[10] Crown Prince Georg, however, now a young man of twenty-two, was serving as an officer in a Prussian Guards Regiment in Potsdam, and there he experienced the turbulent events at first hand. In a series of letters to his mother he wrote very excitedly about the dangers of the situation, especially the revolutionary threat to the monarchies. In early March he judged that it was already too late for the princes to make any concessions; and in any case the notion of progress towards democratic government evidently did not commend itself to him:

if any [concessions] are made, then the people will want to continue and have more, and the *Plebs*, having assumed the task of implementing the will of the people, will gain so much power that eventually it will propose legislation, as has already happened in Paris.

Showing both his firm commitment to monarchical rule and his authoritarian nature, he urged the severest repressive measures in defence of what he believed to be a sacred cause:

I hope that the fullest force will be used mercilessly against the precious rabble . . . At the present time it is foolish to show indulgence to the rebels; if Paris had been bombarded and half the city reduced to ashes, that would have been better than the weakness, thanks to which the whole world might yet be overtaken by revolution.[11]

Very soon Georg had an opportunity to put his resolve to the test by taking part in the military actions against the insurgents in Berlin; but, despite his son's desire to remain there and play an active rôle in the defence of the thrones, his father abruptly curtailed such involvement in Prussian affairs and ordered him home.[12]

   This paternal restraint did not arise from any liberal inclinations on the part of Duke Bernhard. The idea of German national unity, which was very much in the air in 1848 and 1849, and which came to occupy a prominent place in liberal thinking in the following decades, did not have his support. Seeing in Prussia the greatest threat to the independence of the smaller states, he reacted with increasing antipathy to the policies of Bismarck, and looked with increasing sympathy towards Austria.[13] Not so his son who, in 1849, had led a battalion from Meiningen on the Prussian side in the conflict with Denmark over Schleswig-Holstein; who continued to serve in the Prussian army; who, in 1850, had married a Prussian princess, Charlotte, a niece of King Friedrich-Wilhelm IV; and who, since his marriage, was spending a great deal of time at court in Potsdam. His growing insight into political developments made him – like his father – see the need for Meiningen to choose between the two major German powers as they moved inexorably into conflict; but the Crown Prince's letters reveal an understanding of the situation that is both more realistic, given the geographical and economic circumstances of the Duchy, and at the same time closer to the inclinations of its overwhelmingly Protestant population in its leaning to its powerful northern neighbour:

Nor do I believe that the small states will be able to choose their own politics if it should come to a regrettable war between Prussia and Austria . . . In this case, at any rate, Meiningen would not be able to take Austria's side, because it is too close to Prussia . . . It would therefore be in the political interest of Meiningen to do with good grace what it would have to do anyway.[14]

These cautionary words were not heeded by Duke Bernhard, who allowed his son no influence on the politics of the Duchy before 1866; who protested as alliances, in the form of military pacts, began to be forged between Prussia and neighbouring territories, such as the Duchy of Saxe-Coburg under its liberal and pro-Prussian ruler, Ernst II; and who took a consistently pro-Austrian and separatist line in foreign-policy matters until 1866, when Austria and Prussia came into open conflict over the Schleswig-Holstein question. Among the Thuringian states, which constituted the 12th *curia* of the *Bundestag*, Meiningen alone voted for the Austrian proposal and in favour of mobilisation against Prussia. The Austrian proposal was, however, carried by the assembly as a whole, whereupon Prussia declared the Confederation dissolved.

In the war which followed the regiments from Meiningen were found a non-combatant rôle in garrisoning Frankfurt am Main; whereas the troops from neigbouring Saxe-Coburg and other parts of Thuringia fought on the Prussian side against the Hanoverians at Langensalza, where Duke Ernst II played a prominent and controversial part in the negotiations before the battle.[15] In contrast, Duke Bernhard was obliged to flee with his government to the safety of Bamberg in Bavaria. Recognising the untenability of the isolated position into which his father was moving, Crown Prince Georg had, before the outbreak of hostilities, requested permission to rejoin the Prussian army; after the victory of the Prussians at Sadowa (Königgrätz), which, for all the rapidity with which it was accomplished, had not by any means been a foregone conclusion, Georg repeated his request:

Now that so and so many weeks have passed, and now that the situation has, from your point of view, become so hopeless, I am resubmitting my request to you to permit my entry into the Prussian army.[16]

Again the Crown Prince's request was refused, and Duke Bernhard, fearing his son's ambition, continued to exclude him from any involvement in negotiations with Prussia, although he finally, and reluctantly, attempted to make use of him as a mediator when it became clear that it was going to be difficult to save anything. In fact the King of Prussia and his Chancellor, Bismarck, refused to negotiate; in effect they treated Meiningen as a defeated enemy, demanding that the Duchy cede territory to Prussia and pay a financial indemnity. Finally Bismarck lost patience with Bernhard's unrealistic attempts to bargain for some last vestige of power from a position of weakness; Prussian troops were ordered into the town of Meiningen on 19 September 1866, and Bernhard was forced to abdicate in favour of Crown Prince Georg. The circumstances surrounding the abdication caused deep and lasting bitterness between father and son, and the breach was a decisive one. The situation, as Georg saw it, required the complete exclusion of his father's separatist voice from the councils of state:

I would be . . . ill advised to make you my principal adviser, dear Papa, for you detest the situation in which we North Germans now find ourselves after this great historical event;

and it did not allow for anything other than total political submission to Prussia:

We are now entirely in the power of Prussia. She will do with us as she pleases. It is hard to have to admit this, but it is completely true.[17]

The new ruler very soon began to see that he was not going to make his mark in the political sphere.

The peace treaty of August 1866, the Treaty of Prague, required Meiningen and the other Thuringian duchies to enter the North German Confederation (*Norddeutscher Bund*), which constituted one further step down the road to German unity under Prussian leadership. In his accession speech of 27 September the new Duke urged enthusiastic assent to the arrangements:

The German Confederation has been dissolved. It is necessary to secure a new basis for the political position of the Duchy and its relationship to the German fatherland. By its glorious victories, and by its intelligence and culture, Prussia has shown itself worthy to assume leadership in Germany. An alliance has been offered us, the interest of Northern Germany requires it. Let us enter this alliance joyfully.[18]

This speech echoes the Bismarckian sense of Prussia's mission to lead Germany to political unity, which, after the spectacular military success of 1866, had become something of a commonplace. Interestingly and characteristically – and this is not untypical of liberal sentiment during these years of political realignment – the new ruler of Meiningen justified his appeal to his people with special reference to the intellectual and cultural traditions of Prussia. Here remained a sphere within which there was still room for the unfolding of the creative energies of the Duchy.

A year later Georg II took up another of the great unifying themes of the day, the fear of hostile neighbouring powers, resentful and suspicious of Germany's increasing unity and strength.[19] Such feelings may not have been directly inspired by Bismarck, but they were certainly exploited by the Chancellor with consummate skill in his foreign policy between 1866 and 1870. They found their fiercest expression in the outburst of patriotic fervour which greeted the declaration of war between Prussia and France in the summer of 1870, and further elaboration in the justification of the post-war annexation – supposedly for defensive purposes – of Alsace and parts of Lorraine. The war of 1870–71 was experienced as a great national event, for it united all shades of political opinion in the common cause; and it even brought the young Nietzsche back from the safety of neutral Basel to serve voluntarily as a medical orderly with the German armies.[20] Like so many poets, good as well as bad (though mostly the latter), Georg II made his personal contribution to the patriotic lyric which the war inspired; and like so many of his fellow princes who, as Moltke's staff-officer, Bronsart von

Schellendorff, acidly observed, could so easily be spared by their fortunate principalities, he set out himself to follow the campaign.[21]

Georg's letters from the front indicate that he very much relished the sense of close involvement in the fighting, of having been under fire with his men; and he seems to have carried out his duties as commander of 32nd Regiment very conscientiously. Not only did he take part in the battles of the July and August *Blitzkrieg*, up to the Battle of Sedan, but he remained with his regiment for the more protracted and frustrating war in the provinces. He witnessed significant fighting in the Loire region, most notably a five-and-a-half hour battle for Châteaudun, which the French National Guards and *francs-tireurs* stubbornly defended against a full-scale attack; and he experienced the bitter winter of 1870–71. His letters to his second wife, Feodora, contain detailed comment on the progress of the campaign and the performance of the soldiers from Meiningen, whom he observed closely and judged critically; they are frequently illustrated with plans and drawings.[22] Although he had his sketchbook with him – as indeed he did in Schleswig in 1849 – and although he could not but respond to his favourite subject matter, the dynamic scenes of battle with which he was confronted, it is quite clear that he took the historical and political aspects of the war very seriously, and that, like many friends and contemporaries, he felt that he was witnessing a

1   Georg II of Meiningen, Battlefield of Sedan, 1870.

dramatic turning-point in the history of the modern world. Of the battle of Sedan he wrote: 'This is indeed the finale of a terrible national combat, the curtain [*Aktschluß*] on an epoch-making action.' This was a subject to which he was to return in the early 1900s, when he recorded his own memoirs of the Franco-Prussian War.[23]

In his renunciation of sovereignty and his eagerness to serve the new German *Reich*, Georg II displayed a realism which had its counterpart in the flexibility – many would call it opportunism – of the German liberal movement. In response to the military successes of the Prussian army, and the diplomatic and political successes of Bismarck, the liberals had very largely abandoned the opposition which had led to the constitutional crisis of the early 1860s. In the writings of the liberal right the emphasis now came to be placed firmly on unity, which had been imposed from above, at the expense of the libertarian ideals of the earlier period of German liberalism; theorists such as Baumgarten and Rochau now saw this as a period of sterile opposition and failure.[24] In giving explicit support to the national unity achieved by Bismarck's policies at this time they were joined by historians such as Droysen, Treitschke, and Sybel, and by literary historians such as Rudolf Haym, Julian Schmidt, and Wilhelm Scherer; and the change of direction is almost immediately reflected in the scholarly work of these men.[25] Among the organs through which such views were further propagated was the Berlin paper, the *National-Zeitung*, whose drama critic, Karl Frenzel, made extensive use of its columns to draw attention to the achievements of the Meiningen Court Theatre, and the monthly journal, the *Deutsche Rundschau*, edited by Julius Rodenberg, whose drama critic was also Karl Frenzel.[26]

During the 1870s Bismarck governed with the support of the National Liberals. It is interesting to note just how closely the development of the Meiningen Theatre reflects the fortunes of this political grouping: its theoretical reorientation in the late sixties in preparation for its emergence as a national force in the early seventies, and its loss of momentum (in fact its virtual disintegration) at the end of the decade. It is a further indication of the thoroughly representative position of Saxe-Meiningen in the Germany of this period that the leading National Liberal parliamentarian and constitutional expert, Eduard Lasker, was returned to the *Reichstag* as deputy for the second constituency (Sonnenberg–Saalfeld) of the Duchy. He represented it from 1871 until his death in 1884, surviving the anti-liberal swing of the late seventies. His standing as a national politician, who did not reside in the Duchy and did much of his campaigning by proxy, did not adversely affect the loyalty of his constituents. In politics, as in the cultural sphere, Meiningen proved an effective base from which to gain a wider reputation.[27]

This accommodation with the realities of Bismarckian Germany, combined with the ardent desire to participate in the life of the newly unified state as fully as possible, was not entirely free from a certain awkwardness. This is

just as true for the ruling Duke of Meiningen as it was for that intellectual –
professional élite (*Bildungsbürgertum*) which was, by and large, represented
politically by the National Liberals. Conrad Ferdinand Meyer, although a
Swiss, can stand for many as an illustration of the equivocal position in which
a number of writers of his generation found themselves in the later sixties and
early seventies. A poet and novelist, and an almost exact contemporary of
Georg II, whose historicist tastes and whose love of renaissance Italy he
shared, Meyer saw himself forced in the 1860s to make a clear choice between
the two national cultures in which he had grown up. He opted for Germany,
disposing of his French library, writing poetry in support of the German
cause, and moving close to the German nationalist circles around François
Wille and Mathilde Wesendonck in Zurich.

During this period, however, Meyer experienced considerable discomfort
in his relationship with his publisher, Haessel of Leipzig. He wrote apo-
logetically of the crude '*Realpolitik*' which seemed to have come to dominate
contemporary political life, and which is, of course, every bit as dominant in
the actions of the ruthless characters who people the stories which Meyer was
now beginning to publish with Haessel and in Rodenberg's *Deutsche
Rundschau*.[28] The embarrassment which Meyer displayed in his relationship
with the Saxon, Haessel, resembles the discretion which the Meiningen
company displayed in withholding one of its most celebrated productions,
Kleist's virulently nationalistic drama, *Die Hermannsschlacht*, from its non-
German public. Such considerations were not, however, powerful enough
actually to prevent either Meyer or the Duke of Meiningen from fully
exploiting the popular appeal within Germany of such unscrupulous and
energetic forgers of national unity as Jürg Jenatsch or Arminius.

The reservations about the morality of his heroes, which Meyer expressed
directly in the private context, did find their way into his literary work. They
are evident in the subtle and complex use of narrative perspective, by means
of which Meyer prompts his reader to observe the doubts, hesitations, and
compromises of a story-teller closely involved with the hero; and they are
evident in the suspicious insight we are given into the psychology of the will
to power, which frequently recalls the analyses of Meyer's contemporary,
Nietzsche. The ambivalence between attraction to, and repulsion by, these
heroes, however, remains unresolved.

Both of these aspects of Meyer's technique have parallels in the productions of the Meiningen Theatre. The former, the narrative distance, is
echoed in the detachment with which the celebrated Meiningen crowd was
presented as an object for observation, rather than as a group of people in
whose excitement the audience was encouraged to participate directly; while
the ambiguity of Meyer's approach to his characters has a counterpart in the
remarkable and controversial production of Kleist's *Prinz Friedrich von
Homburg*, with the young Josef Kainz, who was already beginning to develop

the nervous, psychologically penetrating style of acting for which he was to become famous.

There is another, less obvious parallel between attitudes during the politically transitional years of the late sixties and early seventies. Meyer, still finding the character of the hero of his first novel morally repellent, temporarily gave up work on *Jürg Jenatsch* and found creative release in a verse epic with Ulrich von Hutten as its central figure. In the religious reformer he believed he had found a hero who shared the energy, patriotism, and effectiveness of the Bismarckian Jenatsch, while at the same time preserving the older virtues of a more chivalrous age: in short 'ein Ritter ohne Furcht und Tadel', ' a fearless and spotless knight'. During these years the Duke of Meiningen, with other of the lesser German princes such as the Dukes of Saxe-Coburg, Baden, and Oldenburg, was attempting, rather nostalgically, to revive an older notion of German unity, under an Emperor, to ensure the pre-eminence of a single authority in the state, but within a conservative constitution, which would preserve for the princes some influence on the business of government. Their hope was that such an arrangement would facilitate a reconciliation with the southern states, especially Bavaria, and would mitigate the influence of any more narrowly Prussian ambitions by appealing to a wider conception of nationhood, for, Georg argued:

With a German Emperor southern Germany would also be brought in, and we would cease to be more or less vassals of Prussia, for the German Emperor is something quite different from the King of Prussia. The specifically Prussian element would gradually fade into the background. The constitution could stay as it is.[29]

At this particular time such ideas did not fit in with Bismarck's plans; and the situation, as it developed after 1870, when Bismarck himself took up and implemented the *Kaiser* idea, did not correspond to the hopes cherished by the Duke of Meiningen and his friends. Similarly Friedrich Theodor Vischer, a south German and a liberal, travelling with Theodor Fontane to France at Easter, 1871, declared himself to his Prussian companion a supporter of current political developments, especially the reconstruction of the German *Reich*; he did, however, regret that the architect should have been Bismarck.[30] Such men belonged to a generation which looked to Crown Prince Friedrich, who had a reputation as a liberal, for the fulfilment of their ideas; but Kaiser Wilhelm I lived on until 1888, and his son died within a year of succeeding him. He, in turn, was succeeded by the young Kaiser Wilhelm II, who adopted a style of government and a set of political and cultural ambitions that were alien to the survivors of the pre-imperial generation. The decision to put an end to the tours of the Meiningen Court Theatre in 1890 was both a tribute to the crucial importance of Ludwig Chronegk for the success of the enterprise and, at the same time, a further indication of the political sensitivity and historical understanding of Duke Georg II. It is a sign of his recognition that his achievement was part of a culture that had experienced a remarkable swan-song within the space of two very special and transitional decades, and whose destruction was soon being openly prepared. In 1891, he wrote sadly to his old friend and dramaturgical adviser, Professor Karl Werder:

It is very doubtful whether we shall preserve the calm which has prevailed since the war against France; we could be heading for terrible storms, which may perhaps break during my reign. It seems to me that an increasingly chauvinistic attitude is being adopted in the very highest place – perhaps because it can be seen that the state of armed peace is gradually ruining us, but perhaps also because the frequent sight of great German armies strengthens the confidence in one's own power.[31]

On 18 January 1871, when King Wilhelm I of Prussia was proclaimed Kaiser Wilhelm I, Georg II of Meiningen was present among the German princes assembled in the Hall of Mirrors at Versailles, playing a walk-on part in a splendidly costumed theatrical display, in a historical setting, pedantically accurate in its timing (on the 170th anniversary of the coronation of Friedrich III, Elector of Brandenburg, as Friedrich I, King of Prussia, in Königsberg): a piece of *Meiningerei, avant la lettre*.[32] One of the main actors, however, was absent.

Politically the most significant direct consequence of the Franco-Prussian War had been the unhesitating acceptance by the south-German states of their treaty obligations to come to the aid of Prussia when war was declared, that is to say their recognition that this was a national war. Consequently Bavarian troops had fought in the 3rd Army alongside regiments from Prussia – and two regiments from Meiningen (32nd and 95th) – under the command of Crown Prince Friedrich. When this national unity was formalised it was the King of Bavaria, the senior of the south-German rulers, who made the offer of the imperial title to the Prussian King. These events would probably be of little interest to the theatre historian were it not for the fact that the Bavarian King, who was not present at the ceremony, was Ludwig II.

From his predecessors, Ludwig I, to whom Munich owes its university, its great art collections, and much of its reputation as an international cultural centre, and Maximilian II, Germany's leading patron of science and literature in the middle of the nineteenth century, Ludwig inherited a vigorous tradition of royal patronage on a grand scale. He surpassed both his forebears in enthusiasm, extravagance, naivety, and eccentricity. Almost as soon as he succeeded to the Bavarian throne in 1864 Ludwig II had sought out Richard Wagner and, over a long period, he supported the work of the composer with devotion and generosity. His interests, and the commissions which followed from them, extended from music and drama to architecture and applied arts, but the unifying element was theatre. Here he shared the taste of Georg II of Meiningen and their contemporaries for historically accurate and visually attractive effects, and, inevitably, they employed some of the same people to create these effects for them, for the artistic world of mid-century Germany was a tightly interlocking one. When the scandal involving his first wife, Cosima, and Richard Wagner broke, Hans von Bülow left Munich; after some years of touring as a piano-soloist and an appointment in Hanover, Bülow became *Hofkapellmeister* in Meiningen. At about the same time the young Josef Kainz left Meiningen for Munich, and soon afterwards began to take a significant part in the *Separatvorstellungen*, the private theatrical productions mounted for King Ludwig II.[33]

The methods of spectacular theatre applied to the arts of opera, drama, architecture, and interior decoration, so as to bring about the most literal and most concrete realisation of an idealised historical past, proved extremely costly of both time and money. But, at a time when the political influence of the minor and provincial courts was rapidly waning, and the absolutist claims which Ludwig, as a monarch, still defended were beginning to look distinctly anachronistic, it was in the imaginative and aesthetic sphere that the Bavarian King's priorities came increasingly to reside. It was, moreover, precisely in the late sixties, that is to say after the defeat of Austria in 1866, after the capitulation of German liberalism in the face of the Prussian solution to the problem of German unity, and at the very time when Georg II was beginning to immerse himself into his own theatre, that Ludwig II began to withdraw into his most private ventures, the *Separatvorstellungen*, and his most extravagant and fantastic projects, the castles of Neuschwanstein, Linderhof, and Herrenchiemsee. This is the background against which we have to consider Ludwig II's involvement in the events of 1870–71.

The letter offering the title and status of *Kaiser* to the King of Prussia had been secured by patient and careful negotiation, and it was essentially the work of Bismarck. It was followed, from the spring of 1871 onwards, by a series of secret annual payments, totalling four million marks, made to the Bavarian King by Bismarck from the *Welfenfonds* (the confiscated resources of the Hanoverian crown). To speak of direct bribery and corruption would be far too crude, but it would be perverse to ignore the political significance and the political motive of payments such as these. Not only was King Ludwig useful to Bismarck in the matter of the letter offering the title of Kaiser to Wilhelm I, but, as the Chancellor was well aware, Ludwig II was likely to be a far less committed and energetic spokesman for Bavarian separatism than any probable successor, for his particularism was already finding expression in the cultural sphere. His abdication – and it was known to Bismarck that he had been considering abdicating in the autumn of 1870 – would not have been helpful to Prussia.[34]

In short, however indirect the connections, it remains in a limited but important sense true that King Ludwig was trading some of his remaining political power and independence for the means to create for himself in the rapidly changing circumstances of those years, a private dream-world, in which he could continue to live as an absolute monarch. The obsessive reference of the Bavarian royal castles to an absolutist past: Neuschwanstein to the Germanic middle ages, Herrenchiemsee (a replica of Versailles) to the France of Louis XIV, Linderhof to the France of Louis XV; and the concentration in the repertoire of the *Separatvorstellungen* on pre-revolutionary France, provide spectacular corroboration of this interpretation of his development.[35]

The much smaller Duchy of Saxe-Meiningen had never enjoyed or aspired to the same level of cultural activity as Bavaria, or, for that matter, its other close neighbour, Weimar, but its rulers were no philistines. There was a long tradition of theatrical interest and activity on the part of the ruling house, and in 1776 the ruling Duke (Karl) had set up a theatre in the Great Hall (*Riesensaal*) of the castle, where – as in Weimar – members of the court themselves participated in theatrical productions; these had included dramas by Diderot (*Le Père de famille*), Voltaire, Wieland, and Leisewitz, in whose *Julius von Tarent* (12 June 1780) the Duke himself played the title rôle.[36] The theatre was particularly supported and encouraged by Duke Georg I, grandfather of Georg II, who was probably responsible for a plan to establish a permanent company, jointly serving the courts of Meiningen, Coburg, and Hildburghausen, which – possibly because of the Napoleonic Wars – was not carried out. During the reign of Duke Bernhard II a theatre building was erected on its present site and opened in 1831 with a production of Auber's *Fra Diavolo*. During the following years music rather than drama continued to be the principal focus of cultural life and the Court Orchestra established for itself a high reputation, particularly after the appointment of Jean Joseph Bott as *Kapellmeister* (1857–65); it frequently gave concerts under the direction of Spohr and Liszt. The ducal collection of paintings included a Raphael Madonna, and was regularly increased by commissions; its quality was noted by the sculptor, Adolf von Hildebrandt, when he visited Meiningen in 1891.[37] Local literary figures, such as Ludwig Bechstein, a poet and editor of folksong and popular legends, benefited from the Duke's support, as did the more important figure, Otto Ludwig, albeit only briefly and in the pursuit of his musical interests. Behind this activity lay the traditional belief in the ceremonial and representative function of the arts within court society, and an enlightened-absolutist sense of the educational responsibilites of the ruler to his subjects. In nineteenth-century Germany this latter notion derived further impetus from the idea of *Bildung*, so cherished by the German liberals, and it is very much in this spirit that Ernst II of Saxe-Coburg explained his cultural policies to the prominent liberal writer, Gustav Freytag.[38]

An equally important factor in the cultural activity of this area at this time was the undoubted artistic talent of the ruling houses, which meant that their interest in the arts was a genuine and active one. Duke Bernhard II of Meiningen was a violinist, which partially explains the privileged position enjoyed by music during his reign; Ernst II of Saxe-Coburg was also a musician and composed a number of operas; while his brother, Albert, also composed, before exercising a wide range of talents as consort to Queen Victoria.[39] Georg II of Meiningen was a talented graphic artist, and from an early age he was given instruction in drawing. During his studies he was encouraged to pursue and deepen his interest in the visual arts by visits to the Academy in Düsseldorf, to various German collections, and to Paris. Many of the letters he sent to his mother while he was studying are illustrated with careful and detailed pen or pencil drawings. Throughout his life he sought the company of artists, from Peter Cornelius and Andreas Müller in the 1850s, to Adolf von Hildebrand in the early 1900s; 'It is a pity', the painter Wilhelm von Kaulbach is said to have observed, 'that you are a minor prince, otherwise you might have been a great artist.'[40]

On his marriage to Princess Charlotte in 1850 Georg acquired the Villa Carlotta on Lake Como as a wedding present, and along with it a substantial collection of paintings and sculptures. Lacking the resources, one must suppose, to increase the art collection, he did not remain idle, but devoted himself to the enrichment of the gardens, which now constitute the greatest glory of the villa.[41]

After his accession Georg II continued the cultural traditions of the Duchy, but from 1871 onwards there is a distinct intensification of activity, ambition, and quality. Art no longer simply has the function of decorating, or even cultivating the Duchy; it assumes the function of representing first the Duchy, and then the new Germany, and enabling it to make its mark on the world outside. From the beginning, the tours of the Meiningen Theatre represented a conscious challenge to the pre-eminence of Berlin and, as we shall see, the official cultural institutions immediately recognised this. The two most important areas of activity were to be orchestral music and spoken drama. Georg II did not neglect the plastic arts, but the more important commissions, the monuments sculpted by Hildebrand, date from after the end of the theatrical tours.

In orchestral music the achievement is closely associated with the person of Hans von Bülow, who was appointed *Hofkapellmeister* in 1880 and remained in this post until 1885. Thanks to the favourable conditions under which the Duke allowed him to work, to the quality of the orchestra, which had already performed under Wagner and had provided the basis of the orchestra for the Bayreuth *Ring* productions of 1876 and 1877, and to the experience and ambition which Bülow was able to bring to Meiningen, he was able, in a very short time, to fulfil the aim he had set himself, and to accomplish with the Meiningen Orchestra what the Duke and his collaborators had already done in the theatre.[42] By profound analytical study of the musical score, by a radically different and far more intensive approach to rehearsal, and by developing the notion of the orchestra as an ensemble under the direction of an interpreter-conductor, Bülow here laid the foundations of modern orchestral practice. After serving Wagner, the orchestra and its conductor contributed significantly to the recognition of Brahms as a major composer, and many of his works, including the Fourth Symphony, were given their first performances in Meiningen. As it was to do with the theatre company, the emphasis on the ensemble principle militated against the emergence of great solo performers, but – again as with the theatre – not absolutely: an outstanding clarinettist, Richard Mühlfeld, served in the Meiningen Orchestra from 1884 to 1907. It was for Mühlfeld that Brahms extended his career as a composer and wrote the late Clarinet Trio (opus 114), the Clarinet Quintet (opus 115), and the Clarinet Sonatas (opus 120).[43]

The orchestra, like the theatre company, sought definitive recognition by going to the capital. It gave its first Berlin concerts in the *Singakademie* in January 1882; Brahms appeared as soloist in his own B-flat-major piano concerto and then as conductor, with Bülow as soloist, in the D-minor concerto.[44] The success achieved by the theatre in 1874 was repeated; the correspondent of the *Neue Berliner Musikzeitung* wrote of 'a visit which, in its success and its effects, is comparable to that of the Meiningen actors'.[45] Bülow was well aware that the presence of this provincial orchestra in the capital represented a challenge: 'our appearance in the so-called imperial capital is, that is to say is considered, an affront; and so there will be no lack of fault-finding, or even abuse', he wrote to his mother. In particular the challenge was felt to be directed at the *Hofoper* (Royal Opera House), which, like the *Hoftheater*, was under the direction of Botho von Hülsen. The outspoken and temperamental Bülow did not allow the challenge to remain an implicit one, but created a public scandal by criticising the 'Circus Hülsen' in a speech in the Philharmonic Hall in March 1884. Bülow was formally reprimanded, but informed opinion seems to have supported him, as it had supported the theatre.[46] Finally Bülow took the Meiningen Orchestra on a series of exhausting tours, first of the major German cities, and then more widely on the European mainland, performing in Vienna, Budapest, Brno, Graz, and Amsterdam in that same spirit of cultural imperialism which is evident in the tours of the Meiningen Theatre. In his resignation letter of 23 November 1885 Bülow wrote to the Duke: 'By its moral conquests and their influence on the musical life of all the places it has visited, the Court Orchestra has participated in the process of real annexation'; and a contemporary historian of Meiningen culture wrote of the orchestra: 'They were the apostles of musical art . . . who, in the eighties and nineties . . . undertook a victorious campaign in Germany and abroad in order to make peaceful conquests.'[47]

By the end of 1884 Bülow regarded his task as completed, although it was not until December 1885 that he left Meiningen. He was succeeded by the 21-year-old Richard Strauss whom he himself had recommended, and who filled the post of *Hofkapellmeister* for the short period from December 1885 to April 1886.

With Fritz Steinbach and Max Reger as subsequent musical directors, Meiningen continued to play an important rôle in the musical life of Germany, but it was, of course, in the theatre that the most significant and most personal achievement of Georg II of Meiningen was made. Here he was more than just a patron and consumer, and, unlike his Coburg cousin, Ernst II, he was not satisfied to assume the rôle of dilettante, except perhaps in that very special sense in which Adorno, following Nietzsche and Thomas Mann, applied the word to the Duke's contemporary, Richard Wagner.[48] His early experiences of the theatre, and his first efforts to raise the standard of his own company, taught him that, with the right support, he could implement his ideas more successfully than the professionals. By sending his productions out into the world, he secured confirmation that this was true.

2　Art and literature: the historicist style

. . . the only thing I want is to be sure that the historical occurrence is accurately represented.
　　　　Ludwig II of Bavaria to Ernst Possart

T HE YEAR OF THE FIRST TOUR by the Meiningen Court Theatre, 1874, was also the year of a famous essay by Nietzsche, 'Vom Nutzen und Nachteil der Historie für das Leben' ('On the use and disadvantages of history for life'). This essay began with an attack on what Nietzsche saw as the major malaise of contemporary Germany, an all-consuming historicist fever. Although this had been fuelled by the atmosphere of self-satisfaction and philistinism, which prevailed in Germany after the victory in the Franco-Prussian War and which had been the object of his scorn in the preceding essay of the *Unzeitgemäße Betrachtungen* (Thoughts out of season), Nietzsche was well aware that the historicist style – in which he, however, could recognise only eclecticism and stylelessness – had played a dominant rôle in German artistic and intellectual life for at least two decades. It had been very much to the fore in the 1850s in great national events such as the Munich industrial exhibition of 1854 and the Schiller centenary celebrations of 1859.

The effect of the historicism manifest in such spectacles, Nietzsche argued, was to undermine the moral strength of the individual personality by calling forth an entirely passive response to the sensual stimuli being provided by contemporary historicist art. Making a slight chronological adjustment to the popular comparison between Bismarckian Germany and the Rome of Julius Caesar, and thereby subverting it, Nietzsche drew an analogy with the decadence of Imperial Rome:

The Roman of the imperial period became un-Roman as he beheld the world which lay at his feet . . . and the same must be happening to modern man, as he continually causes his historical artists to prepare for him the festival of an international exhibition; he has become a spectator who walks around and enjoys, and has assumed a condition which even great wars or great revolutions can scarcely alter even for a moment.

Anticipating the style of theatrical production that was soon to make such an impression in Berlin, he warns against it, citing Goethe:

18

No one had more scorn of material costume than [Shakespeare] did; he knows the inner, human costume very well, and in this respect all men are alike. People say his depiction of the Romans is excellent; I do not agree, they are Englishmen through and through, but they are, of course, men, men from the very roots, and so the Roman toga fits them too.[1]

Nietzsche, it might be argued, was being less than just, for this was the age of the great German historians, and some of their most enduring achievements. It saw, for instance, the publication of Ranke's *Französische Geschichte* (1852–1861), Droysen's *Geschichte der preußischen Politik* (1855–1885), and Mommsen's *Römische Geschichte* (1854–1885). For many, however, the achievements of German historiography, especially during the last quarter of the century, were tarnished by the use to which they were put, usually with the connivance of the historians themselves. The historicist trend, based on the principles of moderate liberalism and displaying an increasing nationalistic tendency, was given added impetus by the events of 1870–71, as the newly founded German Empire sought to establish its identity as the legitimate heir to a long tradition. We have noted evidence of this in the ceremony and the timing of the proclamation of the Kaiser in 1871; it was very much in the same spirit that Barbarossa, in an analogy to the venerable and bearded Kaiser Wilhelm I, came to enjoy a privileged place in art and literature in Imperial Germany.[2] The Italian Renaissance, as a period of great, assertive heroism, also enjoyed something of a boom; but that historical eclecticism which Nietzsche deplored, continued to manifest itself in the gothic post offices, romanesque railway-stations, and byzantine banks which sprang up in so many German cities, nowhere more prominently than in the garrison and frontier town of Metz, in the annexed territory of Lorraine. The plastic arts, painting, architecture, and monumental sculpture, were, in fact, the media in which the historicist style found its most prominent expression. These were the media in which the Kaiser himself had most interest, both because, without possessing the talent of his brother, Friedrich-Wilhelm IV – or, for that matter, the Duke of Meiningen – Wilhelm I had, in his youth, shared his interest in pencil-sketching, and also because of his recognition of the cultural–political value of the visual arts.[3] So widespread was this recognition, and so vulgar the works it stimulated, that this period virtually killed the public monument as a respectable art form in Europe.[4] Ironically, therefore, in an age whose characteristic sense is that of the eye rather than the ear, we have to look for the most enduring artistic expression of the historicist style to music, the art form least capable of the concrete realisation of heroic gestures which official and public taste seemed to require.[5] Almost immediately after the accession of Georg II historicist principles were introduced into the planning of concert programmes in Meiningen: the pieces were arranged in chronological order and their dates given;[6] and the same tendencies are reflected in a variety of ways in the work of composers who were close to Meiningen: in the Germanic mythology of Wagner's operas (although here, of course, the visual sense is also involved);[7] in the revival of baroque and classical forms in the symphonic music of Brahms; and in the subject of an early composition by Richard Strauss which dates from shortly after his Meiningen period, opus 16, *Aus Italien*.

Besides being very prominent in the visual arts, historical subjects, especially Germanic subjects, received extensive literary treatment; and at the same time styles and genres, such as classicism and the epic, associated with great historical and national developments, came back into favour.

Very frequently choice and treatment of subject reflected the widespread tendency to the actualisation of the past and the legitimation of the present. Of the large number of second-rate and third-rate historical dramas produced during these years, a few came to be included in the touring repertoire of the Meiningen Theatre: works by Minding, Lindner, and Fitger; while dramas by Ernst von Wildenbruch were performed before the local audience in Meiningen. The touring repertoire was, of course, dominated by *first*-rate historical dramas. In the narrative genres long historical novels by writers such as Dahn and Ebers enjoyed a certain popularity, and Gustav Freytag was inspired by unification and the foundation of the German Empire to write a cycle of novels, *Die Ahnen* (The ancestors), tracing the development of one German family over many generations up to 1848. But the most important exponents of the historical narrative during this period are probably Conrad Ferdinand Meyer, a favoured contributor to Julius Rodenberg's *Deutsche Rundschau*, whose close affinity to Georg II has already been noted,[8] and Theodor Fontane, who, as a theatre critic, was particularly responsive to the visual aspect of the achievements of the Meiningen Theatre.[9]

The talent of Georg as a visual artist lay in drawing in pencil and ink. The greater part of his surviving sketches, whether they be for the theatre or not, are monochrome, and there is no evidence of his having worked extensively in oils or any other coloured medium. Many of the costume designs and sketches for sets contain instructions on colour, but execution was left to the scene painters, and it has been observed that the colouring of the theatre decorations, with its predominant brown hues, is characteristic of the Brückner studio. This, in turn, looks back to Goethe and his preference for restrained backgrounds: 'In general decorations should have a tone . . . like those of Beuther, where the brown hues are inclined to be dominant and the colour of the costumes stands out in all its freshness.'[10] It was also remarked by a number of contemporary observers that the colouring was rather crude.[11] This is probably a response to the use of new materials, including recently developed aniline dyes; the negative judgment is only partially confirmed by the examination of such material as has survived. Some of the restored sets, hung, it is true, under modern lighting conditions, which bring

out the contrasts (and the subtleties) of the colour to a higher degree than the
gas lighting of nineteenth-century theatres, show up very well, with brilliantly coloured flowers and bright green foliage over the red-brown base.[12]

As a young man Georg received instruction from Friedrich Paul Schell-
horn, a history and portrait painter appointed to the court by Duke Bernhard, and Wilhelm Lindenschmitt the Elder, also a historical painter, and a
pupil and assistant to Peter Cornelius.[13] This contact with the Nazarene
school, who were linearists rather than colourists (painters who could not
paint, observed Otto Brahm),[14] was probably a further factor which confirmed Georg in his loyalty to his chosen medium. Certainly the very lofty
conception of the artist's calling, which was central to Nazarene doctrine,
was passed on to Georg, and it is reflected in his consistent and passionate
criticism of the very successful historical painters of the next generation,
colourists, with whose work the productions of the Meiningen Theatre were,
nevertheless, frequently – and understandably – compared.[15]

Historical subjects, however, Georg did not reject; on the contrary, they
always figure very significantly in his drawings and in the sketches which
accompany his letters. Almost equally prominent are careful and detailed
drawings of uniformed figures, and sketches of dramatic or violent actions,
such as a series of illustrations of a mishap while riding.[16] These elements are
not kept separate; they figure simultaneously in drawings such as one of the

2   Georg II, sketch for Kleist, *Die Hermannsschlacht*, Act v, scene 4, encounter of
    Varus with the Alraune, 1875.

3   Max Brückner, Quintilius Varus in the Teutoburg Forest by moonlight, 1909.

battle of Kappel, involving the reformer, Zwingli, or the sketches from the campaign of 1870–71.[17]

Also to be found among Georg's earlier drawings are a number of sketches of fantastic prehistoric creatures, probably dating from the 1840s. Together with a number of drawings of a distinctly Gothic character, and the recurrent depiction of grotesque and distorted trees, such as will appear in the Teutoburg Forest scenes in *Die Hermannsschlacht* and the Bohemian Forest in *Die Räuber*, these throw an interesting sidelight on the psychology of the artist, who was, perhaps, not so much of a realist as is generally believed.[18]

An anecdote from Georg's childhood illuminates this aspect of his artistic personality further. In 1835, when he assumed his responsibilities as tutor to the Crown Prince, Moritz Seebeck was very critical of the education his charge had hitherto been receiving from a certain Frau Hermann, believing that it had produced an excessive stimulation of the boy's imagination: after taking part in a re-enactment of an episode from the life of the Prussian cavalry general, Seydlitz, the young Georg had declined an invitation to go and see some real horses as much too boring.[19] The situation described here recalls that of the young Conrad Ferdinand Meyer who – for different reasons – spent much of his childhood and youth in sheltered and isolated circumstances. During this time he developed a rich imaginative life by reading voraciously in history books, which offered an excitement remote from his own situation and alien to his own character.[20] The evidence that, in his youth, Georg acquired the habit of sublimating his creative energies in this way, lends some support to the psychological component in the explanation of his subsequent profound immersion in the theatre after the events of 1866 and the loss of political power which they entailed.

The specific historicist style that dominated the German artistic scene at the time when the Meiningen Theatre began to make its mark first came to prominence in Germany in the 1840s. The development which then took place is strikingly illustrated by a change in direction in the work of the major German painter of the period, Adolph Menzel. In 1848 Menzel was working on his *Aufbahrung der Märzgefallenen*, an oil-painting depicting the funeral ceremony of the victims of the March disturbances of that year, and a fairly direct critical comment on their suppression. He did not complete this canvas, and his next important work sees him retreating from this concern with the contemporary world and immersing himself in the idealised past which he had depicted in his illustrations, 400 woodcuts, from Franz Kugler's life of Frederick the Great (*Geschichte Friedrichs des Großen*, 1839–1842); up to 1858 he devoted himself to a series of large-scale paintings on the same subject, the most famous of which is the depiction of a flute recital by Frederick the Great in his palace at Sanssouci (1852).[21]

Menzel, a mature and innovative painter in the 1840s, who became a quasi-official painter of Imperial Germany in the 1870s, but who was to return to the realistic depiction of modern life, is far from being a typical exponent of mid-century historicism. In Germany this style is most evident in the generation of painters whose careers began at the end of the 1840s, when Kaulbach was appointed Director of the Academy in Munich, and Munich is the centre with which they were particularly associated. A significant influence emanated from the Belgian school of history-painters, largely thanks to the exhibition in many German cities in 1843 of two enormous canvases by Louis Gallait and Edouard de Bièfve. Crown Prince Georg saw the paintings and was highly critical; after discussing Gallait's *Abdication of the Emperor Charles V in favour of Philip II* with Peter Cornelius he noted with satisfaction that the German painter shared his view that this painting, and others like it, was lacking the seriousness and substance necessary to genuine historical painting.[22]

The most notable follower of the Belgian painters was Karl von Piloty, who rose to prominence with a series of historical paintings in the 1850s, and was appointed professor at the Academy in Munich in 1856. Piloty's subjects anticipate in detail the touring repertoire of the Meiningen Theatre. He established his reputation firmly in 1855 with *Seni an der Leiche Wallensteins* (Seni with the body of Wallenstein), a painting which both had a theatrical inspiration in the drama of Schiller and was itself exploited in the theatre,

serving as a model for the *tableau* with which Dingelstedt's production of
Wallensteins Tod concluded in 1859.[23] There followed *Ermordung Cäsars*
(The assassination of Caesar) in 1865, *Maria Stuart* (1868), which was
displayed at the Munich International Exhibition of 1869, and *Thusnelda im
Triumphzug des Germanicus* (Thusnelda in the triumph of Germanicus) in
1873. Apart from the riot of colour which they provided, in contrast to the
restraint of Nazarene painting, the principal quality of these works is their
theatricality: the artificial glitter of the illumination; the baroque use of space,
with dramatically crossing diagonals; the stark contrasts of light and shade;
the posing of the characters (Piloty used actors as models); the lavishing of
attention on costume; the virtuosity in the treatment of materials, particularly the luxurious materials of the clothing and drapery (the display of technique in the rendering of the velvet cloak of Seni, for instance, was felt by some
contemporary observers to be out of keeping with the solemnity of the scene

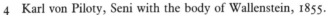

4   Karl von Piloty, Seni with the body of Wallenstein, 1855.

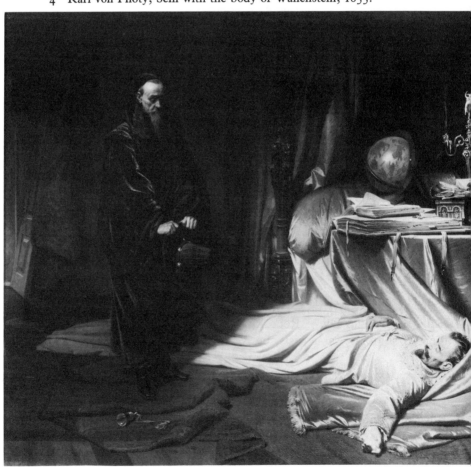

depicted). Comparisons with the theatre were frequently made: the Munich actress, Klara Ziegler, was often mentioned as an exponent of the same style in the art of acting; and at a later date Otto Brahm, advocating a much more ascetic style of *mise-en-scène*, will sum up the naturalists' criticism of their predecessors when he says that Piloty depicted genuine clothes, but not real people, that his works were 'painted Meiningertum'.[24]

This implied criticism of his productions does not do justice to Georg's convictions and intentions, for in 1856 he had anticipated a central aspect of later criticism of nineteenth-century historicist painting, by drawing attention to its essentially sensuous appeal and its failure to provide any moral stimulus: 'art exists . . . in order to do more than charm the senses, its purpose is the awakening of all the noble forces in man'; and he responded contemptuously to the plan of the Meiningen *Kunstverein* (Art Society) to mount its first exhibition: 'There will be nothing to be seen except genre-paintings.'[25] He followed it in 1857 with an exhibition of his own, in the centre of which he placed the most important picture available to him, the Raphael Madonna from the ducal collection, supplemented by works of Cornelius, Schnorr von Carolsfeld, and Andreas Müller. Against the increasing tide of success enjoyed by the historicist painters, Georg's pessimistic view of the cultural situation is intensified as he notes the tendencies evident in the Cologne exhibition of 1861: a lack of composition and form, and an absence of idealism, which he sees as characteristic of contemporary public life:

It is quite monstrous that, to judge by the new pictures on display, Cornelius, Overbeck, Steinle, etc., might just as well not have lived and painted as far as present-day artists are concerned. The shallowest naturalism is now dominant, and our undiscriminating public has allowed itself to be so taken in by Piloty and the rest, that it no longer has any understanding for the old, considered compositions. – I find the much-praised Nero [*Nero auf den Trümmern Roms*, 1860] appallingly vulgar in both conception and execution . . . What is art for, if not to elevate mankind; but nobody is elevated by vulgarity. The same aims are now being expressed in art as in politics and in public life – everything shall be brought down to the same level.[26]

It was to the old masters that Georg always looked. During his visit to England in 1857, for instance, he went to Petworth House to see the paintings by Van Dyck, Rembrandt, Holbein, and Raphael; and when, in the course of the same visit, he went north to see the great exhibition of paintings in Manchester, it was Rembrandt, Van Dyck, Rubens, Murillo, and Velasquez who secured his attention. Unlike Fontane, who visited Manchester at about the same time, he showed no interest in contemporary British painters, not even the Pre-Raphaelites, whose works were being exhibited there, and for whom he might well have been expected to feel a certain kinship.[27]

The follower of Piloty to achieve the most spectacular contemporary acclaim was Hans von Makart, whose decorative and theatrical style exercised an enormous influence on fashion, interior decoration, and design in the 1870s and 1880s. Like Piloty he first made his name as a historical painter with subjects from the Thirty Years War, but he moved on to subjects from Roman history and the Italian Renaissance, where the sensational element takes precedence over the specifically historical (it is characteristic that the painting *Die Pest in Venedig* (The plague in Venice) should also be known as *Die sieben Todsünden* (The seven deadly sins). Makart, too, drew subjects from dramatic literature, and generally favoured the kind of material which was to figure in the repertoire of the Meiningen Court Theatre. Like Piloty, he regularly painted actors posing in costume, most notably the star of Vienna's *Burgtheater*, Charlotte Wolter, whom he painted as Cleopatra.

Among Makart's most celebrated, not to say scandalous, paintings was his *Einzug Karls V in Antwerpen* (Entry of the Emperor Charles V into Antwerp), 1877, which shows the citizens of Antwerp, including prominent naked females, welcoming the Emperor's troops on their triumphal entry into the city. This spectacular depiction of a procession by victorious troops recalls (although not in all its details) the ceremonial entry of the German troops into Paris, Berlin, and other German cities in 1871. It is also connected with another characteristic and theatrical phenomenon of this period, the historical masque or *Kostümfest*, a kind of carnival procession with a particular historical theme. In Munich a 'Festzug Karls V' had been mounted by the *Allotria Gemeinschaft* in 1876, while Makart himself was the chief organiser of such manifestations in Vienna.[28] In England Charles Kean had produced something along these lines within his production of *Richard II*, where the entry of Bolingbroke into London had been presented as an *entr'acte*. Already with Kean such an episode lacked any dramaturgical function, serving only to illustrate a reference in the text, and not to advance the action. Makart's processions, independent spectacles without any reference to a text, develop the means of the *tableau vivant* and the *entr'acte*, but in doing so they betray clearly their exclusively choreographical character; whereas, the Duke of Meiningen will assert, 'the . . . function of the theatre . . . is to present . . . the relentless forward progress of the action'.

The dividing line between the historicism practised by the Duke of Meiningen and the tendencies outlined here is a fairly narrow one, and a number of artists closely associated with the Meiningen enterprise clearly crossed it. Franz von Lenbach, in particular, extended the historicist style into portraiture, allowing his own style to be influenced in its development by the commissions he received from Graf Schack, initially to produce copies of works by great portraitists of the past in order to give historical completeness to the collection which Schack was assembling in Munich. Lenbach's later subjects are the great men of the age: Kaiser Wilhelm I, the Austrian Emperor Franz-Josef, Moltke, Bismarck (most frequently of all), and, in

1878, the Duke of Meiningen. The subjects are presented in the stern pose of the ruler, in the colouring of Van Dyck, and with all the iconography of this tradition of portrait-painting. Lenbach's subsequent experiments with photography did nothing to modify the statuesque quality of his work; formality and monumentality remained the qualities sought, rather than spontaneity or psychological insight.[29]

During the years after 1870 it must have been exceedingly difficult for public and critics alike to make the fairly subtle kind of distinction – which was clearly a fundamental one for Georg II – between serious and responsible historicism, *Meiningertum*, and the sensuous and superficial *Meiningerei* which the Duke himself recognised and condemned in a number of his contemporaries. The difficulty must have been exacerbated by the very success of the Meiningen productions, for they attracted into the theatre contemporary painters, who came to study the decorations, with a view to making use of them in their own work.[30] Moreover, the same style of detailed and painstakingly accurate realism was the style adopted by official and semi-official artists of this period, by Anton von Werner, Georg Bleibtreu, and Louis Braun, in their paintings of battle scenes from the Franco-Prussian War and, above all, in the highly popular re-creations of these scenes in historical panoramas. These manifestations of patriotic art engaged the interest of a wide public, which included both the Kaiser and the Crown Prince, who responded with that same concern for detailed accuracy which was evident among the audiences of the Meiningen productions; there were, indeed, occasions when the Emperor and his son were members of these

5   Hans von Makart, Cleopatra, 1875.

audiences.[31] It should, however, be stated, that the wholesale recruitment of the visual arts into the service of the new *Reich* – and despite the ravages of the Second World War and the disappearance from public view of many once-celebrated paintings, there are still traces of this in the cities and galleries of Germany – called for a style that was found alien by a handful of significant artists, who marked their protest by withdrawing.[32]

One such artist was Anselm Feuerbach, who completed one of his best-known paintings, *Iphigenie*, in 1871. As his contemporaries, Piloty and Makart, so often did, he took a subject that was familiar to his German public from the theatre. *Iphigenie auf Tauris* was performed fourteen times by the Meiningen theatre, and was the only play by Goethe to figure in the touring repertoire. Feuerbach's painting, with its heavy classical drapery and the sculptural treatment of the statuesque seated figure, has that monumental quality to which the official art of the period aspired; while the reference to Dürer's engraving, *Melencolia I*, in the pose of Iphigenie, head resting in hand, and in the distant horizon of the sea, reinforce the historicist appeal of the picture. In its most striking and essential feature, however, Feuerbach's painting departs from this model: the solitary Iphigenie, whose longing is directed to her Greek homeland beyond the horizon, has her back to the observer. The provocation inherent in this pose is not aimed at Dürer, for Feuerbach has done no more than radically intensify the self-*absorption* that is central to Dürer's depiction of the female figure which, in his engraving, embodies melancholy; it is aimed rather at the essentially *theatrical* quality of so much contemporary painting. On this subject Feuerbach wrote as follows:

I hate the modern theatre . . . I hate all the business of decoration from the depths of my soul. It is ruining the public, driving out the final remnants of decency, and creating a barbarism of taste from which art is turning away . . . True works of art have always had sufficient inner power to create situations without having recourse to un-worthy and anti-artistic means . . . Modest suggestions are needed, not confusing effects . . . Would I have been able . . . to create my *Iphigenie* if I had felt differently.[33]

Whereas artists such as Makart and Lenbach revelled in the public culture of the *Gründerzeit*, Feuerbach viewed it with a hostility reminiscent of Nietzsche:

As far as I am concerned the German *Reich* no long exists [Whitsun, 1874] . . . the barrel-organ of patriotism is being turned and turned until cultivated people take flight [June 1874] . . . In Germany cretinism has become so great that I have no hopes for my pictures. Great wars make people stupid [May 1875].[34]

To escape the 'barbarism', Feuerbach set up his studio in Italy, distancing himself from the *Reich* – again in the manner of Nietzsche. Hans von Marées, with the generous support of his patron, Conrad Fiedler, and the stimulus of work on the frescoes in Naples, was able to do the same. The career of the sculptor, Adolf von Hildebrand, illustrates even more clearly the tension between the demands of public art and the concern of the serious, reflective artist for the development of his medium, which led Hildebrand to settle in Munich rather than Berlin after his return from Italy. The residual separatism of the Bavarian capital provided a favourable atmosphere for progressive artists who were at odds with prevailing official taste, and here he was given a number of important commissions, beginning with the Wittelsbacher Brunnen, completed in 1894. Support for Hildebrand also came from Meiningen in the form of commissions for, *inter alia*, a memorial to Otto Ludwig, which stands in the municipal park; a statue of Marsyas, for the palace of Altenstein; and a fountain, the Herzog Georg Brunnen (now destroyed), in the market-place. Hildebrand's correspondence shows that a warm relationship with the Duke developed during his work on the various commissions, and the sculptor took a direct interest in the rebuilding of the theatre after the fire of 1908.[35]

The extreme introversion of works such as Feuerbach's *Iphigenie* and Hildebrand's celebrated *Young Man* is not even remotely aspired to in the work of the official and semi-official artists of the period.[36] They all signally lacked the highly developed formal sense and theoretical insight of Hildebrand. Nevertheless there is, at least among some contemporary critics, evidence of concern for the integrity and independence of the world depicted on the canvas, and for the primacy of formal values over striving for effect.[37] Writing in the *Deutsche Rundschau* (the journal to which Conrad Fiedler was to contribute) in 1874, Bruno Meyer had adopted such criteria in his criticism of Georg Bleibtreu's depiction of the Battle of Sedan:

all of the persons are presented as portraits, and they are so arranged that each individually is shown to the greatest possible advantage, one might almost say without any regard for coherence and unity of action, or for a composition representing a complete scene. Among these several portraits some are strikingly characteristic, the majority are easily recognisable, above all in their appallingly unnatural poses, which verge on the theatrical.[38]

But the criticism stops short; the formal understanding is not developed to a radical conclusion. The reasons for this timidity probably lie in the cultural–political atmosphere. After years of disappointment and frustration, there was among the liberal intelligentsia a strong desire to claim the *Reich* as its own, to participate in its achievements, and to hold back criticism. This is not only true of Werner and Bleibtreu, who, like Gustav Freytag, accompanied the campaign of 1870 in an official capacity, but also of Menzel and Fontane, Marées and Mommsen. It explains why Hildebrand, who had long been resident in Italy, should have chosen to offer a design for a memorial to the very Kaiser who had ruled over the Germany from which he had voluntarily exiled himself. His humiliation and subsequent bitterness bear a certain resemblance to the experiences of Fontane who, over a decade previously, had been deeply disappointed at the cool reception given to his history of the Franco-Prussian War by the Kaiser.[39]

A genuinely radical alternative to the anachronistic artistic and literary practices of the *Reich* was, of course, available, and was being employed by Germany's defeated neighbour. This is most spectacularly evident in the arrangement of the exhibition in the *Neue Pinakothek* in Munich, where the visitor moves directly from the paintings of Marées and Feuerbach (not to mention Kaulbach and Piloty) to the seemingly remote and quite different open-air world of the French impressionists. The development of Menzel, curtailed, as we have seen, at the end of the 1840s, indicates that he, for one, was aware of this. His painting of the *Departure of King Wilhelm I for the Army on July 31 1870* (1871) uneasily combines precise and purposeful reference to the historical momentousness of the occasion with the casualness of Manet or Degas, in the choice of a subsidiary scene and a division of attention in the composition of the picture.[40] It thus shares the ambiguity of Fontane's war reporting, when he turns away from considerations of strategy, tactics, and their execution, and his eye comes to rest on the debris in the train of the Crown Prince, the dead sheep scattered over the fields before St Privat, or the factory chimney bearing the date 1870 at the burned-out village of Bazeilles. Both artists will develop their style further in works on contemporary subjects, but, to a greater or lesser extent, they remain ambivalent: oblique and sceptical rather than forthright and critical.

In France, too, the older style of historical and military painting survived in the work of the artist known and admired by Menzel, Meissonier, who recorded the Parisian resistance of 1871 in that very combination of the realistic and the allegorical which Fontane had rejected as inappropriate for the illustration of his account of the war.[41] Not so Manet, who, like Meissonier – but unlike Monet and Pissarro who fled to England (and Cézanne, who ignored the war) – served in the National Guard during the siege of Paris. Demonstratively excluding any sense of participation or commitment to a national cause, he records death and misery in his etchings and lithographs on this subject with a coolness and detachment that would have been scarcely conceivable in the jubilant atmosphere of victorious and united Germany. The same discrepancies in style (and artistic merit) and the same time-lag are evident when one compares French and German literature on the theme of war: the casualness of Daudet's *Contes du Lundi*, the detachment of the stories of Maupassant and the *Journal* of the Goncourts, the unrelenting detail with which Zola exposes the senselessness of war and the anachronism of the Napoleonic myths in *La Débâcle*, have proved more enduring than the epic treatment of military exploits by the likes of Ernst von Wildenbruch and Karl Bleibtreu.

It was not, however, until the 1890s that the new impressionist and naturalist styles began to make any kind of headway in Germany. The reprieve which was thereby given to an older historicist style provided a space of two decades within which the Meiningen Theatre could bring this style a final and unprecedented public success. Its very lateness contributed to its success, for the Meiningen Theatre was able to exploit the technical progress and the cultural–political changes of an advancing industrial society, to apply to the production of historical drama a style which had hitherto enjoyed its major successes in opera, ballet, and spectacle, media which did not often pretend to realism.

The very success of the enterprise, however, proved to be a factor which inhibited its flexibility and further development. In the 1880s the voices of younger critics, whose sympathies lay with the emergent naturalist movement, began to point to impressionist, and then to symbolist, painting as an appropriate inspiration for modern scenic design. However, the convictions, habits, and loyalties of the Duke of Meiningen tied him to the Brückners, the scene painters who had served him so well since his first productions, and who were just as much a product of the historicist ethos of the nineteenth century as was the Duke himself. The same factors, of course, lay behind the loyalty of Bayreuth, which continued to use the designs of Max Brückner until well into the twentieth century, and was, in consequence, very slow to respond to the revolutionary projects of Adolphe Appia.[42]

That Duke Georg II of Meiningen did not develop his ideas significantly beyond the position he had reached in 1874 should not be regarded as a failure. This, too, is a consequence of a characteristically realistic appreciation of his own talents, which were developed entirely within the context provided by the historicist culture of the nineteenth century; and it shows a reasonable understanding of just how much reform could be achieved by a theatre such as his, operating with limited resources, from a provincial base. Seen only in its immediate cultural–historical context, his achievement might look like no more than the late flowering of a tendency to which – with its excess, its bombast, and its nationalism – posterity has been understandably unsympathetic. Nevertheless the Meiningen style and the Meiningen methods contained many elements that were eminently susceptible to exploitation and development by precisely those artists who rejected many of the assumptions that had been self-evident in Meiningen, and who sought to change the conditions under which their ducal predecessor had worked.

3   Theatre: the realist tradition in Germany

In the present age, a theatre which sets out on its travels with all its bag and baggage in order to be seen and heard in strange cities, is an unusual phenomenon. One could almost say an outdated one. It is unanimously agreed that the rise of the dramatic arts in Germany is intimately connected with the establishment of permanent theatres.

Ludwig Speidel, Vienna, 1875

THE GERMAN THEATRE of the modern period has its roots in two traditions: that of the *Hoftheater*, the court theatres, under the direct control of the princes and scattered about the numerous states; and that of the *Schauspielergesellschaften*, travelling theatre companies, under the control of actor-managers.[1] In the context of court society the former had a ceremonial function which was best served by a repertoire of opera and the formal and stylised drama of French classicism and its imitators. The hierarchy of the court was reflected in the architecture and seating arrangements of the theatres, the distribution of places corresponding to social rank. Aside from this representative function, the court theatres were not public institutions; they enjoyed a monopoly position within their own area; they were administered by a court official appointed by the ruler; and they provided for the wishes of a limited and exclusive audience. Only from the middle of the eighteenth century onwards did they gradually come to be open to a paying public. Among the consequences of these special characteristics were a frequently changing repertoire, which meant no more than minimal rehearsal; freedom from competition; and, despite the engagement of professional actors, an amateur administration and artistic direction. This was the situation in Meiningen until the end of the 1860s, when Georg II himself assumed active control of his theatre. Even during the later part of the nineteenth century, at the time of the Meiningen tours, the Berlin royal theatres still bore the imprint of this tradition; the general director, Botho von Hülsen, a Prussian officer, was subjected to fierce criticism from younger men of the theatre, self-consciously cultivating a new professionalism, and at this time, of course, in direct competition with the increasingly anachronistic court theatres.[2]

The *Schauspielergesellschaften* were also subject to state control of an only slightly less direct kind, for they had to apply to the relevant ruler for a *Privileg*, that is to say a licence to give theatrical performances within a particular area. The touring companies did not, however, compete with the court theatres, for they performed before a quite different section of the public, offering popular entertainment to the lower strata of society. Made up of professional actors, the *Schauspielergesellschaften* operated on strictly commercial lines, although they were far less well equipped and their members enjoyed a far lower social status than the artists employed by the courts. Ironically, it is the actors from the touring companies, Caroline Neuber, Schönemann, Koch, Ackermann, Seyler, whose names are remembered for their contribution to the development of theatrical art in Germany, even on the higher, literary level.

Towards the end of the eighteenth century a significant convergence took place between these hitherto parallel, but quite distinct, strands in the German theatre, as there developed a middle-class audience whose appetite for serious theatre was not met by either of the established institutions. From the 1760s onwards the actor-managers began either to settle in potential theatre centres, where some of them built their own playhouses, or they were absorbed into the court theatres. During the final part of the century the old itinerant companies died out completely.

6   View of the old theatre in Meiningen.

As far as the writing of drama and the development of the theatre to perform it are concerned, the situation in the earlier part of the nineteenth century was the opposite of that which prevailed in the period between 1860 and 1890. The years which saw the creation of a sizeable part of the canon of German dramatic literature: Schiller's late plays, the dramas of Kleist, and the works of Grillparzer, Büchner, and Hebbel, were not a favourable period for the institutional development of the theatre in Germany. Whereas it had been the wish to establish a national theatre, as a *public* institution, which had inspired many of the initiatives taken since 1770, it was the courts which reasserted themselves in the period of restoration after 1815. Stein's reform proposals of 1808 would have placed the theatre in Prussia under the aegis of the Ministry of Culture and Education, confirming the status it had begun to acquire in the eighteenth century as an opinion-forming institution in the public sphere; except for the royal theatres, however, which continued to be directly responsible to the court, the Prussian theatres remained subject to control by the police, the *Gewerbepolizei*, which restricted their growth according to the ruler's understanding of the country's need.

As a symptom of a widespread defensiveness before the emancipatory and national trends of the era of reform, the title of *Nationaltheater* fell out of favour, and was replaced by either *Hoftheater* (Court Theatre) or *Königliches Theater* (Theatre Royal); the *Herzoglich-Meiningensche Hoftheater* (1831) is a characteristic example. The absence of a capital city, serving as a national cultural centre, meant that there was no counterbalancing force to such separatist tendencies. Liberal writers and men of the theatre such as Gutzkow, Laube, and Prutz continued to work against the pre-eminence of the court theatres in the period before the revolution of 1848; and they were joined in their efforts by Richard Wagner, who submitted to the Dresden court a memorandum on the subject: *Entwurf zur Organisation eines deutschen Nationaltheaters für das Königreich Sachsen*; his proposals were not, however, implemented. More progress was made in Prussia, which saw the most important initiative to arise from the liberal revolutionary movement of the middle of the nineteenth century. A detailed set of proposals was worked out by Franz Kugler, designed to regulate the position of the theatre as a national cultural institution; and Kugler was successful in securing the interest of the Prussian minister, Ladenburg. A model for the rest of Germany would have been established by the proposed legislation of December 1850, but, too soon, the brief period of liberal hopes came to an abrupt and disappointing end; Ladenburg was replaced in the Manteuffel ministry and the reforms were shelved. Only after some sixty years of gradual evolution were the ideas behind them fully implemented.[3]

Prior to 1848 Berlin had only three theatres, and over the next two decades there was only very limited growth. However, this period did witness the establishment of several important theatres: the *Friedrich-Wilhelmstädtisches*

Theater, for the opening of which, in 1848, F. W. Deichmann was granted the first concession to be given since 1842, after he had given the assurance that it was not his intention to compete with the royal theatres (in fact his theatre came to concentrate on operetta and musical comedy); the *Wallner-theater* (1858), which specialised in popular comic forms; and the large *Victoria-Theater*, with a capacity of 1,432, which opened in the Münzstraße, in 1860, and was to provide the stage for the Berlin production of the first three parts of *The Ring* in 1880.[4]

An important change took place in 1869 with the passing of trade laws which introduced the principle of 'allgemeine Gewerbefreiheit' (the general freedom to practise trade); paragraph 32 of the new legislation referred expressly to the theatre, so that establishments could from now on be opened with almost total freedom; when the south-German states were incorporated into the *Reich* in 1871 the legislation extended further. Its effect was to break the monopoly of the court theatres and put an end to most (but not all) of the advantages they enjoyed.[5] This brought Germany to the position that had been established in England by the Theatre Regulation Act of 1843, when the patents of Charles II, which had limited the legitimate spoken drama to the theatres of Covent Garden and Drury Lane, were revoked, and the way was cleared for the significant expansion in theatre building which took place in London in the second half of the nineteenth century.[6] At the same time the rapid growth of towns, most notably the capital city of Berlin, during Germany's delayed industrial revolution, meant that a new audience was coming into existence. In the speculative atmosphere of the post-war period these two factors gave rise to frenzied activity: the first year of 'allgemeine Gewerbefreiheit' saw the building of ninety new theatres; and the next fifteen years saw the total number of theatres in the *Reich* rise from some 200 to some 600.[7]

The situation was, therefore, a highly competitive one, both in the metropolis and on the margins of the Empire. Some rash attempts were made to exploit it and, as in the commercial world at large, there were a number of financial failures.[8] Theatres concentrating on the spoken drama could, however, be run at a profit. During his tenure of the *Königliches Schauspielhaus* von Hülsen never had a deficit; and during the years from 1880 to 1886 he had monthly profits of the order of 30 – 50,000 marks. Although he clearly derived a considerable proportion of this profit from popular plays by writers such as Lindau and Lubliner, he did nevertheless keep the standard classics in his repertoire, and with a performance of a classic drama he could clear between 900 and 1,900 marks.[9] It must have seemed that the theatre, as an institution, was flourishing, even if drama, as a literary form, does appear to have been at a rather low ebb. From the vantage point of a major theatre centre the benefits to be derived from any reversion to the practice of touring cannot have seemed at all self-evident; and the disadvantages of the practice

must have seemed proportionately greater the more the public demanded –
and the more the touring company depended on – effects of decoration and
production, rather than the distinctly more transportable talent of the individual actor; hence the irony with which Ludwig Speidel greeted the Meininger in Vienna.[10]

On the other hand, however, there were in existence at this time only a
limited number of theatres which had any tradition of classical production:
the private theatres were new, and the municipal theatres were financially
weak and in many cases unable to respond very rapidly either to the new
situation or to the emergent taste for detailed and decorative realism. In
contrast the Meiningen Theatre, forced by the scope and nature of the
Duke's ambitions to look for a larger audience than the local community
could provide, and after the careful work which had been undertaken since
1866, was in a very strong position to exploit the opportunity which had been
opened up in the German theatre in 1871. Far from being an anachronism,
the Meiningen theatre, by going out on tour, was assuming an advanced and
evangelical rôle in a theatrical tradition which had only begun to develop in
Germany in the latter part of the eighteenth century, when the itinerant
companies had settled in their own playhouses. It employed, refined, and

7   Georg II, sketch for Schiller, *Fiesko*, Act I, scene 4.

extended the techniques and practices of this theatrical tradition in addressing itself to the same problems as had exercised stage-designers and managers in those early days of theatrical realism.

The type of stage in almost universal use in the second half of the nineteenth century was the *Kulissenbühne*, with scenery painted on a backdrop, wings, and flies. As compared with the theatre of the renaissance, this baroque development introduced a greater sense of space, a greater illusion of depth, and a greater degree of dynamism to the stage. The renaissance style employed an architectural background, which reduced the available acting space, so that movement by the actors was restricted to the transverse direction; action was therefore confined to a relatively shallow space at the front of the stage and the possibility of dynamic expressiveness correspondingly reduced. This style was reintroduced in the classical sets of Schinkel in the earlier part of the century. It received articulate theoretical support from Ludwig Tieck: 'that depth, which spoils everything in our theatres and makes the set . . . unpainterly . . . ought to be abandoned . . . everything ought to be presented, as it were, in profile'; and it received practical support from Immermann, who experimented with Tieck's ideas in his Shakespearean productions in Düsseldorf in the 1830s.[11] With the baroque-style stage the use of perspective in the design and painting of backdrop and wings led to the opening up of the rear part of the stage, and permitted greater scenic variety; in particular it permitted the alternation of the action between scenes played downstage, sometimes in the shallow space in front of a dividing central curtain, and those played with this curtain open to reveal an inner room or a distant panorama. This particular technique had been anticipated (exceptionally) by Racine in the *tableau* scene of *Athalie*; it was also used by Goethe in his production of *Proserpina* (1814); but the dramatist who makes most consistent and spectacular use of the new possibilities is Schiller: for instance in several scenes in *Fiesko* and *Die Jungfrau von Orléans*, and in the overall structure of *Wilhelm Tell*, a play with a large number of scene changes.[12] It is no accident that these plays were among those most successfully produced by the Meiningen Theatre.

Certain fairly significant restrictions remained, however, and prevented the full exploitation of the stage space. In the early part of the period theatre lighting was not adequate; indeed, it was not until towards the end of the eighteenth century that techniques were sufficiently advanced for performances generally to be scheduled to begin at seven or eight in the evening.[13] In the course of the nineteenth century rapid progress was made with the introduction of gas lighting; without this new and brighter illumination the detail and splendour of the décor of the realist theatre would not have been conceivable.[14] At the same time the number and variety of special lighting effects which could be created, sometimes with the help of early developments in electric lighting, increased significantly. The pioneer of these techniques in Germany was the firm of Hugo Bähr in Dresden, whose work is credited in the Meiningen playbills. Theatres in Germany, however, did not begin to be equipped with full systems of electric lighting until towards the end of the Meiningen touring period. Thanks to the enterprise of its machinist, Karl Lautenschläger, the *Hof- und Nationaltheater* in Munich was the first to have a complete electrical installation.[15] Despite initial suspicions, the possibility of reducing the risk of fire increased the attractiveness of the new technique.

By illuminating, and so opening up, the deeper recesses of the stage, the improved lighting made the problem of perspective more evident. As we shall see, this is something which exercised the Duke of Meiningen very considerably, for it is at the centre of his deliberations on the use of stage space. However much care was exercised, the juxtaposition of actors and painted scenery in the rear part of the stage could easily break the illusion created by the use of perspective. If the action was not entirely confined to the front of the stage, as in the classicist theatre, it had to take place well forward from the backdrop; movement, therefore, continued to be constrained, to be lateral and lacking in depth. Stage-designers during the earlier part of the nineteenth century, accepting the restrictions of the contemporary theatre, had, by and large, been content to maintain the separation between actor and set, as figure and ground. This habit is reflected in the work of the Meiningen scene painters, the Brückners, who continued the practice of using light colours for the costumes of the actors, in order to make them stand out against their red-brown backgrounds. Evidence of this can be seen in the published illustrations of the Brückners' sets for Bayreuth, and it is confirmed by the report by a Meiningen actor, Aloys Prasch, of a performance of *Die Räuber* (The robbers) in Düsseldorf:

The famous painter Camphausen . . . moved uneasily in his seat and finally whispered to his neighbour, 'I don't know what it is, but there is some colour missing from this scene which would make it complete.' In a few minutes he said, 'I have it; there should be some white in the picture.' At that very moment the door opened and Hermann entered, dressed from head to foot in a white Croatian cloak.[16]

There is also evidence, however, that the Duke, like a number of his contemporaries, was anxious to overcome this dichotomy. Many of the sets produced for his productions do contain bright colours, and the use of back-lighting in landscape sets, such as those for *Wilhelm Tell* and a very late production, *A Midsummer Night's Dream*, has the effect of lightening the background and giving it added depth. Contrasting light and dark colours were, moreover, often used in costumes to create contrasts between characters rather than to make the actors stand out against the background. It was a similar consideration, the desire to bring some action and movement into the rear part of the stage, that prompted the Duke to use children dressed as adults in the production of *Wilhelm Tell*, although he found this experiment unsatisfactory, and did not persevere with it. Many of his sketches show evidence of the wish to make use of upstage and downstage movement, rather than restricting his performers to movement in a lateral direction; and this search for greater freedom in the use of stage space would seem to be confirmed by his enthusiastic response to the dancer, Lucille Grahn, whom he saw in London in 1846 (although it should be noted that what can be done in the stylised context of the ballet cannot be immediately taken over into the realistic theatre).[17] His preference for diagonal movement and obliquely constructed, asymmetrical sets is also characteristic of the aspiration of the nineteenth-century theatre to the integration of figure and ground, actor and set, exemplified in England in the productions of Charles Kean.[18]

A further problem arose from the shape of the auditorium in theatres built in the traditional style. The horseshoe shape, with tiers of balconies or boxes, meant that there was one single position in the theatre which enjoyed an exclusively privileged point of view; this would normally be that of the royal box in the centre and at the rear of the auditorium. All the other places were more or less disadvantaged as far as perspective, and so visual illusion, was concerned; while the spectators in the extremities of the theatre did not even have an uninterrupted view of the stage. The hierarchical ordering of the seating, which reflected and perpetuated existing social divisions, had not appeared at all problematic in the context of court society and in court theatres. It was given a new lease of life in Berlin by Langhans' rebuilding (after a fire) of Knobelsdorff's opera house in the 1840s, and elsewhere by Garnier's Paris *Opéra* (1874; designed 1860). But for those men of the theatre for whom absorption in the theatrical illusion was paramount, such designs were becoming more and more evidently anachronistic, and it was their concerns which found expression in the progressive theatre designs of the late nineteenth and early twentieth century. The most notable example was, of course, Richard Wagner's *Festspielhaus* at Bayreuth, where the wide arc of the amphitheatre-like auditorium is intended to permit all members of the audience an equal privilege in their view of the stage.

It is another indication of the transitional position of Georg II in the history of the theatre, that despite his commitment to the illusionist principle, he was not able to make this move. In 1908, when he had the opportunity to rebuild his theatre from scratch, and notwithstanding the fact that at least one modern, amphitheatre-style design was submitted to him, he chose to erect what was essentially a court theatre, in both name and conception. This theatre was planned with great care so as to permit to all an unrestricted view (and with additional care to ensure the closest possible proximity of the ducal box (a proscenium box) and the visitors' box to the stage), but with its horseshoe-shaped auditorium, its separate tiers with their own staircases, vestibules, cloakrooms, and exits, it remains an elegant compromise, like the

Deutsches Volkstheater designed by Fellner and Helmer in Vienna (1889), a court theatre only slightly adapted to the bourgeois age.[19]

The itinerant companies of the eighteenth century had, for obvious practical reasons, managed with a very limited amount of scenery and stage furniture, but the situation began to change fairly rapidly once the drama, like the already well-equipped opera, came to be housed in its own permanent buildings. The problems of perspective inherent in the theatre designs and the available stage space restricted the use of practicable units and free-standing stage furnishings or decorations, especially in open-air sets, where trees, doorways, or balconies towards the rear of the stage might suddenly be dwarfed by an approaching actor. For interiors, the box set, with three walls and a ceiling, which had been developed in France, was first used in Germany by Schröder in 1790; it was, of course, eminently suited to the intimate scenes of domestic tragedy, such as Diderot's *Le Père de famille*, or the plays of Lessing. It did, however, have significant disadvantages: it made scene changes much more difficult, and it seriously reduced the illumination of the stage by eliminating the wings as sources of light. It was not until half a century later that it came into more general use, particularly in the productions of Heinrich Laube at the *Burgtheater* in Vienna. Box sets with side walls, decorated ceilings, and (much admired) practicable doors were normally used for interiors in Meiningen decorations;[20] but painted backdrops, wings, and flies continue to be a principal resource in the German theatre until after the end of the Meiningen tours. These were, however, produced with increasing sophistication and 'correctness' (in terms of historicist criteria); and they were used with increasing subtlety and in increasing quantity. The surviving Meiningen decorations illustrate impressively the effects of depth and plasticity that could be produced with painted scenery, but none of the practicable units, with which the Duke sought to break up the stage area, has survived. Contemporary accounts suggest that the Meiningen sets were exceptional, certainly for Germany, and even in post-Kean London they received a fair share of praise.[21]

Georg II's scenery certainly represents a brilliantly intuitive response to the increasing public appetite for the fullest, most literal and concrete realisation of the situation of the drama, and it rapidly established itself as the standard by which other theatres were judged; thus Fontane observes with reference to a new production of Schiller's *Die Räuber* at the *Königliches Schauspielhaus*: 'Anybody who still has the strength and the desire to see the play has . . . become more demanding.'[22] Of course this created difficulties for other theatres, both large and small. In 1880, after the first visit of the Meininger in June and July, the director of the Municipal Theatre in Düsseldorf, Schirmer, appealed to his financial committee for additional funds so that he could equip the theatre with new decorations:

this seems all the more necessary now, after the visit of the Meininger with their splendid decorations. What a difficult task I shall have, after this visit, in the new season, hardly needs to be mentioned.[23]

It also made the Meiningen Theatre less than popular among its rivals, especially the *Königliches Schauspielhaus*, which suffered most from direct comparison. In 1876 von Hülsen, smarting under the taunt of dilettantism in the design and use of decorations, complained bitterly to Julius Rodenberg about the inaccuracy of the reports by Karl Frenzel, published in the *Deutsche Rundschau*. Not really getting satisfaction, for Frenzel had been carefully inexplicit in his criticisms, von Hülsen wrote again to Rodenberg with a (revealing) two-fold justification of the practices of his theatre, appealing firstly to the authority of Ludwig Tieck, as a champion of the view that decorations are subordinate rather than essential elements in production, and, secondly, drawing Rodenberg's attention to the difficulties which prevented a large theatre, with an extensive repertoire, from achieving the consistency of detail, accuracy, and harmony which was recognised as the hallmark of the Meiningen productions.[24]

Problems such as those encountered in Düsseldorf and Berlin had led, in the earlier part of the century, to the establishment in France of specialist suppliers, *ateliers*, which provided decorations, furnishings, and equipment to order or from stock. The centralised administrative structures of France and the concentration of cultural life in the capital had favoured such a development; it is no accident that it was during a visit to Paris in 1857 that Georg II discovered the firm of Granget et Cie, which was later to supply armour and weapons for some of his productions.[25] After 1870, when the situation in Germany began to develop in a similar way, the Parisian *ateliers* provided a direct model, although there was never the same degree of centralisation. Outside the metropolitan centres, Berlin and Vienna, the town of Coburg rapidly established itself as a major supplier of theatre decorations. As in neighbouring Meiningen, the reason lay in the combination of individual talent, enlightened patronage, and the favourable historical circumstances we have described.

The talent was that of the Brückner family, who had been employed as scene painters in Coburg since 1834, Max Brückner having joined his father in his studio in 1861. After studying at the Academy in Munich, the major centre of historicist painting in the 1850s, where his teacher had been the landscape painter, Albert Zimmermann, Max Brückner had worked with Carl Wilhelm Gropius in Berlin.[26] He had also travelled in Europe, visiting London in 1858, where he had had an opportunity to study the decorations used by Charles Kean. His familiarity with Kean's style was deepened to intimacy in 1867 when Ernst II of Saxe-Coburg commissioned Friedrich Haase to mount a production of *The Merchant of Venice* closely based on Kean's London production, and Max Brückner assumed responsibility for the decorations. Georg II was invited to the Coburg theatre by his cousin and was able to see – though perhaps not for the first time – the work of his subsequent collaborator, Max Brückner.[27] In 1872, together with his younger brother, Gotthold, Max Brückner founded an independent *atelier* in Coburg. His work for the theatre required a fairly wide range and considerable versatility. In his paintings and earlier sketch-books architectural subjects are represented but his real love was clearly for mountain landscapes with rocks and trees; his brother's speciality was romantic landscape. By personal inclination and experience the brothers were ideally equipped to provide decorations for dramas such as *Wilhelm Tell, Die Räuber, Die Hermannsschlacht, The Winter's Tale, The Pretenders* and *A Midsummer Night's Dream*. The easel paintings of Max Brückner, which he continued to produce, betray the influence of his work for the theatre in the choice of subject, the dramatic lighting, and the stark contrasts, but his independent work differs from that of Georg II in that the overpowering Brückner landscape invariably dwarfs the human figure.

The administration of the business and the artistic direction seem to have been largely in the hands of Max Brückner, and it is to him that the correspondence from Meiningen is normally addressed. Within a very short time after its foundation the firm of *Gebrüder Brückner* of Coburg had received the two major commissions of the latter part of the nineteenth century: the decorations for the Meiningen tours, and the decorations for the Bayreuth Festival.

The superiority of the *ateliers* over the stage-designers and the scene painters employed by individual theatres lay in their specialisation: the accumulated technical skill and expertise which, with few exceptions (such as the team which worked for Ludwig II in Munich), could not readily be matched by a single institution. This was becoming exceedingly important with the growing demand for authenticity and historical accuracy. The durability of the decorations prepared by the Brückners for the Meiningen Theatre, which have survived unfavourable conditions of storage, is a tribute to the technical perfection of the work of this particular *atelier*; moreover, within the limits of the illusionist period style, the technique is matched by the artistic quality of the work, both as renditions in paint, on large expanses of canvas, of ideas conceived in the form of ink or pencil sketches, and as detailed and convincingly realistic stage sets.

The disadvantages of the *ateliers* lay also, of course, in their specialisation. It would be exaggerated to talk of mass-production, but, clearly, as an *atelier* begins to develop a characteristic style, independently of the stage productions it is intended to serve, so it becomes more difficult for these productions to attain their own stylistic unity. An interpreter-director, seeking to express a personal and unified vision of a drama, would be likely to require a more individual style. As long as the public were expecting, and the stage-directors seeking to provide, a copy of reality that was correct according to widely accepted criteria of historical accuracy, then the position of the *ateliers* as suppliers remained secure. There was, in this respect, a high measure of agreement between the Brückner *atelier* and its major clients, Georg II and Richard Wagner; for both subscribed to the principle of authenticity, based, wherever possible, on real models. It is also clear that neither Wagner nor the Duke of Meiningen was the sort of man to assume the rôle of passive customer. In the exchanges with Max Brückner it is the Duke who is the dominant partner; although it is occasionally through Ludwig Chronegk that the most forthright criticisms of the work of the *atelier* were made.[28]

Costume, a more portable adjunct to performance, and a more personal possession, had been more important to the actors of the itinerant companies in the eighteenth century than decoration. In this respect, too, the French and English theatres were well ahead of the German theatres, although attempts had been made by Gottsched to introduce criteria of historical accuracy. A notable experiment was made in Berlin in 1774 by Heinrich Koch, with a production of Goethe's *Götz von Berlichingen* in authentic costume, based on designs by the engraver Johann Wilhelm Meil; to judge by the reports of Lessing and Nicolai, this production anticipated the effect to be achieved a hundred years later by the Meiningen Theatre on its first appearance in Berlin:

> *Götz von Berlichingen* has been performed in Berlin and has attracted large audiences; perhaps the clothes and equipment, which were quite new and entirely in the style of the period, had as much as anything to do with the response.[29]

Actor-managers, such as Eckhof and Schröder, applied slightly different criteria to the matter of costuming: the appropriateness of costume as an expression of character, and its suitability in relation to the social status and the situation of the *dramatis personae*; although these criteria are in no way incompatible with the demand for historical accuracy. Contemporary accounts suggest, however, that there was no significant progress until the nineteenth century. In Berlin Graf Brühl, *Intendant* at the royal theatres from 1815 to 1828, an early exponent of historical realism in costuming, attempted to introduce some degree of consistency and to assert a measure of directorial authority.[30] Although he encountered resistance from actors and actresses, who managed in practice to preserve an element of freedom of choice, Brühl was clearly an important forerunner of the Duke of Meiningen in this particular aspect of theatrical production. Its growing significance led to a widespread demand for more basic information, which was met in 1860 by the publication of an important reference work on the costumes, buildings, and equipment of antiquity, Hermann Weiß's *Kostümkunde: Handbuch der*

Geschichte der Tracht, des Baues und des Geräths der Völker des Alterthums. This is the work which the Crown Prince is reported to have sent to von Hülsen, a successor of Graf Brühl at the royal theatres, after seeing the first Berlin performances of the Meininger in 1874, although von Hülsen disputed the accuracy of this widely repeated anecdote.[31] It should, however, be noted that von Hülsen's own designer, Albert Kretschmer, was no ignoramus in this field, for he had himself published two books on costume in Germany and other countries: *Die Trachten der Völker* (Leipzig, 1864) and *Die deutschen Volkstrachten* (Berlin and Leipzig, 1870). The policy of the *Königliches Schauspielhaus* nevertheless remained less radical, and so less fashionable, than that of the Meiningen Theatre; as von Hülsen explained to the Kaiser:

> [Kretschmer] always understood how to capture the essential character of the costume of an epoch, for instance a particular century, without allowing himself to be unduly influenced by the rapidly changing manifestations of fashion; a touring company, such as the Meininger, can afford such extravagance, but not the *Königliches Schauspielhaus*.[32]

Contemporary accounts draw attention to a number of absurdities in the productions of von Hülsen's theatre: fashionable crinolines in classical and historical drama, enormous animal skins in *Die Hermannsschlacht*, high Viennese boots for the Amazons in *Penthesilea*, which suggests that the artistic directors at the *Königliches Schauspielhaus*, Julius Hein and Arthur Deetz, lacked the authority to impose consistency. Some progress seems to have been made in the 1880s, for in 1883 von Hülsen reprimanded Hellmuth-Bräm – who, having served several years with the Meininger, ought to have known better – for changing the details of his costume for *Hamlet* in a way that critics (rightly, observed von Hülsen) had described as senseless (*widersinnig*).[33] This new severity is symptomatic of a tendency, now coming to a climax, for the artistic director to assert his control over all aspects of dramatic production. Beginning with Eckhof in the eighteenth century, this had led to the formulation and codification of sets of rules governing the conduct of actors and actresses, and their obligations to the theatre which employed them.[34] Unlike Goethe's *Regeln für Schauspieler* (Rules for actors), such rules were not concerned with questions of interpretation and performing style, although they clearly had implications for this aspect of the actor's work. They covered such things as casting, attendance at rehearsal, participation in walk-on parts, and the memorisation of lines; and they were backed up by sanctions, consisting largely of fines, but including immediate dismissal for certain offences. It is difficult to tell how rigorously they were enforced, but it was certainly a slow process. In this respect the theatre in Meiningen was at an advantage, for it first began to establish a permanent company in the 1860s, and was very soon provided with a set of published rules, *Dienstregeln für die Mitglieder des Herzoglich-*

Meiningenschen Hoftheaters (Meiningen, 1868), which were revised and made slightly firmer in 1880. In Meiningen the rules were implemented strictly, on occasion very strictly.

The increasing subordination of the actor to the requirements of the production as a whole, as conceived by a director, led also to the phasing out of the old system of casting by character type. In this system the actor or actress was engaged to perform a particular category or categories of rôle, and was given the contractual right to such rôles in the company's productions. The composition of a company was determined by the need to cover all the basic categories in comedy and tragedy, and so in the eighteenth century a company would need to consist of about sixteen members. This was clearly a system which might work simultaneously in two ways, both reflecting drama already in repertory and influencing writers in their exploitation of the resources of the theatre. Even so important and original a writer as Lessing worked within such constraints, without thereby becoming a lesser dramatist;[35] but it is easy to see how this system could have been felt to be an obstacle to the development of dramatic literature and the art of acting.

The attack on conventions by the younger dramatists of the 1770s, the entry into the repertoire of the German theatre of Shakespeare's plays and, subsequently, the mature dramas of Schiller, which required a wider range and greater psychological subtlety in the art of acting, are reflected in the increase in the size of the average ensemble to about twenty-five to thirty by the beginning of the nineteenth century. The process continued so that in the 1880s the *Königliches Schauspielhaus* had a permanent ensemble of thirty-eight, although it was, in fact, rather on the small size for the time; from 1873 its actors were engaged simply as *Schauspieler*, without reference to character category in their contracts.[36]

The old system, nevertheless, proved fairly tenacious, and individual casting was far from universal even in the later part of the nineteenth century. The mentality created by years of operating within the constraints of the system could affect a relative newcomer, like the Duke of Meiningen, although he is credited with having made a more radical break than even a progressive forerunner like Dingelstedt.[37] Quite apart from this element of inertia, there were certain practical factors which conspired against all-too-rapid change, and which actually inhibited the established theatres more than newer ventures. At the time of the appearance of the Meiningen Theatre in Berlin, the *Königliches Schauspielhaus*, for instance, still had on its books a number of actors whose contracts dated from well before 1873, and who therefore still had contractual claims to a specific class of rôle. The more distinguished the actors, and the more important they were to the company, the longer the term of their contracts; Theodor Liedtke, a great favourite of the Berlin public, had a life-contract dating from 1853, and he was to remain an active performer at the *Königliches Schauspielhaus* until 1889. In a period

of increasing competitiveness this gave a further advantage to the newer
theatre companies; for the older performers wanted to hang on to the great
rôles of their youth, and this blocked the way for younger actors, who might
develop their own talents and revitalise the ensemble. After only a year at the
Königliches Schauspielhaus, the gifted young Paula Conrad wrote to von
Hülsen complaining of the limited opportunities she had been given, and
asking to be released from her contract:

> apart from my three initial rôles, the only artistically rewarding task I have had has
> been the part of Puck; all the other rôles have been of the second or third rank, and
> Your Excellence will understand that such inactivity must have a discouraging effect . . .
> In the rôles which I have generally been performing I do not feel that I can learn
> anything new, and instead of making progress I could slip back. I am therefore resolved
> to go on my travels.[38]

The same slow, irregular, but, over the period as a whole, consistent
progress is characteristic of most aspects of the emergent realistic style of
acting. The reforms and practices of the last quarter of the eighteenth
century, most particularly the contributions of Eckhof and Schröder, anticipate much of what was to be done in the following century by Immermann,
Laube, Eduard Devrient, and Dingelstedt. In certain respects the classicism
of Goethe during his years of practical work in the Weimar Theatre, with its
reversion to a formal and rhetorical style, obstructed this development; but
in many other respects his conception of the art of acting was consistent with
the general line of development, for respect for the literary text and careful
preparation of the performance had not been high priorities among the
Schauspielergesellschaften, nor, for that matter, in the court theatres, with
their frequent changes of repertoire. In fact rehearsal tended to be minimal,
and extemporisation was widely – and in the early part of the eighteenth
century probably skilfully – practised.[39] Gottsched's influence had done a
little to increase respect for the integrity of the printed text although probably at the expense of vitality in performance; and, as early as 1775, extemporisation was formally forbidden in Gotha, as, a century later, it was in the
Meiningen *Dienstregeln*.[40] From around the same time contracts began to
stipulate that actors must be present at rehearsals. Goethe, in keeping with
his literary orientation, made extensive use of the *Leseprobe* (reading rehearsal), although he was by no means alone in doing so. In the first instance
rehearsals in the theatre, with costumes and decorations, remained very
limited, although they became more extensive as more theatre buildings
became available; most rehearsal, however, was carried out without costumes and properties. In these circumstances, and so long as the individual
actor enjoyed a relatively high degree of independence vis-à-vis the artistic
director, the possibility of developing a genuinely integrated ensemble
scarcely existed; too often the relationship of actors and actresses to each
other was marked by rivalry and competitiveness, although Eckhof, Les-

sing, Dalberg, and Goethe all actively championed the ensemble idea and understood its implications for rehearsal. They were followed in the nineteenth century by most of the major directors, including Immermann, Devrient, and Laube. The slowness of progress can, however, be gauged by the practices of the *Königliches Schauspielhaus*, where the maximum number of rehearsals for a new production would be seven; and where Kleist's *Die Hermannsschlacht*, mounted to forestall the carefully rehearsed Meiningen production of 1875, opened only three days after its first rehearsal, and even the dress rehearsal was conducted without the full costume.[41]

During the years before the Meiningen tours, while these developments were taking place, the nascent ensemble principle led an uneasy parallel existence with the star system, which involved a visiting artist performing his choice rôles with a local company, after minimal rehearsal. It is therefore not a coincidence that the first Meiningen season in Berlin in 1874 was preceded directly by a series of guest performances by the great Italian virtuoso, Ernesto Rossi; just as in London in 1881 and Prague in 1888 the company was preceded by Sara Bernhardt. In April/May 1878, within the space of one week, the Berlin public was able to see three different, but characteristic, performances of Schiller's *Die Räuber*: a new production with the familiar actors of the *Königliches Schauspielhaus*; the touring production with which the Meiningen spring season opened; and a production with Cäsar Beck, from the Municipal Theatre of Strasburg, as a guest-star; 'to look ahead to next week', observed Fontane, 'is to peer into the Bohemian Forest'.[42]

While the contradictions between the guest appearance and the developing ensemble style may seem evident in retrospect, in mid-nineteenth-century Germany the two phenomena do not seem to have been felt to be mutually exclusive; nor did Georg II reject the star system totally and consistently. In the 1850s he had shared the admiration of many of his countrymen for the black American actor, Ira Aldridge, who was touring Germany and performing in English with German-speaking companies; Georg even persuaded his father to invite Aldridge to perform in Meiningen in 1858.[43] In early 1870, when he had already begun to assume an active rôle in the artistic direction of his own theatre, he was attempting to engage Klara Ziegler to play the part of Cleopatra in Meiningen; and when she proved unavailable he considered approaching the other major female star of the German-speaking theatre, Charlotte Wolter.[44] In May 1885, the month in which she was banned from performing in the German *Reich*, including French-speaking Metz and Strasburg, Georg went to see Sara Bernhardt in the spectacular production of Sardou's *Théodora* in Paris, where he followed her performance, and observed her appearance, with great attention.[45] In his own productions the appointment of *Ehrenmitglieder* (honorary members) to the company for a number of major rôles was not so far removed from the practice of guest appearances; and Ludwig Barnay, fêted in London as 'the

German Garrick', clearly used his appearances with the Meininger in much the same way as the normal guest appearance. In the early tours, attempts were made to mitigate any disruptive effects by inviting Barnay to rehearsals in Meiningen; but Emerich Robert does not appear to have been to Meiningen for rehearsal before joining the company in Berlin for the early-summer tour of 1878.[46] It was not until the 1890s that any real advance was made in Germany in reconciling stars and ensemble.

The principal distinction between the older style of acting and the style being advocated by the champions of ensemble, lay in the relationship to the audience.[47] In the former the actor was, or aspired to be, an independent agent, offering his own 'line of business', or a soloist, performing particular rôles of his own choice directly to the public, with no more than minimal mediation by a director, shaping the production in accordance with his vision of the dramatic work. This is reflected in the response of theatre critics, who clearly recognised, and often indicated in the titles of their reviews, that they were writing about a performance by Rossi or Ziegler, rather than by the company with whom the star was performing; in 1874 Lindau reported on the tour by Rossi as follows: 'Rossi is, without a shadow of doubt, one of the most important living tragic actors. The company which serves as a foil to him does not contribute much to our pleasure in the enjoyment of his art, but at least it does not detract from it.'[48] The directness of the relationship is evident in the manner of addressing the audience, *en face* rather than in profile, and in a declamatory or elevated, rather than a natural or conversational style of speech. This is the style that had been favoured by Goethe in Weimar, 'for the actor should always bear in mind that he is there for the sake of the public';[49] although it needs to be noted that Goethe's reasons derive from the idealising intention inherent in his classicism, rather than any concern for the intimacy of the relationship of the actor to 'his' public. It is further reflected in the practices of audiences which, recognising the directness with which they were being addressed, would applaud at the entrance of a favoured performer in mid act, or after a particularly effective speech; while the actor would respond by bowing in acknowledgment of the applause.

Matters such as these were still very much alive for the Duke of Meiningen, and they are dealt with in detail in the *Dienstregeln*: 'Applause which the public gives to an actor during the course of a scene . . . must not be acknowledged by bowing to the public. An actor whose entrance is greeted with applause may, however, acknowledge this by a gesture in the discreetest possible way' (§56; second edition, §60).

It is interesting to note how the practices of King Ludwig II of Bavaria only represent in an extreme form the aspirations of progressive elements in the theatre committed to a realistic style of production. The effect of his *Separatvorstellungen* was actually to remove the audience, save for the shadowy presence of the King himself, and so compel the actors to perform before an empty house without any opportunity of playing to the gallery or, indeed, of receiving any direct response at all to their performance. In an account which strikingly illustrates the confrontation of two conceptions of theatre, Charlotte Wolter described her unease at what was, for an actress such as her, a very strange situation indeed:

Originally a performance of Sardou's *Théodora* had been planned, but as I had not yet prepared this rôle [Brachvogel's] *Narziß* was chosen. The performance was scheduled for midnight. At half past eleven the actors assembled on the stage. There was total silence; the stage hands wore felt slippers. All that was to be seen through the peephole in the curtain was the illuminated proscenium; the auditorium was completely dark. At twelve o'clock precisely a bell rang: the King is leaving his palace and proceeds by a corridor, which remains in semi-darkness, to his spacious box, and immediately the curtain is raised. When the curtain was up no one dared to speak and I began to tremble with nervousness. How was I to perform before this dark and empty room? Finally I made my entrance. I, who am accustomed to playing before packed houses, found myself facing a void. Vainly I made every effort to discern through the darkness the merest outline of my sole spectator. There was nothing. There was none of that electrical contact which exists between public and artists. It was the first time I had found myself in such a strange situation, and it took great courage not to lose one's head. What kept me going was the thought that the invisible spectator really possessed an enormous artistic sensibility and that in the depths of his soul there resided a true passion for my art. I was both flattered and calmed by this thought. I knew that the King was not taking his eyes from me, that he was sitting in his box with complete concentration and attentiveness, and he was so completely absorbed that he even held his breath, so as not to betray his presence or disturb himself. All of this was new and strange to me. I seemed to be performing my rôle in a dream, and I believe that I never played in such an excited mood. What almost made me lose my nerve was the fact that at the end of the act the invisible King gave no sign of approval. However, one adapts so quickly to the most unaccustomed impressions that I felt grateful to him for his silence. The King's penchant for having plays performed exclusively for himself has provoked a great deal of mockery, but I must admit that I understand it completely. In this way the King keeps at a distance everything which might disturb the artist and his listener. In these circumstances there are no loudly spoken critical remarks, no rattling of seats, no rustling of fans; there is nothing but the dramatic work, its performers, and the solitary spectator, whom we transport so completely into the world of the illusion that he takes the fiction for truth. To be frank, I should not like always to perform in such circumstances; but I am glad to have undergone this experiment, for it has shown me my art from a new angle. At about four o'clock in the morning, when the curtain had fallen on the last act, we were ordered to remain motionless on the stage so as not to disturb the King. He usually remains in his box for some time to reflect on the performance, like someone who has difficulty in returning to reality.[50]

A decade and a half later Rudolf Rittner, some thirty-five years younger than Wolter, and one of the most reflective and intelligent of the new generation of naturalist actors, will attempt to incorporate the illusion that the actor is not performing before an audience into his acting style. Otto Brahm claimed to have engaged him entirely on the strength of an exit he had seen him make, and it was just such an exit that was at the centre of the controversy surrounding Brahm's production of Schiller's *Kabale und Liebe*, with Rittner as Ferdinand, at the *Deutsches Theater* in 1894. At the end of Act I the hero has a particularly strong curtain-line, in which he expresses his scorn for the corruption of the court and the machinations of his father, who is seeking to arrange his marriage with the discarded mistress of the ruling prince, an English émigrée, Lady Milford. The line combines the defiant expression of youthful revolt, which had been the central feature of Kainz's by now celebrated interpretation of the rôle, with a national assertiveness which might well have been expected to strengthen the immediacy of its impact in Wilhelmine Germany; but Rittner threw it away casually, almost as an aside, while he pulled on and buttoned his gloves as he prepared to leave the room and go out to do his job as an officer in the army.[51]

Such stage business, outside the author's text, in which the audience is apparently disregarded, is an essential part of the new style of acting as practised by such performers as Irving and Duse.[52] It is an expression of the *absorption* of the character in the action, and the actor in the rôle. In Rittner's case it was an expression of a consistent directorial policy adopted by Otto Brahm, and designed to eliminate *theatricality*, in the pejorative sense it had had since the eighteenth century, from the theatre.[53] There is an interesting contemporary parallel in the visual arts in the relationship of Hans von Marées to his patron, Conrad Fiedler. The latter's conception of the rôle of the patron was a modest one: he provided the painter with financial independence, without the need actually to sell pictures. Fiedler remained an essentially passive patron, and Marées even excluded him from his studio, so that he, the self-absorbed artist, could create his work without any direct relationship to, or pressure from, a public.[54]

As Michael Fried has shown, in his important book on eighteenth-century painting, the major theorist in the debate on absorption and theatricality is Diderot.[55] It is his simultaneous concern with both the visual and the performing arts which enables us to see more clearly the relationship between the development of painting and theatre. In his writings on art Diderot attacked the theatrical qualities of rococo painting, as exemplified in the work of Boucher, and, instead, championed a kind of painting which treats the beholder as if he were not there. The pre-eminent exponents of this latter type of painting were Chardin and Greuze, and their paintings of blind men, *L'Aveugle* and *L'Aveugle trompé*, epitomise this painting of absorption in a particularly radical way. At the same time, in his writings on theatre, Diderot (like his German follower, Lessing) was critical of the older style of acting, in which there is direct contact between actor and audience. He argued that the classical *tirade* should not be addressed to the spectator, who should be treated as if he did not exist; that, on the contrary, the attention of the actors should be focussed on one another, and that the footlights should constitute a barrier between stage and audience, who should imagine a fourth wall separating them. In contrast to the rhetorical and stylised acting of the French theatre, Diderot commended the practice of the Italian actors, for whom pantomime and other visual aspects of theatre were of primary importance, but who took little evident notice of the audience, and so whose pictures remained within their frame. It is a coincidence, but a very revealing one, that a virtually blind actor, Josef Weilenbeck, was able to extend his career and assume a number of leading rôles in the early tours of the Meiningen Theatre. He was, Grube observes, totally dependent on the discreet assistance of his fellow actors; their absorption in his actions therefore had to take precedence over any concern for their relationship to the audience.[56]

In Germany the pictorial conception of theatre was given a further boost by the acting of Talma, as described by Wilhelm von Humboldt.[57] It came to have considerable importance for the development of acting, even in Weimar, although here the emphasis was shifted towards the static or statuesque and away from the dynamism which is preserved in Diderot's idea of theatre as a succession of continuously changing *tableaux*.[58]

The dynamic emphasis is restored in the work of Büchner, whose own dramas would readily lend themselves to production as a succession of images. His profound awareness of the issues underlying the debate initiated by Diderot is clear from the discussion between Lenz and Kaufmann in his *Novelle, Lenz*;[59] but the lack of resonance enjoyed by Büchner's dramas before his rediscovery by the emergent naturalists towards the end of the nineteenth century is one symptom of a continued preference for the static classical style, at least on the level of the serious literary drama, where firm 'architectural' structures were favoured.[60] The combination of the visual and the dynamic continued to develop, but it tended to be confined to the melodrama and other popular forms, which were cultivated as a speciality by certain of the non-monopoly theatres, such as the *Wallnertheater*, whose admirers included Georg II of Meiningen.[61] The formal preferences of the serious theatre in the period after 1848 are associated with that political quietism, that resigned turning-away from revolutionary manifestations, which is simultaneously evident in the painting of Menzel. In 1851 the liberal literary historian, Hermann Hettner, wrote to Gottfried Keller on the subject of dramatic form:

basically what I am insisting on is nothing other than that on which all writers since the *Sturm-und-Drang* period and Romanticism have insisted: greater calm and simplicity, a reaction against the haste, the expansiveness, the restlessness of *Götz von Berlichingen*.[62]

The same manifestly conservative tendency is evident in an essay of 1879 in *Die Gartenlaube*, in which the reviewer, setting his general assessment of the achievement of the Meiningen Theatre in a historical context and coming to the contribution of Lessing to the development of German drama, regrets the 'excesses' which followed from his liberating influence:

> he did much and he achieved much, but in the German theatre naturalness finally turned into barbarism, the cult of Shakespeare into the *Sturm und Drang*, the liberation from rigid forms into formlessness and hostility to the laws of language and morality.[63]

In the theatre of the nineteenth century the preference for the static manifests itself in its most extreme form in the widespread use of the *tableau vivant*, and in the convention of holding the final scene of an act or a drama as a living picture, not infrequently modelled on a specific and easily identified painting.[64] As a parallel manifestation of the public enjoyment of such *tableaux*, living pictures were being performed in private houses and theatres throughout Europe; the practice is described in – and its popularity was increased by – Goethe's *Die Wahlverwandtschaften* (Elective affinities).[65]

In Germany the Franco-Prussian War and the establishment of the Second Empire in the aftermath of victory gave further nourishment to this long-standing interest in the *tableax vivant* and similar hybrid forms. It was, as we have noted, in the visual arts rather than in literature that the recent triumphs were most prominently celebrated, and it was thus that the visual aspect of theatre came into its own. Official war artists, who had accompanied the armies in the field, used their own experiences and eye-witness accounts to reconstruct the great moments of the war in paintings and in historical panoramas, which provided the models for numerous *tableaux vivants*; and they employed their skills in the processions and pageants which were organised to celebrate the homecoming of the victorious troops.[66] Such visual spectacle also found its way into the theatre proper in two particular forms of dramatic production: the very popular contemporary military drama, which frequently included a *tableau vivant*; and the *Festspiel*, an occasional and ceremonial form, adopted to commemorate directly the events of 1870–71;[67] the Meiningen theatre paid its tribute with a performance of Elsner's *Die Wacht am Rhein* in the 1870–71 season, and three performances of Hopfen's *Festspiel* in the Berlin tour of 1887. Official support for such theatrical productions was strong and explicit, especially on great national occasions, such as the centenary of Kaiser Wilhelm I (an occasion now best known from the satirical account of the unveiling of the monument in Heinrich Mann's *Der Untertan*), and the annual commemoration of the Battle of Sedan, which prompted the following appeal by the *Deutsche Bühnengenossenschaft* (German Theatre Association) in 1874:

> All theatre administrators should ensure that on 2 September this victory and its consequences be remembered in a worthy fashion! All directors should note that this glorious epoch is to be recalled by prologues, festival-plays, *tableaux vivants*, and the choice of dignified plays! All actors, especially all members of the Theatre Association, should endeavour to participate in this celebration with love and devotion.[68]

The context in which the tours of the Meiningen Theatre took place is one of mediation between picture and dramaturgy; it is a period of convergence between the visual and the dramatic arts. Slower to gather momentum in Germany than in France and England, it drew on very much the same sources as it did in these countries, and represented a response to the same changes in taste. It received additional impetus and reached its climax in the early years of the Second Empire, still early enough for it to exert – in its German manifestation – significant influence on the last stages of spectacular theatre in other European countries. It corresponded to the personal interests of Georg II of Meiningen, and was crucial to the success of his endeavours, for, unlike those more ascetic and very literary directors, Heinrich Laube, who preceded him, and Otto Brahm, who followed him, the Duke of Meiningen came to the theatre from a background in the visual arts. The process outlined above was not, however, a simple or straightforward one: that much is indicated by the receptiveness of the classical Goethe to ideas deriving from the realist, Diderot; it is further evident in the paradox, which Goethe himself demonstrates through the person of Luciane in *Die Wahlverwandtschaften*, that *absorption* can well be the most *theatrical* device of all, and the fact that the creation of an ensemble and the careful direction of supernumeraries might be just another way of focussing attention on a star performer.[69] This does not exhaust the possible inconsistencies in the theatrical reforms of the Duke of Meiningen, nor the discrepancies between his aspirations and their practical consequences; but if we are to understand his contribution to the development of German and European theatre at a vital transitional stage in its history, it is important not to lose sight of the underlying current beneath the contradictions.

4 Emergence and development of a touring company

The guests from Meiningen under the command of their Chief of Staff, Director Chronegk, have carried the day with a total and glorious victory.
Leipziger Theater- und Intelligenzblatt, 17 January 1878

T HE FATHER AND SON who, between them, ruled as dukes of Meiningen throughout almost the whole of the nineteenth century each presented the Duchy with a theatre, the only two purpose-built theatres the town of Meiningen has ever known. The first was built by Bernhard II in that same spirit of enlightened absolutism which was to be proclaimed by his son in the inscription carved above the portico of the new theatre which he erected to replace his father's, when the latter was burnt down in 1908: 'Georg II to his people, for their delight and edification'.

The old theatre had been opened on 17 December 1831, but it did not have a resident company until about thirty years later.[1] Before this troupes had been engaged on an annual basis to perform opera and drama during the winter season (from mid November to mid April), playing on three nights a week with a repertoire that took into account the needs and wishes of the court. During the reign of Duke Bernhard this meant the performance of one opera a week, and the avoidance of any plays which were regarded as offensive, such as Schiller's *Die Räuber*. Initially theatrical matters were administered directly by the court through the *Hofmarschallamt*, but in 1858 Duke Bernhard established the theatre as an independent unit with a budget of its own, although it continued to receive a generous subsidy. An *Intendant* (administrative director) was appointed by the court to manage the theatre, and he was assisted by an *Oberregisseur*, who was responsible for the artistic direction. The first *Intendant* was Carl, Freiherr von Stein, an equerry to the Duke.

This fairly common practice of appointing a court official, who had no experience of the theatre, appears to have worked out fairly well in this particular case. Von Stein took his responsibilities seriously and, in order to make good his deficiencies, he visited important theatres, including those run by Dingelstedt (Weimar) and Eduard Devrient (Karlsruhe).[2] Encouraged by the Crown Prince, and, from 1864, assisted by an able *Oberregisseur* in the person of Karl Grabowsky, he brought about a real improvement in

54

the standards and the repertoire of the theatre. Immediately after his accession Georg II was therefore able to pursue his own personal interest in the dramas of Shakespeare, and launch an artistically more ambitious and more serious policy than the Duchy of Meiningen had previously known. An article by Wilhelm Roßmann (tutor to Crown Prince Bernhard of Meiningen) appeared in the Yearbook of the German Shakespeare Society announcing these changes, and, for the first time, reviewing the productions of the Meiningen Theatre in a national journal. The plan to take the theatre company on tour was still some way from formulation, but Roßmann's article can be seen as the first pointer in that direction:

It is my privilege to inform you that with the accession of Duke Georg the Meiningen Court Theatre . . . has joined the ranks of the Shakespeare theatres. From now on it will apply very special care to the presentation of Shakespearean plays, select its actors and actresses with this in mind, and make it a matter of pride to compete with the foremost theatres in extending the German Shakespeare repertoire . . . while still Crown Prince, the reigning Duke acquired for the theatre a wardrobe which is probably among the finest and most correct in Germany.[3]

Georg had, in fact, prepared himself for the production of Shakespeare's plays by other means than assembling a wardrobe. As a student in Bonn he had been introduced to a number of the dramas. His correspondence with his mother indicates a fairly intense concentration on Shakespeare in the autumn and winter of 1844–45. He took part in discussions with Professor Johann Wilhelm Loebell on the relative authenticity of the two versions of *King John*, and he attended lectures by Loebell on this play and *Richard II* (two plays which were to figure in the Meiningen programme for that first season announced by Roßmann in 1866); a few weeks later he wrote of readings organised by Dahlmann (also a professor in Bonn) of *Romeo and Juliet* and *Julius Caesar*, and, a year later, *Coriolanus* (three further plays to which his attention was to return when he became more actively concerned with the theatre).[4]

Even more important were the journeys he made to London in 1846 and 1857. His numerous visits to the theatres there took him to opera, ballet, and the multifarious spectacles which were so prominent a feature of the Victorian cultural scene. He was also able to see the spectacular style applied to the work of Shakespeare in the 'Revivals' of Charles Kean at the Princess's Theatre, and wrote:

The day before yesterday we were . . . in the British theatre; in the evening we went to the Princess's where Shakespeare's *Richard II* is being performed. The scenery is of an extraordinary splendour, the costumes extremely authentic, but the acting leaves a great deal to be desired; the only exception is Kean, son of the famous Kean, who performs very well as Richard II.[5]

During his residence in Berlin he had seen Shakespearean productions by Samuel Phelps, whose Sadlers Wells company had visited the city in 1859.

This company had been brought over by Friedrich Wilhelm Deichmann who had organised several visits by complete ensembles to the *Friedrich-Wilhelmstädtisches Theater*, where, some years later, the tours of the Meininger were to begin.[6] In 1864 Georg had travelled to Weimar in order to see the complete cycle of Shakespeare's Histories (from *Richard II* to *Richard III*) which had been mounted in ambitious and spectacular productions by Dingelstedt to celebrate the tercentenary of Shakespeare's birth.

It is, however, important to note that there is no evidence of Georg's having seen, during these formative years, a significant or impressive production of any play – by Shakespeare or any other dramatist – which was to figure prominently in his own subsequent touring repertoire. Between 1869, when Georg himself took over the artistic direction of the theatre, and 1890, the end of the touring period, the only two of the Histories to be performed by his company were *Richard II* and *Richard III*: each play was performed only once, in Meiningen and not on tour. The Tragedies, which formed the basis of Phelps's programme for the Berlin visit, fared only a little better. *Macbeth* was given ten performances in the Meiningen tours, five each in Berlin and Breslau; while *King Lear*, *Othello*, and (especially) *Hamlet* were frequently performed during the winter season in Meiningen, but were never taken on tour.[7] The rather surprising absence of the Histories from the touring repertoire has both practical and aesthetic reasons, which will be discussed further. The absence of the Tragedies is less surprising; it almost certainly reflects the Duke's consciousness of a weakness in the composition of his company, and the recognition that he did not have, and could not expect to secure, the services of actors who could vie with the likes of Ernesto Rossi in the great tragic rôles.

The influence of Charles Kean's production of *The Merchant of Venice* on the productions of the Duke of Meiningen has been the subject of much discussion, and must not be overlooked.[8] Not only was this play to become, along with *Julius Caesar*, *The Winter's Tale*, and *Twelfth Night*, one of the Duke's four major Shakespearean productions; but Friedrich Haase's replica of the Kean version was seen by Georg in Coburg at an important moment in his development as a man of the theatre. It must, however, also be borne in mind that the Duke of Meiningen's own first production of this play was a failure. In Berlin in 1874 it was performed only twice, and only three times more in the following year: Georg conceded ruefully to Frenzel: 'With *The Merchant of Venice* I have, it seems, made myself more or less ridiculous.'[9]

The realism which the Duke displayed in his choice of repertoire had become immediately apparent in 1866 when he almost entirely abandoned the production of opera, the form traditionally preferred by the court theatres, in order to concentrate his limited resources on the drama and the concerts of the Meiningen Court Orchestra. Out of seventy productions in the season 1865–66 there were eighteen operas, one operetta, one ballet, and

two *Liederspiele* (dramas with songs); in 1866–67 there were sixty-two productions of (spoken) drama, and one *Liederspiel*.

As a further step in strengthening his theatre and raising its status as a
'Shakespeare theatre', Georg invited Friedrich von Bodenstedt to become
Intendant in place of von Stein. Bodenstedt, who had been a member of the
circle of writers assembled by King Maximilian II in Munich, enjoyed a
fairly high reputation as a poet and translator, but he lacked experience of the
theatre. It was as an authority on Shakespeare that he was appointed,
specifically as a champion of textual authenticity and an opponent of the then
current practice of heavy adaptation, of which the chief exponent was
Dingelstedt.

The latter, regretting the neglect of Shakespeare's plays by the German
theatres, had begun the process of adapting Shakespeare in the 1850s.
Responding to the conditions and conventions of the nineteenth-century
stage, and to his own acute sense (which, of course, was fully shared by Georg
II of Meiningen) of the contemporary need for external means to support the
theatrical illusion, he aimed at simplification and clarification, starting with
adaptations of *The Tempest* and *Macbeth* in Munich in 1855. He took even
greater liberties in Weimar in 1859 with *The Winter's Tale*, with music by
Flotow; and again with the Histories, rewriting extensively to produce a
continuous cycle for his Weimar production of 1864, repeated in Vienna in
1875.[10] Bodenstedt, on the other hand, had argued vigorously against any
cuts or alterations other than those which were dictated by practical
considerations.[11] There was, however, an important difference between the
Duke of Meiningen and his new *Intendant*. This lay not in the degree of their
belief in textual authenticity, but in the reasons for this belief. In the Duke's
case it was but one aspect of an all-embracing historicism, and so it did not
always have priority: if the dramatist were *historically wrong* he might have to
be corrected. For Bodenstedt, on the other hand, it reflected an essentially
literary orientation, and a corresponding lack of interest in visual and production values.

Bodenstedt continued with his other literary activities as poet and translator, but clearly committed himself fully to his new job and to the Duchy;
his son, incidentally, enlisted voluntarily in 1870 with 32nd Regiment and,
to his father's great pride, was awarded the Iron Cross for his exploits in the
Franco-Prussian War.[12] To begin with, the arrangement went fairly smoothly; the productions of 1867 were not only well received, but attention was
already being drawn to Meiningen as one of a number of provincial theatres
which could serve as an example to Botho von Hülsen and the *Königliches
Schauspielhaus* in Berlin:

It is necessary to go to Weimar, Meiningen or Karlsruhe to enjoy accomplished performances of the works of the great master who has inspired the revival of the German

national theatrical art . . . This advice is directed particularly at the theatre in the capital of North-German intellectual life.[13]

But the differences between the Duke and his *Intendant* soon became apparent, and Bodenstedt, a figure of some repute, who had come to Meiningen from a larger court and a more important cultural centre, was not the man to take criticism quietly. In answer to the Duke's remarks about his lack of practical sense and experience in theatrical and administrative matters, he complained, in effect, that he lacked the independence of a modern theatre director because the Duke interfered too much, and that he was *Intendant* in name only:

If, along with the title [of *Intendant*] I also had the corresponding powers, the theatre would look quite different; everything would then be organised according to firm principles rather than constantly changing influences, and the theatre, the box-office, and the public would all benefit.

For his part, the Duke complained of Bodenstedt's insolence, and insisted – with characteristic authority – on the traditional rights of the ruler and paymaster within the court-theatre system; only in this particular case the insistence derives at least as much from an informed interest in the theatre as from an interest in the maintenance of authority:

If you had . . . before accepting the post of *Intendant*, informed yourself about the extent of your powers, you would have perceived, before assuming your responsibilities, that during my lifetime you would hardly secure 'the most important prerogatives of an *Intendant*, choice of repertoire and engagement of personnel' . . . Since I provide a budget of 26,000 fl. for the theatre, it is right and proper that plays which do not appeal to me should not be presented, and that persons whose acting offends me should not perform before me.[14]

At the end of 1869 Bodenstedt ceased to function as *Intendant*, although he retained a formal connection with Meiningen. From this point on Georg II assumed personal responsibility for the productions of his theatre and for matters of general policy. Over the next twenty years the importance of the Meiningen Court Theatre, first as a national, then as an international, institution, was to grow rapidly and consistently.

Coming to the theatre from the visual arts, and himself lacking practical experience in matters of staging and the direction and training of actors, Georg was in need of advisers and assistants who would help him to implement his ideas and give expression to his firmly held views. Such collaborators were close at hand in the persons of two actors in the company, Ellen Franz and Ludwig Chronegk.

Ellen Franz, the daughter of an English mother and a German father, had studied music from an early age and had been accepted as a piano pupil by Hans von Bülow, little knowing that she would encounter him in very different circumstances in Meiningen in the 1880s.[15] On the advice of von Bülow's first wife, the redoubtable Cosima, she gave up music in order to go on stage. She began her career in Gotha and, after engagements at Oldenburg and Mannheim, she was invited by Bodenstedt to join the theatre in Meiningen in 1867. Almost immediately she established herself as one of the company's leading actresses, eliciting praise from Oechelhäuser and Frenzel in the earliest national reviews of Meiningen productions, and being mentioned by the Duke in the same breath as the two most prominent German actresses of the day, Klara Ziegler and Charlotte Wolter.[16] When Georg took over artistic direction of the theatre she began to play an increasingly active part in rehearsals, but her influence did not stop there. During the course of this collaboration she and the Duke developed such personal rapport and sympathy that Georg, whose second wife, Feodora, had died in February 1872, decided to marry her morganatically in March 1873, giving her the title of Freifrau (Baroness) von Heldburg. The marriage of the reigning Duke to an actress caused further ill-feeling between Georg and his father; it occasioned some disrespect in the Duchy; and it met with disapproval in Berlin.[17] The following years, however, saw the Baroness taking a varied and active part in the work of the theatre: in the choice of repertoire, in the editing of texts for performance, in extensive correspondence with the theatre's two literary advisers, the theatre critic, Karl Frenzel, and the Berlin professor, Karl Werder, and in correspondence with Chronegk while the company was on tour. She came to assume special responsibility for the preparation of actors, and for training in declamation, although this was, perhaps, the area in which she had the least success. She herself had been trained by Heinrich Marr, an actor of the first half of the century, who enjoyed a high reputation as an instructor of younger performers.[18] However, although Marr is reputed not to have favoured the rhetorical style associated with classical Weimar, it may be that even his style was becoming dated in a period of increased realism, for the declamation of the Meiningen actors is one of the most widely criticised aspects of the touring productions. The complaint of the drama critic of *The Saturday Review* is typical of many: 'Their acting was distinctly stagy and their elocution monotonous. It suggested a lesson mechanically repeated after a master'; it is echoed a year later by a German reviewer: 'Few of them understand how to speak naturally. There is too much evidence of mechanical schooling, bombastic, artificial, lifeless declamation, and empty, stilted pathos.'[19]

In view of the collective nature of the enterprise, it is difficult to be exactly certain of the extent and significance of the contribution of the Baroness. Her letters do not reveal any broad interpretative vision, but they do show a considerable understanding of practical aspects of theatre, and a perceptive eye for details of production. They also testify to a very strong personal commitment to her work with the company, and a deep concern for the public reception of its productions, occasionally manifest in discreet, but unmistakable, attempts to prompt or guide Frenzel in his published comments.[20] She was clearly quick to recognise the exceptional qualities of both Josef Kainz and Amanda Lindner when they came to Meiningen as rather raw talents; and in the case of the former she stood firmly by her initial judgment when the actor was savaged by certain of the Berlin critics. After rehearsals it was often she who wrote down the Duke's criticisms and instructions (*Inszenierungsvorschriften*) for transmission to Chronegk, but these are clearly the comments of the Duke himself; just as it was the Duke's own comments which went, usually directly, to Max Brückner.

The second assistant who worked alongside the Duke throughout the whole of the touring period, Ludwig Chronegk, was a Jewish actor who had joined the company in 1866 and had played a large number of secondary rôles, specialising in comedy.[21] After the withdrawal of Bodenstedt, Chronegk was appointed *Regisseur* (later *Intendant*, with the title of *Hofrat*), and he shared the task of direction with the Duke. In rehearsals it was Chronegk who was on stage, where he controlled the production and communicated the impressionistic instructions of the Duke in the language of the professional theatre. Over and above this task – itself demanding enough in view of the exacting rehearsal schedules in Meiningen – he carried a large administrative burden, which included negotiating with managers and agencies in Germany and abroad in order to set up the tours. The Duke and the Baroness did not accompany the theatre on its travels, and only rarely did they visit the house or even the city in which their troupe was playing; on tour, therefore, Chronegk had complete authority. From the account of Stanislavskij it is clear that he exercised this authority very sternly; the sternness was felt particularly by actresses who did not attend rehearsal or who declined to play walk-on parts.[22] Invariably Chronegk was backed up by the Duke. In one particular respect he showed himself to be an organiser of genius, recruiting and directing large numbers of extras, whose native language was not always German, to produce those crowd scenes on which the success of many of the productions depended.

To assess precisely the extent of Chronegk's contribution to the success of the Meiningen Theatre is even more difficult than assessing that of the Baroness. The major contribution is certainly that of the Duke, the visual artist among the three, and it derives – as historians of the theatre such as Simonson and Bablet have eloquently argued – from his interest in the relationship between the actors and the stage set, between the human figure and the space within which it moves;[23] but the rôle of Chronegk in eliciting, prompting, modifying, and implementing his ideas is not recorded, because the correspondence shows him only as the recipient of instructions, not as the initiator of discussion. In the accounts of actors who worked with the company he figures – one senses in a rather stylised fashion – as little more

than a faithful servant of his master; but it is difficult to believe that a man
who occupied such a potentially influential position for some twenty years, in
circumstances which demanded so much exercise of independent judgment
in matters so central to the ultimate character of the work in which he was
involved, did not leave a very deep personal imprint on the whole enterprise.
Chronegk already held an important position in the Meiningen Theatre
when the proposal to go on tour was first formulated, and the Meininger
never toured without him. When the years of touring took their toll on him,
as they did on Hans von Bülow, and after he had collapsed, for a second time
in mid tour, in Odessa in 1890, the Meiningen Court Theatre ceased to be a
touring company.[24] Chronegk, whose life's work was complete, died shortly
afterwards, at the age of fifty-four. His grave can be seen in the Jewish
cemetery in Meiningen.

Practical preparations by the nascent production team for the first tour by
the Meininger began, it can be seen in retrospect, in the winter season of
1869–70. Considering the radical nature of the change that was to take place
in the policy, methods, and ambitions of the company, and considering that
from late summer 1870 to Easter 1871 preparations were interrupted by a
major European war, in which the Duke played a full part, the activity in the
remaining part of these preparatory years must have been very concentrated
and purposeful. Without yet mentioning the possibility of taking his theatre
to Berlin, Georg wrote in December 1869 to a leading Berlin theatre critic,
Karl Frenzel of the liberal *National-Zeitung*, explaining that the public in
Meiningen was small (the population of the town at this time was around
8,000 and its theatre had a capacity of 721), and not really appreciative of the
merits of its theatre. Frenzel was invited to attend performances of *Julius
Caesar* and *The Taming of the Shrew* on 1 and 2 January 1870, and to publish
reviews, which would give some encouragement to his actors and some
reward for their efforts. The Duke was already well aware of the things which
he and his company could do well and which might bring about their success
in a wider forum; the two productions had been chosen, he explained to
Frenzel, because of their effectiveness in terms of ensemble, costume, and
mise-en-scène.[25]

   An immediate consequence of this particular emphasis was a significant
increase in the time spent and the effort expended in the rehearsal of those
plays which were to be the company's display-pieces. For a new production
there would be twenty to thirty rehearsals, lasting from five to six hours, with
costumes, decorations, and properties in use as far as possible from the
beginning; the *Dienstregeln* (§27) are strict about attendance and
punctuality.[26]

   A secondary consequence was a reduction in the size and range of the
repertoire, which was necessitated by the time spent during the winter

season in Meiningen on preparation of the major (touring) productions; and this, in turn, led to an erosion of the company's function as a court theatre serving a small duchy. In the season (November–March) 1866–67 the number of productions, including revivals, dropped from seventy to sixty-three, which is explained by the fact that the season got off to a late start after the turbulent events of September. In 1867–68, Bodenstedt's first season, the number of productions was back to seventy, and it increased to seventy-eight in the following year. A week's programme would normally consist of one serious drama and two or three lighter plays.[27] The lengthy repertoire is a consequence of the small size of the potential audience: no production would be presented more than twice in the course of a season, so that the seventy-eight productions of 1868–69 together yielded a total of only 114 performances. In 1869–70 the number of productions fell back to seventy, but, as a result of more repeats, the number of performances rose to 121. Among the plays repeated were *The Taming of the Shrew*, *Julius Caesar*, *Papst Sixtus V* (four times each), and *The Merchant of Venice* (three times), that is to say those plays which were being prepared for a wider public; other repeats were necessary in order to release rehearsal time. Despite some minor fluctuations, the number of productions per season continued to fall, whereas, once the tours began, the number of performances given by the company in the course of a year rose significantly. In 1873–74 there were sixty-five productions, of which seven were seen in Berlin, and a total of ninety-four performances; but this was, in effect, the last full season in Meiningen until after the end of the tours in the season 1890–91, when, in line with pre-touring practice, no play was seen more than three times.

From 1874 onwards the number of new productions and revivals per season never exceeded fifty-nine (1876–77); in the 1870s the number averaged fifty-four, and in the 1880s it fell to thirty-seven. From 1880 the annual touring programme began to include revivals which were performed only on tour, without having been presented during the immediately preceding winter season in Meiningen. This marks a clear separation of function between court theatre and commercial theatre. The increasing concentration on the latter function is further reflected in the theatre's accounts. At the beginning of the 1880s the budget assumes an income of 60–70,000 M. from each of the two annual tours, and only 23–24,000 M. from the sale of tickets in Meiningen.[28]

In 1870 the Duke also began to turn his attention to the playhouse itself, and he undertook substantial rebuilding. The plans were drawn up by the court architect, *Baurat* Hoppe, and were submitted to the Duke personally for approval; the correspondence shows a close and active involvement on his part.[29] It was principally the non-stage area which was extended on this occasion, reflecting, on a modest scale, that European tendency of which the greatest monument is Charles Garnier's Paris *Opéra*.[30] The construction of a new foyer, corridors, and a *bel-étage*, emphasises the ceremonial function of the theatre for the audience, who came to the theatres of the later nineteenth century in order to be seen as well as to see. The capacity of the auditorium was also increased by fifty-two seats, to a total of 773; but this was carried out selectively, in a way which probably reflects the desire to make this theatre a national institution rather more than it reflects the social composition of the population of Meiningen. The number of standing places (*Stehparterre*), which the Duke considered excessive, was reduced by four to sixty-six, while the pit (*Parterre*) was upgraded to rear stalls (*2es Parkett*), and increased by thirty-four seats; the other increase was to the dress-circle (*1er Rang*), by twenty-two seats to 108. The interior was refurbished in such a way as to express the integration of the Duchy and its theatre into the North German Confederation and, subsequently, the *Reich*; samples of illuminated decorations provided by the Berlin firms of Schaefer and Hanscher, and Schaeffer and Welcker consist very largely of victory chariots, Prussian eagles, Germanias, and suchlike patriotic symbols. These objects were, of course, still to be illuminated by gas.[31] Only in 1887, following the example of the Court Theatre in Munich, did the Duke of Meiningen begin correspondence with AEG, and Siemens and Halske about the possible installation of a permanent electric lighting system in his theatre; and it was not until around the turn of the century that Meiningen was equipped with such an installation.[32]

The alterations undertaken in 1870 must not, however, be considered solely in relation to the social and political function of the theatre as it became adapted to a new situation. The changes in production style which the Duke was introducing brought with them more scenery, more costumes, more equipment, and more personnel, and so required an extension to the backstage area. Dressing-rooms were built in the new extension for the principal actresses, the *Hofschauspielerinnen*, leaving the old rooms for subordinate actresses and the far more numerous extras; and three rooms were found below stage for 'spear-carriers' and other male extras, with their own access, so that all the performers were kept out of the foyer and corridors. This last point is particularly symptomatic, for the sight of costumed actors and actresses, rubbing shoulders with the public, would have seriously undermined that illusion of reality which the Meiningen productions were designed to create.

In the meantime preparations continued. Frenzel accepted the invitation and came to the performances on 1 and 2 January 1870, writing an encouraging report in the *National-Zeitung*, in which the production of *Julius Caesar* was commended as a model of authenticity to the major theatres, with their greater resources. In particular he drew attention to those aspects of the productions on which the Duke was counting for their success: ensemble, costume, and *mise-en-scène*, but he remarked on a certain unevenness in the quality of the acting. He was full of praise for the scenery which, on this occasion, had been produced partly by the Brückners and partly by Händel of Weimar, and he was dismissive of the notion that splendid decorations must necessarily distract from the literary text. Discreetly he referred to the importance of the contribution made by the Duke personally to the character and quality of the production; his comments demonstrate just how closely connected are the arts of painting and theatre in the mind of one representative observer: the authenticity of the latter is, it seems, guaranteed by its resemblance to the former.

The Taming of the Shrew transports us, by its decorations, the streets and rooms, the costumes of its figures, directly into the Italy of the early Renaissance. Several of these figures could almost have stepped out of paintings by the two Lippis or Pollaiuolo; it is evident that a painter's eye, taste, and expertise have all been at work here.[33]

The Duke wrote personally to Frenzel, thanking him for his review, as did both Ellen Franz and Ludwig Chronegk who, along with Josef Weilenbeck, were mentioned particularly favourably; he also invited him to the performances of *The Merchant of Venice* and Julius Minding's *Papst Sixtus V* in February.[34] For a second time Frenzel came to Meiningen, and again he wrote an encouraging review in the Berlin *National-Zeitung*. Although there was, as yet, no explicit reference to a visit by the company to the capital, the involvement of Frenzel, as an expert adviser on the standards and expectations of the public theatre, and as a friendly critic and spokesman, represents a further strengthening of the enterprise. In 1872 Frenzel and his wife were invited to spend part of August at Bad Liebenstein, not, the Duke explained, in connection with the theatre, but in order to take a break from his exhausting literary activities;[35] from then on he was a regular visitor to Meiningen and a regular correspondent of the Duke and his wife. In October 1872 he returned for a performance of the new production of *Twelfth Night*, which the Duke – now clearly thinking of a tour – considered good enough to be taken to Berlin.[36] In detailed letters dating from the same month Frenzel was consulted about aspects, including stage design, of a proposed production of *Macbeth*; a year later, with the first Berlin tour now firmly planned, discussion returned to *Julius Caesar*.

The outstanding problem was now casting. This reflects a weakness in the composition of the company which Frenzel had pointed out in his first review; the Duke himself will return to it in a long and, in this respect, rather despairing letter written shortly after the completion of the first tour:

Better actors! That is more easily said than done! Where can one find a romantic leading-lady (*erste Liebhaberin*), a romantic male lead (*erster Liebhaber*), a romantic hero (*Heldenliebhaber*)? All the good actors have firm engagements, and the training of young actors is a risky business, since it is impossible to know how a young actor will develop. I would pay a high salary for a romantic leading-lady – but so far there has not been the slightest chance of finding one. It is also difficult to find romantic male leads; I have two romantic heroes, both with good qualities alongside many bad ones . . . I would gladly get rid of both of them if I could find a man like Barnay.[37]

Throughout the touring period this will continue to be the main point on which criticism is focussed.

Of the three actors whom Frenzel had singled out for praise in 1870, Ellen Franz, now Freifrau von Heldburg, could no longer perform in public; Chronegk, never a leading actor and now fully occupied in stage-direction, could only assume a few minor rôles; only Weilenbeck was available for the 1873–74 season, and he was ageing and nearly blind. Nevertheless the Duke was still prepared to consider him seriously for the rôle of Mark Antony; indeed Weilenbeck played this rôle in the preparatory performance in Meiningen on 9 November 1873; although it is clear from a letter of 12 November that Georg was looking for a suitable alternative.[38] In the final casting arrangements for this season Weilenbeck did not play Antony, but he carried a considerable burden, taking on three major rôles, Cardinal Montalto in *Papst Sixtus V*, Argan in *Le Malade imaginaire*, and Shylock. He was widely praised, although some of the praise was clearly intended as a reflection on the quality of the rest of the acting:

among the exceptions [to the general mediocrity] are two men of whom one may once have been an excellent actor . . . He, Herr Weilenbeck, is without any doubt the most outstanding member of the whole company, but, blind and with a rather feeble voice, he can only be put on the stage with caution.[39]

This important weakness was not caused by the size of the company: in the seven plays performed in Berlin in 1874 speaking parts were taken by a total of forty-two different actors and actresses; in London in 1881 the touring company numbered over eighty.[40] Nor was it caused by rigid adherence to the *Fach* system, for although the Duke still thought – as his letter to Frenzel indicates – in terms of this system, he was quite prepared to break with it; indeed, he did so by casting Nesper (a *Heldenliebhaber*) as Julius Caesar in the first touring production. Moreover, according to their contracts the Meiningen actors and actresses were engaged (in line with general practice after 1873) as *Schauspieler* or *Schauspielerinnen*; the standard form used included the following paragraph (§3):

The management shall have the right to direct the artistic activity of the member of the Ducal Court Theatre entirely according to its judgment, but only within the art forms – not, however, within a particular category of rôle – for which the said member has been engaged.[41]

To judge by the delighted response of Kainz when he first joined the company in 1877, salaries were evidently not uncompetitive;[42] although, as is to be expected, they were substantially lower than those paid by the *Königliches Schauspielhaus*. There, a top actor, Theodor Döring, was receiving an annual salary of 15,000 M. in 1875; and the scale was approximately

9,000–13,000 M. for the leading actors, plus 24–30 M. per appearance; 6,000 M., plus 15–24 M., for those in the middle of the range, and this was the salary paid to Wilhelm Hellmuth-Bräm when he left Meiningen and joined the *Königliches Schauspielhaus* in 1879; and 3,000–4,800 M., plus 9–15 M., for a beginner.[43] In 1878 Josef Nesper, who must have been at the top of the Meiningen scale, was on an annual salary of 6,000 M.; Marie Berg was receiving 4,000 M., and Paul Richard, who also served as assistant *Regisseur*, 3,000 M; a newly engaged actor or actress would receive 100 M. per month, rising to 160 M. in the third probationary year. All members of the company received double payment while on tour, and Nesper received a special bonus of 100 M. for every performance after the twentieth, with a guaranteed minimum of 1,000 M. for each tour.

The attitude of Kainz illustrates one source of the problem with which the Duke had to reckon. Although pleased with his starting salary of 360 M. per month (720 M. plus travelling expenses while on tour), his status as a *Meiningenscher Hofschauspieler*, and his first rôles (Ferdinand in *Kabale und Liebe*, Lorenzo in *The Merchant of Venice*, Brackenburg in *Egmont*, Kosinsky in *Die Räuber*) it is quite clear from his letters to his parents that, for the self-confident and ambitious young Kainz, Meiningen represented no more than a step towards an engagement at the *Burgtheater*. Within five months of his appointment at Meiningen, and before he had played a significant part in any tour, Kainz was already in correspondence with Dingelstedt; and he viewed his first Berlin tour as a means of making his name known in Vienna.[44] It was difficult for the Duke to secure and to hold talented and ambitious actors, for whom the real laurels, and more substantial rewards, were to be won elsewhere. The difficulty was exacerbated by the rapid expansion of the theatre in the 1870s; it was definitely not a buyer's market.

To overcome the problem of filling certain important rôles Georg had previously invited prominent actors down for short visits to Meiningen: in 1870, for instance, Siegwart Friedmann and Ludwig Dessoir had come from Berlin to take part as Cassius and Brutus in *Julius Caesar*.[45] For the first tour the Duke had recourse to the same expedient, strengthening his company by the addition of Ludwig Barnay as an 'honorary member'. It is not clear exactly when he decided he needed Barnay, but it must have been at a fairly late stage, for in the previous autumn he had been considering Teller (whom he had cast as Cassius) as an alternative to Weilenbeck in the important rôle of Antony.[46] The Duke's letter informing Chronegk is dated 3 February 1874, and states that Barnay is coming to take part in five performances between 1 and 15 March. The list of plays includes *Bluthochzeit* and *Julius Caesar*, in which Barnay was to appear in Berlin; other possibilities mentioned were *Wilhelm Tell*, *The Taming of the Shrew*, *Macbeth*, and Laube's *Graf Essex* (The Earl of Essex).[47] Barnay, of whom the Duke thought highly, continued to appear regularly with the company, achieving, perhaps, his greatest success on his last tour, in London in 1881. In 1878 Emerich Robert took part in the spring tour as an honorary member. He was not reinvited, and the practice was not extended further; possibly because of the obvious difficulties of integrating the guest artist into the company; possibly also because – as a result of such changes as the extension of the ensemble principle in the theatres of Germany, and the opening of the *Deutsches Theater* in Berlin – there were fewer suitable actors free to enter into such arrangements.

On 16 April 1874, with preparations complete after a final performance of *Julius Caesar* on 9 April, the Duke of Meiningen wrote to Karl Frenzel in the following terms:

Yesterday was the end of the winter season in the theatre here, and the time is approaching for my company to be sent out to Berlin. Sometimes I am afflicted by a certain anxiety when I think of the many ill-disposed . . . elements which there may be among the Berlin public, particularly where this enterprise is concerned, but then I think of the encouragement which you so firmly expressed to allow my theatre to visit Berlin, and I remember that you are really the father of the enterprise, and I look forward to May with confidence.[48]

For the month of May he had leased the *Friedrich-Wilhelmstädtisches Theater* at a rental of 225 M. per evening. The theatre, which had been chosen partly because its stage area was similar in size to that of the theatre in Meiningen, had had an interesting past under the enterprising management of Deichmann.[49] Since 1872 it had been owned by a consortium of business-men, which included Albert Hoffmann, the proprietor of the satirical jour-nal, *Kladderatsch*; it was responding to the fiercely competitive situation of the early 1870s with a repertoire of operetta: Offenbach, Strauss, and Suppé.[50] It was to have a remarkable future, for this theatre was to become the birthplace and home of the early modern theatre in Germany. A sequence of debuts by the major modern ensembles began here on 1 May 1874, when the visitors from Meiningen opened with Shakespeare's *Julius Caesar*. After being sold by its consortium of owners to Adolf L'Arronge and after exten-sive rebuilding, it reopened on 29 September 1883, with a production of Schiller's *Kabale und Liebe*, and with aspirations to national status, as the *Deutsches Theater*. Starting in 1894, L'Arronge leased his theatre for two successive terms of five years to Otto Brahm, who set out to develop further those modern, realist intentions which had not come to fruition under L'Arronge, nailing his colours to the mast with an opening production of *Kabale und Liebe*. A decade later, sensing that the tide was turning away from Brahm's naturalism, L'Arronge declined to renew his lease. After a year's interval the theatre was taken over by Max Reinhardt, who opened in September 1905 with a play that had figured prominently in the Meiningen repertoire, Kleist's *Das Käthchen von Heilbronn*.[51] Since 1874 the *Deutsches*

Theater has been much extended, rebuilt, and restored. It still stands on the same site in the Schumannstraße, now in East Berlin; all that remains of the theatre in which the Meininger played is the cellar of the theatre restaurant and the F–W–T motif on the buffet doors.[52]

The opening production of this first tour created a division among the theatre critics of Berlin that was not to be repeated until the première of Gerhart Hauptmann's *Vor Sonnenaufgang* (Before sunrise) fifteen years later; it provoked a debate about principles that was to accompany the Meininger throughout the whole of the touring period, and was to be repeated in the theatre capitals of Europe, even in Paris, which the company did not visit. Karl Frenzel, who, fifteen years later, was to be one of the leading opponents of Hauptmann's naturalist drama, responded to the Duke's explicit appeal to his sense of paternity and became the most prominent apologist for the visiting company. He wrote both in the *National-Zeitung* and in the monthly journal, *Deutsche Rundschau*, when it began publication in the autumn of 1874. The great majority of the Berlin critics joined with Frenzel in assenting to the principles they recognised in the Meiningen productions; a representative example is provided by the critic of the *Berliner Bürger Zeitung* of 3 May:

it is something quite different, something quite new, it is the realisation of a *principle*, namely that art must be higher than the artist, the effect of the whole . . . higher than the admiration of the individual . . . and if there is anything that can bring salvation to the German theatre, then it is the path being trodden by the Court Theatre of Meiningen.

In the opposite camp, voicing strident criticism of the emphasis on external aspects of production and deficiencies in the art of acting, was Hans Hopfen, writing for a Viennese public in the *Neue Freie Presse* of 30 May:

in the crowd scenes we come to the *principle* of the Meiningen method of producing tragedies, which does not base its effects on the value and significance of the acting achievement, but employs all possible means to divert the attention of the listener from it . . . Here it is not the actor who counts, but the archaeologist, the historian, the scene painter, the tailor, the machinist, and the stage-manager. The stage has become a peepshow, an exhibition of rare objects, a museum, a waxworks. This is no longer a tragedy, but a spectacle.[53]

At first Hopfen was supported by Paul Lindau, editor of the weekly, *Die Gegenwart*, although within a fairly short while Lindau was able to overcome his reservations. Not only did he become a supporter of the Meiningen Theatre and its methods, but he developed a close personal relationship with the Duke, who mounted a special performance of one of his plays, an adaptation of José Eschegaray's *El gran Galeoto*, in December 1886. For a period of five years, beginning in 1894, he actually joined the theatre in Meiningen as *Intendant*. His place among the hostile critics was more than adequately filled by Oskar Blumenthal, who cultivated a particularly vitriolic style of reviewing in the *Berliner Tageblatt*, about which the Baroness became particularly angry in 1878.[54]

The first season was, however, enthusiastically supported by the public, and traffic problems were created in the Friedrichstraße. The costs were covered by 20 May, and the season was extended by two weeks to 16 June. The company played, without a break, on forty-seven consecutive evenings, giving fifty-one performances of the seven plays that had been prepared (there was one double-bill). The Duke, who did not come to Berlin, was delighted and relieved, and he proceeded at once to plan a second tour.

The success of the first tour had been based on a very shrewd appreciation of contemporary theatrical taste. The Duke of Meiningen knew the strengths and weaknesses of his company, and resolved to play to its strengths; but he also knew precisely which of these strengths would appeal most directly to the public of the time; and this and subsequent tours were organised accordingly. On the eve of the first tour the Duke, as we have seen, had been apprehensive about the first encounter with the Berlin public and critics; even so, he was confident that the audience would be carried away by the conclusion of the third act of *Julius Caesar*. It was for this kind of reason that this production had been chosen to break the ice; in the same letter to Frenzel he noted that all the other major productions of the tour contained scenes which could be relied upon to have the same exciting impact.

Apart from *Julius Caesar*, these other plays were: *Papst Sixtus V* by Julius Minding, *Twelfth Night*, *Bluthochzeit* by Albert Lindner, *Zwischen den Schlachten* (*Between the battles*) by Bjørnson, which was performed in a double-bill with Molière's *Le Malade imaginaire*, and *The Merchant of Venice*. Not all of these plays required or received the same detailed and lavish decorations and costumes as *Julius Caesar*, but all the productions transported the audience into a carefully realised, alien world. To take the least obvious example, comparing the production of *Tartuffe* by the *Königliches Schauspielhaus* with the Molière productions of the Meiningen Theatre, Fontane wrote:

> At the performance of the two above-mentioned plays [*Le Malade imaginaire* and *Les Femmes savantes*] by the Meininger I had the feeling that I was moving among people of another country and a different age, and yet also that I was not at all out of place but was chatting cosily to them without any sense of strangeness. And that is as it should be. We should sense the old-fashioned quality in these plays, but in such a way that it gives us pleasure, and does not disturb us.[55]

The historical accuracy of the productions, explicitly indicated in the publicity material and guaranteed by the highest academic authorities, was, moreover, fully recognised for its cultural and educational value. The critic of the *Berliner Bürger Zeitung* wrote:

> the characteristic feature of the tendency pursued by the Meiningen Theatre is that it corresponds to everything that should be required of aspirations in the spiritual and

8   Georg II, costume sketch for Shakespeare, *The Merchant of Venice*, Shylock, 1886.

cultural field: it can make out of the theatre an educational institution, where, as in our museums and art galleries, the best of suchlike treasures as we possess are displayed to the rising generation in a worthy fashion.[56]

This material realisation of the historical past is combined with a strong actualisation of any political implications in its content. This is something to which we shall have occasion to return in the discussion of *Julius Caesar*, but the combination is perhaps most evident in one of the two plays by contemporary authors, *Papst Sixtus V*. Here the Italian renaissance setting that was so popular in Germany in the 1870s was realised in decorations which afforded a view of the interior of the Sistine Chapel and its paintings, including Michelangelo's *Last Judgment* on the end wall; while the action of the drama is centred on a papal conclave in which Cardinal Montalto secures his election to the papacy by the subterfuge of feigning chronic illness.[57] *Bluthochzeit* is the work of a prominent apologist of the annexation of Alsace and Lorraine; like Conrad Ferdinand Meyer's *Das Amulett* (1873), it is set in France at the time of the massacre of St Bartholomew's Eve. In presenting Catholicism in an unfavourable light, and associating it with Latin cunning and treachery, both of these plays drew on the national stereotyping prompted by the recent war, and they reflect the mood brought about by the *Kulturkampf*, the campaign mounted by Bismarck against the Roman Catholic Church during the early post-war years.[58] The Chancellor showed his support by attending a performance by the Meiningen Theatre for the first time; *Bluthochzeit* was also seen by the Kaiser, the Crown Prince, and Field Marshal Moltke.[59]

None of these factors, nor the Duke of Meiningen's personal admiration of the work, nor even the care lavished on the production, with its splendid decorations and unusual stage-effects ('poisonous' candles), was sufficient to rescue Minding's weak play. After four performances in Berlin, it was dropped from the Meiningen repertoire. *Bluthochzeit* fared rather better, and the Duke persevered with it, taking it not just to a number of German cities, but further afield, to Catholic Vienna as well as to Calvinist Amsterdam, and to all four of the Russian cities which the company visited. Like *Julius Caesar*, it remained in the repertoire for the whole of the touring period, making Lindner the sixth most frequently performed author, after five of the major figures of European dramatic literature. After the tours were over the decorations were bought by the Municipal Theatre in Strasburg.[60]

Next to *Julius Caesar*, which was shown on twenty-two of the forty-seven evenings, the most successful production to be launched during the first tour was *Twelfth Night*. This play, which was best known to the German public in the heavily adapted version of J. L. Deinhardtstein used by the *Königliches Schauspielhaus* – as Frenzel provocatively remarked in his review – was given in the unadapted version which the Meiningen Theatre had been using since 1872.[61] The relative failure of the third Shakespearean play, *The Merchant of*

Venice, has already been noted. It is, however, worth recording that, with
Weilenbeck as Shylock, the production seems to have been quite free of
anti-Semitic touches. Indeed, a number of critics expressed regret at this
actor's restraint, the absence of any 'individual ugliness', 'demonic' outbursts of hatred, or vengefulness, noting, sometimes praising, the preservation of a certain patriarchal dignity, verging on heroism, rather than a
concentration on the baseness of the Jewish usurer, as conventionally
portrayed.[62]

The end of the first season in Berlin therefore saw the Meiningen company
with two proven productions of Shakespeare in its repertoire; a play on a
topical subject by a contemporary author, which seemed worth a further
trial; and a production of a comedy by Molière which, because of its brevity,
needed to be combined with another short or fragmentary piece in order to
fill up an evening. This was available in Bjørnson's *Between the battles* which,
although not a great success, was nevertheless kept in the repertoire, but not
frequently performed.

In planning his next tour the Duke's first aim was to consolidate the
success of 1874; 'we must prepare plays of which we can be certain that they
will attract the public in the same way as Caesar'.[63] Prompted, no doubt, by
his success with Shakespeare he considered two plays which share many of
the characteristics which he exploited successfully in the productions of
Julius Caesar and *Twelfth Night*: *Coriolanus* and *The Tempest*; but, in the
event, he proceeded with neither. The factors which prompted this decision
were largely practical ones: the numerous scene changes in *Coriolanus*, the
storm scenes in *The Tempest*, which was not only difficult to stage, but would
have necessitated the loss of fifty seats in the auditorium; there was also the
recurrent problem of casting: where, the Duke wondered, was he to find a
Caliban (or, for that matter, a Volumnia)?

What really needed adding to the repertoire, however, if the company was
to hold on to the sympathies of its public at this time of national assertiveness, was a selection of plays by the major German dramatists. The suggestions of the Baroness, Hebbel's *Maria Magdalena* and Lessing's *Miß Sara
Sampson*, indicate a willingness to extend the range from the historical
spectacle to the domestic interior, and so an intelligent awareness that the
bürgerliches Trauerspiel (domestic tragedy), with its intimate relationship
between actor and setting, might well respond to the Meiningen treatment.[64]
The Duke, concerned for the financial implications of his choice, rejected
Hebbel's play as too solemn for the Berlin public; *Miß Sara Sampson* did not
enter the touring repertoire until 1884.

The dramatists to whom he now turned were, firstly, Schiller, the most
obvious one; and, secondly, Kleist, who, in 1875, was a far from obvious
choice, unless it were to have been with the romantic drama, *Das Käthchen
von Heilbronn*.[65] Of Schiller's dramas he seriously considered *Don Karlos*,

but ruled it out because it would have required three first-rate actors, and two exceptional actresses, more than he had at his disposal; although, he observed somewhat unfeelingly, Weilenbeck could always play the (blind) Grand Inquisitor. Instead he chose the very much less obvious *Fiesko*, which had the added advantage of not having been performed very frequently in Berlin. [66] Its setting in renaissance Genoa, and the tumultuous combat of the final act were also very much in its favour and, like *Julius Caesar* the year before, twenty-two performances of it were given in Berlin in 1875. *Das Käthchen von Heilbronn*, which also had a lot to offer in terms of *mise-en-scène*, was held back until the following year; in 1875 the play by Kleist that was chosen was *Die Hermannsschlacht*, a passionate, but violent and brutal dramatisation of the struggle of Hermann (Arminius) against the Roman legions occupying Germany. The play had not hitherto enjoyed much popularity; the portrayal of the Germans as ruthless barbarians had not proved congenial in the earlier part of the century, and von Hülsen had not taken it into the repertoire of the *Königliches Schauspielhaus*. [67] The most energetic and forthright of Kleist's appeals for resistance to Napoleon Bonaparte, the play had acquired a new topicality in the anti-French climate of the 1870s. The widespread use in art and literature of parallels between Napoleon I and Napoleon III had contributed further to the renewed interest in Kleist's version of this act of national assertion. During these same post-war years the enormous monument, the *Hermannsdenkmal*, overlooking the Teutoburg Forest, the scene of the German victory over Varus and the Romans, on which Ernst von Bandel had been working almost single-handedly since 1814, suddenly received national support, and was completed and unveiled on 16 August 1875; the *Königliches Schauspielhaus* marked the occasion with a performance of *Die Hermannsschlacht*. [68] In these circumstances Kleist's drama was sure of an enthusiastic response from German patriots; moreover, it also gave the Duke the opportunity to demonstrate his adherence to the principle of textual authenticity. On this occasion, however, he compromised; the performance version was based on the adaptation by Rudolf Genée, although some of the scenes which he had omitted or altered, including some of the more brutal ones, were restored for the performances by the Meiningen Theatre. [69]

In choosing his programme the Duke was very conscious of the superior forces at the disposal of the *Königliches Schauspielhaus*. If he seems to have avoided plays such as *Minna von Barnhelm* or *Don Karlos*, which had figured prominently in von Hülsen's repertoire, it was not to avoid confrontation, but either for simple commercial reasons, or else to ensure that the battle was conducted on ground of his own choosing. To come to the capital with productions of classical drama could not but be a challenge to the leading theatrical institution of the *Reich*, which had, until quite recently, enjoyed a monopoly in the production of such plays. The implicit and explicit comparisons between the provincial visitors and the resident company would have been made even without the persistent sniping of Frenzel.

The public criticisms of the *Königliches Schauspielhaus* which followed the first Meiningen tour, and continued for some years after, concentrated on the lack of historical accuracy in points of detail, and the general poverty of the visual realisation in the productions: 'The one remarkable thing was the modest living conditions. Only on the stage of the Theatre Royal are people housed so wretchedly. The anti-Meiningen cult must not be carried too far', observed Fontane of a production mounted in 1878.[70] This seems to place the contrast between the two theatres firmly in the context of the *Prinzipienstreit*, the debate of principle about the relative importance of the art of the individual actor and the *mise-en-scène*, such as will be conducted in the exchanges between Antoine and Sarcey in the pages of *Le Temps* in July and August, 1888, and which will recur in the responses of Brahm and Stanislavskij to the productions of the Meiningen Theatre; but this is not how the Duke of Meiningen saw his differences with the *Königliches Schauspielhaus*. Indeed, as early as July 1874, before there had been time for any reaction, he recognised that von Hülsen was not going to stand firm on principle; to Frenzel he wrote:

I am afraid (although really I ought to wish it) that the Theatre Royal will do its utmost to pay as much attention to the hitherto neglected 'accessories' as I do, and that care and attention will also be paid to ensemble.[71]

The *Königliches Schauspielhaus*, in fact, went much further than Georg had anticipated in its efforts to beat off the challenge. From the 1874–75 season it pursued a vigorously competitive policy, using its advantages as a resident Berlin company to undermine the financial success of the tours. In May 1875, to coincide with the second visit of the Meiningen Theatre to the capital, the *Königliches Schauspielhaus* put on a series of classic dramas from its repertoire at reduced prices, concentrating on Shakespeare, and including *The Merchant of Venice* and *Twelfth Night*. It succeeded in filling the house in what was normally a bad month, although the impact on the financial success of the Meiningen tour was negligible.[72] In its choice of new productions the *Königliches Schauspielhaus* also began a policy of anticipating the Meiningen programme. In response to the success of their rivals' *Julius Caesar*, von Hülsen's theatre mounted a production of *Coriolanus*, and performed it at the end of March 1875; and, hearing of the inclusion of *Die Hermannsschlacht* in the spring programme, the *Königliches Schauspielhaus* hastily prepared a production of its own. In 1878 Fontane observed of this practice:

The visit of the Meininger, which opens on Wednesday with *Die Räuber*, was introduced yesterday, Saturday, by a *Schauspielhaus* production of *Die Räuber*. Our Theatre Royal thus once more assumed the duties of a colleague by drawing the attention of the public to the Meininger in this, now no longer unusual, fashion.[73]

The production of *Die Hermannsschlacht* which opened at the *Königliches Schauspielhaus* on 19 January 1875 is the subject of a long and interesting letter by the Freifrau von Heldburg to Karl Frenzel, dated 29 January, one or two points from which found their way into Frenzel's subsequent review of the production in the *Deutsche Rundschau* (No. 2, 1875). Her response to the rival production was significantly cooler than that of either Frenzel or Fontane, whose characteristic combination of sharpness and flippancy is, on this occasion, matched, if not surpassed, by the Baroness; but her comments are, of course, most interesting for what they tell us about the Meiningen approach to the production of this play.[74] She is not ungenerous in her acknowledgment of the performances of the individual actors, agreeing with Fontane that Berndal as Marbod was outstanding and that Luise Erhartt made an accomplished Thusnelda. Her real interest and her most detailed criticisms, however, focus on decoration, costumes, and stage-direction. Here she sees her husband's fears confirmed: the style is derivative of their own, but lacking in any real understanding of Meiningen principles, and so deficient in both the will and the understanding to implement them properly: 'es war . . . unverstanden gemeiningert'. From the historical–realist position she picks out a number of details which appear absurd because of their inconsistency: Thusnelda's rather ordinary hair, which scarcely seems to merit the fuss made about it in the dialogue; Hermann's vast cloak (also the object of Fontane's sarcasm): 'God knows how many skins had to be sewn together to make this great tent'; his carrying his lance around throughout the evening, in all situations; Germans with black hair, when the text constantly refers to their blond hair ('We are having sixty blond wigs made'); Hermann's rather meagre tent: 'Hermann is not on a journey to Marbod, but in his palace, in the Teutoburg, and so he will surely have had rather more furniture and equipment than two tree-trunks, a table, and a *lute*?' Where the material was good, the Baroness complains, it was not fully exploited because of ineffective stage-direction: the unimaginative use of the set meant that the excellent costumes of the Roman legionaries were inadequately displayed in the final march-past of the Roman army, a scene which was to elicit special praise in the Meiningen version.

The production at the *Königliches Schauspielhaus* was by no means unsuccessful, being given twenty-eight performances in the four years up to 1879; but this was exceeded by the Meiningen production, which ran for twelve evenings (alongside the successful *Fiesko*) in Berlin in 1875, and was presented 101 times in the course of the Meiningen touring period. The general opinion seems to have been that the provincial visitors carried the day, and that, with the second tour of the Meininger, the *Königliches Schauspielhaus* had suffered a further severe blow to its prestige as a representative national institution. A similar blow was to follow in the 1880s when Meiningen, so to speak, opened up the attack on a second front, and the musical arm of the royal theatres was subject to comparison with the Meiningen Court Orchestra.

This rivalry was to continue, and at times it became very bitter. One of the most notable episodes took place during the Berlin tour of 1878, when Therese Grunert, who had been summarily dismissed for refusing to appear as Time in *The Winter's Tale*, appealed to the theatre association, the *Deutscher Bühnenverein*, of which von Hülsen was president, and the judgment went against Meiningen.[75] Von Hülsen was publicly accused of prejudice and his judgment related to the unfavourable comparisons that had been made, most notably in an article in the *Berliner Tribüne* in June 1874, between his theatre and the Meiningen Theatre; but, even if we set such resentments aside, it is not entirely surprising that von Hülsen should have given judgment in favour of the individual rather than the company. It is true that in his own theatre things were changing, but the *Königliches Schauspielhaus* still owed its reputation and its success with the public to its individual actors and actresses, Frieb-Blumauer, Liedtke, Berndal, and Döring.[76] In contrast, the artistic director was not a figure of great significance. This was recognised and stated with great clarity by the Freifrau von Heldburg in her comments on the production of *Die Hermannsschlacht*: 'It is no good considering Hein in terms of the highest conceptions of *mise-en-scène* – he has no sense of the picturesque, and he is totally ignorant of what excitement means.'

Behind the rivalry lies a shift in cultural tastes and theatrical practices to which *both* theatres were responding, but with a different measure of commitment and skill. Meiningen was setting the pace, and was doing so consciously. Far from being the innocent victims of a vindictive establishment, the Duke and his collaborators clearly anticipated, relished, and, in part at least, provoked this ambiguous conflict. At this time of transition the theatre provided an excellent arena in which the residual separatism of a once (indeed, recently) independent and autonomous state could still find expression, paradoxically by exploiting the form of the modern commercial theatre, and so challenging the pre-eminence of a traditional and central representative institution.

The Meininger returned to Berlin for a third tour in the following year, and in total visited the German capital eight times in seventeen years. After this third successful visit, which saw the addition of *Das Käthchen von Heilbronn* and *Wilhelm Tell* to the repertoire, as well as Ibsen's *The Pretenders* (which was performed seven times, and not repeated elsewhere), the Meiningen Theatre had a firmly established position in the theatrical life of the metropolis, with a repertoire based on Shakespeare, Schiller, and Kleist. Following a break in 1877, the Duke and his company reclaimed their place in a tour which included a controversial production of *Prinz Friedrich von Homburg* and a production of *Die Räuber* (anticipated by the *Königliches Schau-spielhaus*) in rococo costume.[77] By now further competition was emerging from other theatres who had followed the Meininger and adopted the practice of touring as a troupe; while the Meiningen Theatre was playing in the *Friedrich-Wilhelmstädtisches Theater* the *Theater an der Wien* was playing in the *Wallnertheater*, whose own resident company was visiting Stettin.[78]

The visit to Berlin in 1882 saw the beginnings of a slightly more critical appraisal of the company, but without – in Germany at least – any renewal of the excited controversy of 1874. This was partly due to the emergence of a group of younger critics sympathetic to the aims of the naturalist movement, and sceptical about historical subjects and their treatment in a spectacularly decorative fashion; and this coincided with a certain loss of creative momentum while the company undertook extensive and important foreign tours with its earlier productions. Between 1878, the year of *Die Räuber*, *Prinz Friedrich von Homburg*, and *The Winter's Tale*, and 1884, the only significant new production (a fairly demanding one, it should be said) was Schiller's *Wallenstein* trilogy. There were visits to Berlin in both spring and autumn of 1882, but the latter visit involved a change of theatre. The *Friedrich-Wilhelmstädtisches Theater*, having just been acquired by L'Arronge, was no longer available for leasing, and the Meiningen company hired the *Victoria-Theater*, further to the east in the Münzstraße. This was a very much larger theatre, with almost 1,500 seats, and a stage which was evidently not so suited to the Meiningen crowd scenes, which depended for their effect less on sheer size and numbers than on breaking up and limiting the stage space, and filling it to overflowing. The *Victoria-Theater* was also the most expensive theatre leased by the company. For the first time a tour resulted in a financial loss, and the deficit had to be made up by 5,100 M. from the Duke's own resources.[79] So far as Berlin was concerned the decline continued in 1884, and the hopes of the younger critics were now focussed on L'Arronge's newly opened *Deutsches Theater*.[80] The *Deutsches Theater*, however, failed to fulfil its early promise, and the Meininger came bouncing back in 1887 with a production of Schiller's *Die Jungfrau von Orléans* which depended for its success equally on its spectacular *mise-en-scène* and on the performance of a new recruit to the company, the young Amanda Lindner, who brought to this familiar rôle a new reading which belied Fontane's lament of seven years earlier at the general absence of actresses with the maidenly qualities it required: 'Es gibt keine Jungfrauen mehr.'[81] The new production dominated the Berlin tour of 1887 in a way no previous production had done, running for a record fifty-five consecutive performances. In the remaining four years of touring, with no further visits to Berlin, it was performed 194 times, overhauling all the other established productions except for *Julius Caesar* (330 performances in seventeen years), *The Winter's Tale* (233 performances in thirteen years), and *Wilhelm Tell* (223 performances in fourteen years). Brahm generously conceded that he had written off the Meininger prematurely, and confirmed that even now, as the naturalist movement was beginning to penetrate the Berlin theatres (1887 was the year which saw the final breakthrough of Ibsen's social dramas), there was still room for the example and influence of the Meiningen Theatre:

When the company . . . last came to Berlin the *Deutsches Theater* was at the height of its success, whereas the visitors seemed to be on the decline; today, having come back in different circumstances, at a time when the situation in the Berlin theatres is moving towards a variety of changes, their effect on our theatrical life can only be fruitful.[82]

Apart from the rather special case of Ibsen's *Ghosts*, which had been performed before an invited audience in Meiningen on 21 December 1886, and was given one performance on tour in Dresden (17 December 1887) and one in Copenhagen (17 May 1889), no major new productions followed *Die Jungfrau von Orléans*; but the company was now armed with a new and fresh weapon for the final stage in its campaign, for two of the most important foreign tours were still to come.

In order fully to realise its status as a national institution after the success in Berlin in 1874 the Meiningen Theatre had to extend its reputation to the provinces and to the major cities of the German-speaking world. The response to this challenge was immediate and direct: the first city to be visited after Berlin was Vienna, where the company performed in the *Theater an der Wien* for a five-week season in the autumn of 1875. It arrived in the Austrian capital to expectations that had been aroused by its reception in its own capital city, but in other respects the situation was less favourable. On the one hand, the Viennese critics and public were traditionally disposed to concentrate their attention on specifically *acting* qualities; Kainz, who had mixed feelings about the skills of his colleagues, was apprehensive about the proposed Viennese tour of 1879: 'I am already looking forward to seeing how our Viennese tour turns out, if we should really have the nerve to perform there.'[83] On the other hand, Dingelstedt, who had the reputation of being a Meininger *avant la lettre*, had anticipated some of the most immediately attractive elements of the Meiningen method in the elaborate decorations of the productions he had been mounting at the *Burgtheater* since 1871.[84]

As in Berlin, the season opened with *Julius Caesar*, which was given ten performances in all; the audience filled the house and included prominent members of the Viennese theatre such as Dingelstedt himself (but not Laube), Charlotte Wolter, and Adolf Sonnenthal.[85] The public responded enthusiastically and the season was again a financial success. Critical debate was less heated than it had been in Berlin and the response was not, on the whole, unfriendly. There was, however, one important exception: Ludwig Speidel, the city's leading dramatic critic, wrote in the influential *Neue Freie Presse* contemptuously dismissing the visiting company for its cultivation of the external aspects of theatrical art, the inadequacy of its actors, and its disservice to the spoken word. Although this reflects the purism of the former *Burgtheater* director, Laube, it is by no means a characteristically Viennese view of theatre, nor is it representative of the city in which the painter Makart was enjoying considerable success; but it is coupled with an insistence on the pre-eminence of Vienna in theatrical matters, and a very deep dislike of the implications of the practice of touring. In the background one recognises the changing situation, and the confrontation of two contrasting models of theatre: the company rooted in its immediate environment, creating and exploiting an intimate relationship between its actors and its public; and the more anonymous company of the modern commercial theatre, presenting its productions rather than its actors to a changing cosmopolitan public. Speidel's voice is raised clearly in defence of the former:

We have always been of the opinion that a theatre . . . is inextricably bound to the soil on which it has grown, that its particularity can be appreciated only on that spot, where even relative weaknesses become strengths. One becomes accustomed to actors, indeed one has first to become accustomed to actors before one can overlook disturbing blemishes and bad habits and understand their true worth; there is many an actor who is, rightly, regarded as a hero in Berlin, and, equally rightly, is not in Vienna. Actors are like strong drinks: the more distinctive they are, the firmer are the geographical limitations to their popularity.[86]

From this point on, the net was spread ever more widely. The first stage, in the 1870s, brought in the theatres of the main German provincial cities, and those cities outside the *Reich* with a significant German-speaking population (1875 Budapest, 1878 Prague). From 1880 the tours were extended to non-German-speaking countries, beginning with a visit to Amsterdam;[87] there followed, in 1881, a visit to London which, at the international level, had the same significance in establishing the reputation of the company as the Berlin tour of 1874.

The task of taking the whole company, its costumes, sets, and equipment, across the Channel created all sorts of practical problems; to do so in order to present Shakespeare in German, in competition with Irving, and with memories of Charles Kean's productions not yet entirely faded, called for enormous efforts and very special preparations, including up-dating and re-painting the *Caesar* decorations. A certain amount of advance publicity was undertaken and a *Comitee von deutschen Kunstfreunden* was constituted among the German residents in London to support the venture.[88]

In court circles in London the activities of this latter body looked like being a source of embarrassment, and the equerry to the Prince of Wales, Holzmann, wrote warning the Duke that it would be counter-productive to allow the tour to develop into a nationalist demonstration.[89] This advice was taken, and the request from Karl Blind, at the time London correspondent of

Paul Lindau's *Die Gegenwart*, that Kleist's *Die Hermannsschlacht* be included in the programme, was rejected. The Prince of Wales was helpful to his cousin, the Duke of Meiningen, in other ways, agreeing to be named as official sponsor to the tour; using his influence with the press to secure publicity, in the form of a picture of Barnay as Mark Antony speaking over the body of Caesar in the *Illustrated London News,* and an article on the Meiningen Court Theatre in *The Times* of 27 May; and suggesting the addition to the repertoire of Wolff's *Preciosa*, with music by Weber, which was subsequently taken to thirteen other cities and ran up a total of fifty-four performances.

For more than a year in advance of the London tour the Duke had been employing the services of the theatrical agents, Bingel and Schumann of St Clement's Lane, and in January Chronegk had been to London to see the situation for himself. There was, however, one major problem that they were not able to resolve satisfactorily: the question of the theatre to be used. Rejecting The Globe, The Gaiety, and the Opéra comique because their stages were not suitable, Schumann narrowed the choice down to Drury Lane and the Lyceum. His sense that the former was too large a house for the German company to fill was shared by Holzmann, but Irving's tenure of the Lyceum left the Meininger with no alternative to the lease of Augustus Harris's theatre, and so Drury Lane was taken from 30 May to 23 July 1881.[90] The fears proved well-founded and, by 4 June, anxious letters were passing between Chronegk and Freifrau von Heldburg lamenting the poor audiences and the low takings.[91] Disappointed, the ducal couple abandoned their plan to come to London, wishing neither to appear in a half-empty theatre nor to add still further to the cost of the tour.

In terms of its artistic impact the London tour was, by contrast, an enormous success. Chronegk reported enthusiastically on the reception of the opening performance of *Julius Caesar*, describing it as unforgettable and without precedent.[92] John Hollingshead, of The Gaiety, wrote to Chronegk:

I have had forty years of experience of dramatic matters . . . I have seen most things, the Macready and Charles Kean Managements in London, the best performances in France, Berlin, Munich and the Ober-Ammergau play, and in point of stage effect I have seen nothing to equal the crowd in the Mark Antony scene over the dead body of Casear. It is a triumph of stage management . . . such a crowd, far from over-lapping the principal actor or actors, ought to inspire them with additional force and spirit.

Congratulations were received from numerous prominent public and theatrical figures, including the Prince of Wales and Henry Irving, who invited all the members of the company to his productions at the Lyceum. The company was invited to give performances in the Theatre Royal, Manchester, and Her Majesty's Theatre, and Mrs Bateman invited them to return in order to give the opening performances at the rebuilt Sadlers Wells Theatre in October. Ludwig Barnay became a much fêted figure in London society; and the 'Gentlemen of the Saxe-Meiningen Company' were elected to honorary membership of the Arts Club for the duration of their stay in London.

The performances in London included a professional matinée for the special benefit of theatre people, and it was attended by Irving, Toole, the Bancrofts, Ellen Terry and others. Irving, who also dined Chronegk at the Beefsteak Club, maintained contact with Meiningen, although, in the absence of precise comparative analyses of the relevant productions, it is difficult to be certain of the extent of any influence on his later work.[93] A self-proclaimed follower in Britain was Frank Benson, whose own Dramatic Company began touring in the 1880s, conducting its affairs, his programmes announced, 'on the Meiningen system'; while a decade and a half later, when the Meiningen tour was far from forgotten, Beerbohm Tree opened at Her Majesty's Theatre with a spectacular production of *Julius Caesar*.[94]

It will, however, be clear that the Victorian theatre, from which Georg II himself had learnt in the past, was well practised in spectacular *mise-en-scène* and not at all unfamiliar with the management of stage crowds. This meant that the methods of the Duke of Meiningen could be absorbed and his techniques adopted without any clash of principle; and this is what practical men of the theatre were eager to do. Hollingshead, for instance, wrote to Chronegk requesting tickets and specifying: 'somewhere where the *crowd* can be seen'. It was probably out of deference to this interest that the London tour included one performance consisting of three single acts, in each case the third act, of *Julius Caesar*, *The Winter's Tale*, and *Wilhelm Tell*. Among the critics there was another lively debate in which the arguments that had taken place in Berlin and Vienna were repeated, but without the same forensic edge. There is an abundance of generous praise, offset by some fairly sharp criticism; the argument is, on the whole, more about precedence and quality: the English critics of the Meiningen Theatre were inclined to argue that it had nothing new to offer; that its style was English in origin, and was more convincingly implemented by London theatres and British actors.[95]

The other three major foreign tours took the Meininger to Moscow in 1885 and 1890, and to Brussels in 1888. These late tours to cities that were culturally more remote than most of those previously visited, did see a more explicit renewal of the debate about principles. In Moscow it was Ostrovskij, about to be appointed director of the Imperial Theatre, who insisted on the pre-eminent importance of the art of acting rather than *mise-en-scène*; in Brussels it was Francisque Sarcey (a veteran of the siege of Paris and the Commune), writing from Paris, who criticised the shift of emphasis from the individual actor and the spoken word to the crowd and the production. In both cities the company also found its champions: in Brussels the Meininger were welcomed by the circle around Edmond Picard and the periodical *L'Art moderne*, which had also championed the work of Richard Wagner, while the prominent critic of *L'Indépendence belge*, Gustave Frédérix, gave a moderate and balanced account of their achievements.[96] In Moscow Ostrovskij's dismissive and often scornful comments were made against a background of almost universal praise for the care and accuracy of the historical detail and the *mise-en-scène*; the much more positive response of two other contemporary dramatists, Lenskij and Kramskoi, who shared the general reservations about the quality of the acting, are probably more representative.[97] More importantly, however, in both cities the Meiningen productions were closely scrutinised by practical men of the theatre, who had come with the express purpose of learning from the Duke's company, in order themselves to initiate major reforms in the theatre of their own countries.

In Brussels the company played in the *Théâtre Royal de la Monnaie* from 2 June to 2 July 1888. As in London, the visit received support from the court, in the form of a small subsidy; receipts amounted to 46,746 francs.[98] The programme was the strongest and most classical that it was possible for the company to mount; it consisted of the four most successful productions of Shakespeare, and the four most successful productions of Schiller's late dramas. It had also been planned to include *Les Femmes savantes* and *Le Malade imaginaire*, but, in the event, neither was performed.

The choice of programme almost certainly reflects the awareness that this was the nearest that the Meiningen Theatre was ever to come to Paris, and that it would be subject to close and critical scrutiny from the French capital. And indeed Paul Porel, Director of the *Théâtre de l'Odéon*, Jules Claretie, Director-General of the *Comédie française*, and André Antoine, travelled to see for themselves the productions of the renowned company. Sarcey, like Laube in Vienna, stayed at home. The first to report was Claretie, in a long article in the weekly, *Le Temps* of 13 July, which is largely critical of what he regarded as an excessive concentration on externals and subordinate aspects of production, at the expense of the dramatic presentation of individual human passion. Running through the whole of Claretie's article, and not always beneath the surface, is an anxiety that extends beyond his concern as a professional man of the theatre. Like the slightly older Sarcey, Claretie belonged to the generation of Frenchmen who had suffered the trauma of the defeat of 1870–71, and who, in the following decades, expressed their revulsion against the triumph of the 'cold method' which they saw as characteristic of the modern German mentality, and which had been most fully exemplified in the strategy of Moltke.[99] The irony with which the drama critic of *The Times* (27 May 1881) had casually observed of the Meininger that 'their training [is] worthy of the country of Bismarck and Moltke', becomes the major motif in Claretie's appreciation, beginning with its detached and patronising acknowledgment of the company's technical skill: 'It would have been interesting for us French to know what was done with our national comedy [*Les Femmes savantes* and *Le Malade imaginaire*] in the hands of these excellent technicians of *mise-en-scène*'; continuing with references to the supposedly military-style recruitment and training practised by the Duke; and reserving qualified praise only for those features of style that could be seen as the product of methodical direction and Prussian discipline.

The much younger Antoine had gone to Brussels in a quite different spirit. Having founded the *Théâtre Libre* in the preceding year, his ambitions were growing. For the 1888 season he was planning productions of the Goncourts' *La Patrie en danger* (The fatherland in danger), Hennique's *La Mort du duc d'Enghien* (The death of the Duke of Enghien), and Ibsen's *Ghosts*; in order to prepare himself for these productions he spent the period from 24 June to 1 July observing the last performances of the Meiningen season in Brussels.[100] When, in the *feuilleton* of *Le Temps* (16 July), Sarcey gave his support to the criticisms of Claretie, Antoine responded with what was to become an important statement of the principles of naturalistic production, and one of the major documents of the modern theatre.[101] His letter to Sarcey is by no means uncritical of the Meiningen company; for instance he condemns the crudeness of the colours, the excessive use of practicable units, the taste of the costumes when they were not directly based on real models, the clumsy deployment of lighting effects, the mediocrity of the acting; however, he clearly recognised in the productions a consistent unity of style, and the illustrations he gives identify this as a style in which the figure is integrated in the ground, the actor absorbed in the action:

Another very characteristic detail is the formal prohibition imposed on the actors and extras against stepping beyond the frame of the stage proper. No one ventures onto the apron . . . and in the course of a dozen evenings I have not seen a single one of them advance his foot to within two metres of the prompter. It is also forbidden to look out into the auditorium, which, incidentally, is darkened. Almost all the principal scenes are played upstage, with the extras turning their backs and observing the actors who are occupied at the rear of the stage.

Taking issue with Claretie, he points out that in all theatres where plays are repeatedly performed, effects are necessarily achieved by means that can be described as mechanical; eschewing stereotyped national comparisons, he makes a contrast between the inefficiency and casualness of the production methods he had encountered in the French theatre, and a *mise-en-scène* in which all the available resources are exploited to produce a unified global effect.

There were Russian tours in both 1885 and 1890, and the company performed in Moscow on both occasions. In 1885 *Julius Caesar* was seen by Vladimir Nemirovic-Dancenko, who published a vigorous attack on the production for its idealisation of the main characters; but, like Beerbohm Tree in London, he chose this same play as the object of an important production of his own. In 1903 he brought it into the repertoire of the Moscow Arts Theatre in a production which shared many of the same concerns, both as to historical detail and the use of stage space, as were evident in the Meiningen version.[102] His production was, moreover, evidently guilty of the same fault as the Meiningen production in relying on effects of *mise-en-scène* to compensate for the lack of outstanding actors. The Moscow Arts Theatre, too, found a resolute defender, significantly enough the choreographer, Diaghilev.[103]

The Meiningen productions in Moscow were also seen by the young Stanislavskij, who had the opportunity to observe the company in rehearsal, and subsequently to imitate the authoritarian methods and style of Chronegk. In a well-known chapter of his autobiography Stanislavskij illustrates and criticises the wide discrepancy between the quality of the acting and the *mise-en-scène*, but he vigorously defends the Meininger against the charge that they were concerned only with externals. In doing so, he attributes to the Meiningen leadership, and specifically to Ludwig Chronegk (whom he had seen at work), that directorial function which the Freifrau von Heldburg had denied to Julius Hein of the *Königliches Schauspielhaus*, insisting that 'the plans of the director were spiritually deep and wide', and that Chronegk, unlike his imitators, was much more than a 'mere producer': 'I valued that good which the Meiningen Players brought us', he concludes, 'their director's methods for showing the spiritual contents of the drama. For this they deserve great thanks. My gratitude to them is unbounded and will always live in my soul.'[104]

The tone of the essay by Claretie gives some indication why Paris was absent from the Meiningen itinerary. Although a great admirer of French culture and the French theatre, the Duke of Meiningen had clearly and understandably judged that the cultural and political relations between Germany and France during the two decades after the war were not such as to permit a French tour by his company. The explanation for the absence of other countries he might well have visited is more straightforward. After the artistic success of the London tour the Americans were particularly anxious to receive the Meiningen Theatre, and preparations were taken to a fairly advanced stage in 1886 and again in 1889. A contract was drawn up with Sisson of Brooklyn in 1886, but, despite assurances that he was ready to do so, Sisson did not deposit the necessary financial guarantee. A further contract was drawn up with Moritz Grau and A. Abbey for 120 performances between 1 January and 1 May 1889, fifty of them to be in New York. The programme was to consist entirely of plays by Shakespeare, Schiller, and Kleist (in fact the eleven most successful plays in the repertoire) and a guarantee of 150,000 M. was to be paid in advance; but, as in 1886, the arrangements were not finalised.[105]

Apart from France, the other European country surprisingly absent from the tours is Italy. This is doubly surprising because of the Duke's strong personal interest in Italian culture, evident in the high incidence of ancient and renaissance Italian subjects in his repertoire, and his regular visits both to the country at large, and to the Villa Carlotta. In fact, on two occasions preparations for an Italian tour were even further advanced than those for America. Arrangements were made in 1885 for a tour to take in Trieste, Venice, Rome, Naples, and Milan, and in May the theatre-agent, Rupert Mahortschitsch, was awaiting only confirmation from Meiningen. The Duke then sought advice from the local consulates about potential audiences, and the arrangements fell through because of continued delay. The process began again in November, and Italian synopses of the plays to be performed were actually prepared; but again caution prevailed, and final confirmation was not forthcoming. The nearest the Meininger came to Italy was in the autumn tour of 1885, which took in Graz and Trieste (not, at that time, a part of Italy).[106]

A brief visit by the Meiningen Theatre to a city in a similar position to that of Trieste, at the very limits of the German-speaking area, merits some consideration by way of a conclusion to this review of the tours, because it highlights the importance acquired by the Meininger as representatives of the *Reich*, and the significance of their activities as a form of cultural colonisation. At the extreme western edge of the *Reich* lay the annexed territories of Alsace and Lorraine, and, situated beyond the Vosges, in the more unambiguously French Lorraine, was the garrison of Metz. During the period after the Franco-Prussian War every effort was made to overcome local resistance to the annexation and colonise the territory, and the German-language theatre had a rôle to play in this process. Accordingly letters were sent out in 1882 from the *Bürgermeister* to a number of German theatres, including that of Meiningen, requesting a visit. With characteristic caution, Chronegk replied, suggesting a short visit while the company was playing in Strasburg. Correspondence was continued through 1883 by the *Intendant* in Metz, Caron, but nothing was finalised, and in December the *Bürgermeister* wrote again, repeating the request and emphasising the special position of the German population of Metz, isolated from the central cultural manifestations of the *Reich*. A little over a month later, having learnt of the planned visit of the Meininger to Strasburg in the summer of 1884, the *Bürgermeister* wrote rather indignantly to Chronegk, complaining that, after himself proposing the combination of Strasburg and Metz, he had failed to inform him of the Strasburg tour. Chronegk replied courteously, explaining that he was not free to book theatres exactly when he chose, but was limited by their availability; Caron, however, persisted in his aim of bringing the Meininger to Metz, and succeeded eventually in making an arrangement with the Municipal Theatre in Strasburg for two performances, *Twelfth Night* and the double-bill of Grillparzer's *Esther* and *Le Malade imaginaire*, in Metz on 6 and 7 June 1884; although it did not prove possible to finalise these arrangements until the summer, when the visitors were already in Strasburg.[107]

In the short time available publicity was hastily mounted in the German-speaking press for the two-day visit; from 22 May to 5 June short notices appeared almost daily reporting on the state of the negotiations, and then, when the arrangements were finalised, these gave way to notices encouraging potential theatre-goers to take out a subscription for both evenings. The *Metzer Presse* published in its *feuilleton* of 7 June an essay on the little-known *Esther*, along with an implicit challenge to its readers in the form of a report that *Twelfth Night* had played to a full house in the course of a similar brief excursion the Meininger had made from Strasburg to Baden Baden, and an assurance that the prices of seats had been kept lower than for performances by the Meininger in any other city.[108] In fact the theatre was not sold out. The *Metzer Zeitung* of 8 June reports that it was the cheaper seats that remained unsold; one can probably assume that – for quite different reasons – the cheap seats would have interested neither the officers of the German garrison nor the largely French-speaking population of the city. More significant still is the reception. Here there is no debate about principles; indeed, there is nothing at all in the way of criticism. In Metz, to be visited by the Meininger was, for a German, confirmation of full membership of the *Reich*, and an occasion not for criticism, but for gratitude:

We feel a deep obligation to express our warmest thanks to director Chronegk for his generous decision to delight the people of Metz with two performances.[109]

5 Two productions

The task of instilling the life of the present into subject matter from the past cannot be avoided, but it is the most difficult task of all.
Conrad Ferdinand Meyer, 16 January 1871

THE TOURS of the Meininger were a mammoth enterprise. They extended over a period of seventeen years, and during this time the company gave almost 3,000 performances of forty-one plays in cities throughout the greater part of Europe. A large number of people were actively involved in these productions, over and above the basic team of Georg II, Freifrau von Heldburg, and Ludwig Chronegk; and detailed preparation for the tours went back at least a further four years to the winter season of 1869–70. In order to obtain an insight into the aims, methods, and style of the Meiningen productions, and before considering the underlying principles in more general terms, it will be useful to narrow the field of investigation and give special consideration to two important but contrasting productions: Shakespeare's *Julius Caesar* and Kleist's *Prinz Friedrich von Homburg*.

Julius Caesar was the most successful and celebrated of the Meiningen productions. It remained in the repertoire for the whole of the touring period, and acquired a reputation as the most characteristic embodiment of the Meiningen style. Subject to constant discussion and criticism, modification, recasting, and redesigning, the production gathered around itself a large body of material, much of it now scattered among a variety of repositories, much of it lost; this material includes sketches for sets and costumes, correspondence between the various participants and observers, and published reviews in several languages emanating from many European cities. Unfortunately the decorations for this important production are not among those which have been preserved; they were sold after the end of the tours, most probably to a theatre in the USA.[1]

Prinz Friedrich von Homburg, on the other hand, was not an unqualified success; indeed, the production provoked a controversy which highlights in exemplary fashion the transitional position of the Meiningen Theatre in cultural and theatrical history. It remained in the repertoire for only three seasons, and was given a total of only thirty-eight performances within a geographically much more restricted area. Because of this it can be more comprehensively documented than most of the other productions. Detailed and extensive comments by the Duke on the rehearsals have been preserved; so too have a large number of sketches for set designs, scenic arrangements, and costumes; and, although not complete, the decorations are among the best-preserved of those to have been saved.[2]

(i)   *Julius Caesar*

On Sunday the theatrical sensation of the present day was performed in the Municipal Theatre: the Meininger were playing in Julius Caesar.
Johannes Wedde, Hamburg, 7/9 June 1879

The subject-matter of this particular Shakespearean drama clearly appealed with great force to Georg II and his contemporaries. There would seem to have been two distinct, but complementary, reasons for this: the Roman setting provided a satisfying focus for the highly developed antiquarian interest of the later nineteenth century; and the figure of Caesar himself, the chief architect of Rome's dominant position in the ancient world, readily lent itself to comparison with the leadership of the Second German Empire, recently established after a series of wars frequently compared with those undertaken by Caesar in securing his political pre-eminence, and he provided an ideal for the aspirations of an important section of the German people.

Georg's antiquarian interest in Roman history dated back at least to the 1840s, when he was studying archaeology at the University of Bonn. In a letter of 2 July 1844 he wrote to his mother describing the recent excavation of a Roman grave and, as was his habit, he accompanied the letter with a sketch, illustrating the contents of the grave: a sarcophagus and three small coins.[3] In Rome itself the period immediately before the Meiningen tours had seen extensive archaeological activity, with German scholars very much to the fore; despite the indifference of Bismarck (who was more disposed to support functional scientific research) the German Archaeological Institute had secured the support of Kaiser Wilhelm I, who valued its contribution to national prestige.[4] As a consequence of the dominant rôle of historical and classical scholarship in German cultural and intellectual life, new discoveries were noted with great interest, and old ideas and images were constantly being updated. Like Weiß's *Kostümkunde* of 1860, which was thoroughly revised and republished in 1881, Franz von Reber's illustrated book on the ruins in and around Rome, *Die Ruinen Roms und der Campagna* (Leipzig, 1863), was extensively rewritten and was republished in 1879. This practice of updating work in order to avoid charges of inaccuracy from eagle-eyed and well-informed contemporaries is also evident in the Duke of Meiningen's revisions of his sets and stage furnishings during this same period. In November 1880, immediately before taking the production of *Julius Caesar* to London, he wrote to his scene painters:

The preparation of the two Forum decorations is a very difficult task, and we shall have to apply ourselves to it very conscientiously, for the English, many of whom have acquired archaeological knowledge on the spot, will subject us to very close scrutiny.[5]

In May 1884, ten years after the first performance of *Julius Caesar* in Berlin, Georg II will still use a visit to Italy to look further into the question of precisely which statue it was beneath which Caesar was murdered.

The principal source for the decorations which were seen in Berlin in 1874 had been a series of sketches provided by the Director of the Vatican art collections, Pietro Ercole Visconti, with whom Georg had been in contact for some years and whom he had visited in Rome in 1869 to discuss his production. Before the performances in Berlin the Meiningen *Julius Caesar* was seen by Hermann Köchly, a leading Roman historian and professor at the University of Heidelberg. As always, the Duke went straight to the top, and, as always, he made sure that the cultural–historical appetite of his audience was satisfied by making sure that it *knew* of the authenticity with which the external appearance of ancient Rome had been realised in the Meiningen stage-set. In 1867 he instructed von Stein to insert an introductory description in the local paper; in 1874 Chronegk was instructed to prepare a handout on similar lines for Berlin, beginning: 'The *mise-en-scène* of *Julius Caesar* is the product of a visit by the Duke to Rome in 1869'; the programme explicitly stated that the costumes were based on the work of Weiß. In 1881 Chronegk was given further such instructions: 'It would be good to state on the programme (*here*), "New decorations etc. etc."', and these instructions are reflected in the programme for the London tour published by the Theatre Royal, Drury Lane, which draws particular attention to the new decorations.[6]

The critics responded to this prompting in different ways. In 1874 Frenzel obligingly followed up by pointing out approvingly that the sets had been designed with the utmost attention to archaeological research and mentioning the collaboration with Visconti. Others, however, were inclined to dismiss such antiquarian concerns as superficial pedantry; Otto Brahm, for instance, concluded his review of the Berlin performance of 1882 as follows:

The new decorations (in Caesar's house and in the Capitol) were a wonderful sight; whether, as the press was informed, they are historically 'authentic' and whether they have, with scholarly accuracy, been brought into line with the latest research, I am, alas, not competent to decide, since I am not a professor of archaeology. 'The problem is too difficult – I shall have to ask a scholar.'[7]

The sketches provided by Visconti for the sets were supplemented by the collections of the Musée de St Germain (the present Musée des Antiquités nationales), where the Parisian *ateliers* which supplied the weapons and armour found their models. These collections included material collected by Napoleon III for his two-volume study of Caesar which had appeared in France and Germany in 1865–66.[8] This brings us to the second source for the contemporary appeal of Shakespeare's play, for while one cannot ignore the antiquarian aspect of Napoleon III's work, it is more significant for its author's implicit claim to an affinity with a classical general and statesman, such as had previously been evident in Canova's statue of Napoleon I, and in Bonaparte's own writings.[9] The exploitation of Julius Caesar as an inspiring model for contemporary nationalism and imperialism was far from being confined to France.

The first three volumes of Theodor Mommsen's *Römische Geschichte*, one of the very great works of German historical scholarship, appeared in the 1850s, offering, in its third volume, an interpretation of Roman history which minimises the achievement of men such as Pompey and Cicero, and presents Julius Caesar as the strong-willed leader who reconciled monarchy and democracy, and brought unity and order to a Rome ravaged by the civil wars. It is difficult not to see in this highly successful work, which won great prestige for its author, an expression of those hopes and aspirations which brought the majority of the German liberals (though not, as it happened, Mommsen himself) into line behind Bismarck in the middle of the 1860s, and which brought the National Liberal party its electoral successes in the early 1870s.[10] It is equally difficult to believe that in 1867, and again in the early 1870s, the production of this play, in which special emphasis was placed on the recent civil war, did not strike a very responsive chord in the Duchy of Meiningen, which had itself been so directly affected by the Austro–Prussian War of 1866, was becoming increasingly incorporated into the militarily powerful and strongly led Prussian state, and had returned a prominent National-Liberal politician to the North-German *Reichstag*.

After 1870 the function of the analogy between the German *Reich* and the Rome of Julius Caesar changed only slightly, the emphasis now being more on the validation of the present than anticipation of the future. Mommsen, himself a National-Liberal deputy in the *Reichstag* (until the liberal 'secession' of 1880) joined many prominent German intellectuals in coming forward as an apologist for the German policy of annexation, offering an historical justification which brought him into direct conflict with his French counterpart, the Roman historian Fustel de Coulanges.[11]

All the while the antiquarian impulse continued undiminished, offering coincidental support to the politically motivated actualisation of the historical past. It was, no doubt, the scruple of the antiquarian in Georg II which prompted him to invite Köchly to give his seal of approval to the production of *Julius Caesar* before he took it to Berlin; but Hermann Köchly was no more a non-political academic than Mommsen. A man of republican sympathies, like his collaborator, Gottfried Kinkel, he had been actively in-volved in setting up the provisional government in Leipzig in 1848, and had fled when the revolution was put down in 1849. He remained in exile until 1864 when, like Mommsen, he returned to a position of academic eminence. Like Mommsen too, he served as a deputy in the *Reichstag*, but for the left-liberal *Fortschrittspartei* (Progressive Party); and he too was disposed to see in contemporary political developments close similarities to Roman history. In 1871 he began a public lecture with a clever adaptation of Cicero's speech of 56 BC urging the Senate to give Caesar a further five years of command in Gaul; by substituting Germany for Rome and France for Gaul he constructed a detailed parallel between Caesar's conquests and the recent German victories in France; although he too shared Mommsen's anti-Bismarckianism, and he concluded with an explicit warning against the militarism of contemporary *Realpolitik*.[12]

The predominance of a foreign author, Shakespeare, with three out of seven plays in the first Berlin tour, did not, despite the nationalistic atmosphere of the time, provoke excessive critical comment among Berlin's theatre critics.[13] Apart from the topicality of the play most prominently displayed, this is an indication of Shakespeare's status as a German author by adoption, which dates back to the writings of Herder, Goethe, and Lenz in the eighteenth century and the translations of Schlegel and Tieck in the early nineteenth century. In the middle of the nineteenth century, however, Shakespeare's position in the German *theatre* was not strong. In 1854, when Dingelstedt assembled a company consisting of the most distinguished actors of the day to take part in the first *Gesamtgastspiel* on the occasion of the Munich Industrial Exhibition, the ten classical dramas presented during the season did not include a single play by Shakespeare. Sixteen years later, when the second *Gesamtgastspiel* took place under the general direction of Karl von Perfall (artistic director: Ernst Possart), Goethe, Schiller, Lessing, and Kleist again supplied ten plays, but a further four by Shakespeare were also included in the programme.[14] The fact that two of the plays chosen (*Julius Caesar* and *The Winter's Tale*) had recently been popularised by the Meiningen tours indicates one reason for the change, but some credit must also be given to Dingelstedt himself, for, in fact, this pro-Shakespearean development antedates these tours, as is evident from the repertoire of the *Königliches Schauspielhaus*. Between 1851 and 1861 von Hülsen's company gave 900 performances of classical drama, of which 263 were of plays by Shakespeare; in the following decade the proportion had risen to 335 out of 968.[15]

Dingelstedt, whose activities as an adaptor and producer, keen to win Shakespeare for the German theatre, have already been mentioned, was further motivated by the sense of Shakespeare as a symbol of national emancipation, which was how he had been seen by the writers of the *Sturm und Drang*. His production of the complete cycle of the Histories in Weimar had something of the nationalist impulse that had been to the fore in the Schiller-centenary celebrations of 1859. The year 1864 had seen a further step in the appropriation of Shakespeare with the foundation of the *Deutsche Shakespeare-Gesellschaft* (German Shakespeare Society), of which Georg, still Crown Prince, became a member.[16] Two years later followed the announcement that the Meiningen Court Theatre had joined the ranks of the 'Shakespeare theatres'.

Before the Meiningen tours *Julius Caesar* had not figured among the more frequently performed of Shakespeare's plays. The *Königliches Schauspielhaus* had first produced it in 1804, but by 1867 the number of performances had risen to only twenty-six. In contrast, *Hamlet*, their most popular Shakespearean production, was performed 259 times between 1797 and 1885. *Twelfth Night*, one of the other two of Shakespeare's plays to be included in the first Meiningen tour, was performed 110 times between 1850 and 1885.[17]

On 20 April 1884, Georg II wrote to Chronegk, who was about to open in Mainz, drawing his attention to the imminence of the 200th performance of the production of *Julius Caesar*, and asking rhetorically, and with some satisfaction, whether any other German theatre had given as many performances of any classical drama within a comparable period.[18] The play came into the Meiningen repertoire before the touring period, during the first season of Georg's reign while the theatre was still under the direction of von Stein; this production was first performed on 10 March 1867. Bodenstedt did not include it among the nine Shakespearean plays he produced in 1867–68, but it was revived for the season 1869–70, with Weilenbeck as Antony and Ellen Franz as Portia. This was the production seen by Frenzel on 2 January 1870. It was performed again (with Friedmann and Dessoir) on 3 April of the same year. In the course of the preparations for Berlin it was performed on 9 November 1873, still with Weilenbeck as Antony; then with Barnay on 8 March 1874, and one last time on 9 April. It opened in Berlin on 1 May 1874; here it was given twenty-two performances and after seventeen years of touring the total had risen to 330. With the exception of Baden Baden and Metz, which received only brief visits while the company was playing in Strasburg, *Julius Caesar* was performed in every city the Meininger visited. It figured particularly prominently in the London tour of 1881, accounting for sixteen out of fifty-six performances (and there were also two separate performances of Act III). In 1887, when the production was seen for the last time in Berlin, in the large *Victoria-Theater*, during a tour dominated by the successful new production of *Die Jungfrau von Orléans*, the receipts for the five performances averaged 4,391 M., compared with an average of 4,181 M.

for this tour as a whole.[19] It was also the most frequently performed play in the two Russian tours of 1885 and 1890, with twenty-four performances in the four cities visited, although in 1890 the newer production, *Die Jungfrau von Orléans*, was given more performances. Its reception in Moscow, where it was seen by Nemirovic-Dancenko and Stanislavskij, and subsequently used (critically) as a model for the Moscow Arts Theatre production of 1903, is a remarkable tribute to its durability.

The version of the text in current use in the German theatre at the time of the Meiningen production was the version prepared by Heinrich Laube for his production of *Julius Caesar* at the *Burgtheater*. Georg II restored some of the material customarily omitted, but his version certainly did not have the completeness and authenticity which some of his champions have claimed. It is, in fact, exceedingly difficult to establish in what way the performance deviated from the text, and it is difficult to be absolutely certain whether the same deviations were maintained throughout the entire life of the production. Furthermore, it can be positively hazardous to speculate about the precise intention or effect of any such deviations.

As the basis for their performance version of *Julius Caesar*, the Meininger used the Schlegel–Tieck translation. The Theatre Museum in Meiningen has a copy of the 1854 edition, with extensive handwritten emendations. In this version the rôles of the tribunes, Flavius and Marullus, are given to the conspirators, Metellus Cimber and Cinna, which corresponds to the cast-list of the first Berlin performance in 1874. In the official Meiningen edition (first published 1879), however, the characters of Flavius and Marullus have been restored; and this corresponds to the cast-lists for the London performances and the last performance in Odessa in 1890.[20] Since there are other differences between the two versions, in respect of dialogue and stage-directions, it would be unwise to regard either as the ideal Meiningen *Julius Caesar*.

As might be expected, the response of contemporary theatre critics, reacting immediately to their experiences in the playhouse, is varied, and their reviews do not normally include detailed consideration of the text. In the eyes of one careful observer, however, whose comments have to be taken seriously, the version used in the performance he witnessed had been edited with a particular end in view, and this aim was supported by the casting policy. After the Moscow performances of 1885 Nemirovic-Dancenko wrote to the journal *Theatre and Life* attacking the Meiningen rendering of the inner substance of Shakespeare's play, and in particular what he considered to be the simplification and idealisation in the presentation of the main characters, a tendency supported by the omission of scenes which add complexity and ambiguity to the actions and motives of Antony, Brutus, and Cassius.[21]

Setting aside, for the moment, the question of casting, and the contribution of the individual actors to the specific performance witnessed by Nemirovic-Dancenko, his interpretation of the intentions behind the omissions is interesting, but far from compelling. His highly sceptical reading of the character of Antony is certainly not served by the omission of the Triumvirs' scene (Act IV, scene 1); but not all interpreters would agree that this scene does indeed reveal 'Antony's practical, spoiled nature . . . in all its nakedness'.[22] In any case, the scene had, in fact, been included when the play was first performed in Berlin, and was dropped (possibly out of deference to the views of Karl Frenzel) for later performances. The omission had clear practical advantages, saving a change of scenery and permitting the whole of Act IV to be played without interruption in Brutus's tent.[23] Nemirovic-Dancenko also criticises the omission of the brief scene of conflict between Antony and Octavius at the beginning of Act V; although this is a scene which is probably of more importance for the characterisation of Octavius than Antony. Its omission is also advantageous to the theatrical presentation of the play, for it permits a direct entry to the battle scenes of the last act. It is, moreover, included in the official Meiningen edition of the text; which suggests that its omission was not a matter of principle, and it may well have been played in other performances.

The significant omissions affecting the characterisation of Brutus and Cassius occur in Act IV, scene 3, after the quarrel between the two men. The suppression of the scene with the poet (ll. 122–41) removes, it is true, a moment of uncontrolled and disproportionate irritation on the part of Brutus, and so reduces the evidence of the breakdown of his stoicism; but it does not affect the substantive point, for this is made explicitly by Cassius: 'Of your philosophy you make no use, / If you give place to accidental evils' (ll. 144–45). These two lines are preserved in the official version of the text (p. 58). Nemirovic-Dancenko also observes sarcastically (and the jibe is characteristic of much criticism of Meiningen productions), 'they have not cut the wine, perhaps to parade an overabundance of external detail: how and from which kind of jug Brutus drinks wine in camp . . . this liberty necessitates having the Shakespearean Brutus demand wine without any motivation'. This, however, is less than just to the editing, for there are, in Shakespeare, *two* occasions on which Brutus asks for wine (ll. 141 and 157), and in the official edition it is only the second of these which is preserved; moreover, this occurs immediately after its motivating factor, Brutus's announcement to Cassius of the suicide of his wife, Portia. The other omission criticised is that of the *second* announcement of Portia's death (ll. 180–94), and – as Nemirovic-Dancenko believes – the play-acting of Brutus, in responding stoically when he pretends to be hearing the news for the first time, and of Cassius, in supporting the pretence. This is almost certainly a case of over-interpretation of the Shakespearean text, for the elimination of this duplication has been justified by successive commentators, who see the second announcement as the original version, which was not cancelled in the manuscript when Shakespeare revised the play by adding the first announcement.[24] In all of these instances the editing removes repetition, and permits the action to advance more rapidly to the climax of Philippi; this dramaturgical factor gains increased importance in the context of a Meiningen production, where the use of elaborate scenery inevitably tends to slow the pace.

Nemirovic-Dancenko's criticism illustrates how much caution needs to be exercised in considering the interpretative implications of textual editing; it does not, of course, mean that there are no such implications. Alongside the realistic decorations, the most significant aspect of this production – in the eyes of both the Duke and his audiences – was the presentation of the crowd. Georg described his aims in a letter to Frenzel shortly before the opening in Berlin:

I hope that the production of *Caesar*, which is to open on 1 May, will correspond to your intentions. At least the effort has been made to do justice to your demands. Even if I might have my doubts about whether this or that scene will be applauded, I have no doubt at all that the third act of *Caesar* will be effective; the conclusion has been made even stronger; I believe the public will be carried away, that it will have the feeling that a revolution is beginning.[25]

Neither the Duke of Meiningen, who had been far from being a supporter of popular uprising in 1848, nor his audiences, whose attitude would most probably have been coloured by the very hostile view of the Commune that was almost universally prevalent in Germany in the 1870s, would have regarded this as anything but a cause for alarm.[26] Examination of the official Meiningen text at this point (pp. 50–52) confirms what therefore might have been expected: namely that the crowd is presented as a wayward rabble, readily inflamed by the oratory of Antony, and then capable of uncontrolled violence. The effects of this mob-violence are intensified by the addition of a few lines which expand the 2nd Plebeian's cry, 'Go fetch fire' (l. 259), and by the return to the stage of others who have carried out his instruction.[27] A further contribution to this effect is made by the restoration of a scene which was normally omitted, Act III, scene 3, in which the poet Cinna, taken initially for the conspirator of the same name, is set upon by the enraged mob.[28] This scene, which was evidently played with great emphasis, was not merely restored; in the official edition it is absorbed into Act III, scene 2, the forum scene, so that it follows directly on Antony's oration, and is witnessed by him. The curtain-line for Act III is Antony's expression of satisfaction at his impact on the crowd: 'Now let it work. Mischief, thou art afoot, / Take thou what course thou wilt!' (ll. 262–63), and a moment of expectant silence is created for Antony's revealing words by bringing forward the servant's announcement that Octavius is in Rome (l. 264). The Duke's instructions for the playing of this scene were very precise:

in the third act the crowd must fall silent when Roßdorff shouts: 'Octavius is in Rome', and must remain silent until Weilenbeck [Antony] has spoken. Everyone is anxious to know how Antony will respond to the great news. But after the words of Antony the tumult must begin again, above cries of 'Octavius in Rome?' Yesterday, when Antony made his exit, the shouting was . . . not loud enough.[29]

Thus strengthened, the Cinna scene is given greater force as a symptom of the dangers of irresponsible demagogy and mob fury; and it surely acts as a corrective to any idealising tendency in the portrayal of Antony. The Duke's subsequent reference to *Julius Caesar*, when he was considering following it up with a production of *Coriolanus*, confirms that this was indeed the way in which he viewed the crowd in the former play:

in this aristocratic play [*Coriolanus*] the crowd comes off even worse than in *Caesar*, and, in order to do justice to the intentions of the author, it would have to be caricatured to some degree, so that the hero of the drama, with whom one ought to sympathise . . . remains more or less in the right.[30]

The other important aspect of the editing of the play, the division into acts and scenes, was directly determined by the decorations, and therefore needs to be considered together with them. It took the following form:

Act I		Forum with view of the Capitol
Act II	scene 1	Garden of Brutus
	scene 2	In the palace of Caesar
Act III	scene 1	Before the house of Brutus[a]
	scene 2	The Curia of Pompey
	scene 3	Forum with a view of the Palatine
Act IV	(scene 1	In the house of Antony)
	scene 2	Tent of Brutus
Act V		Plains of Philippi

[a] Includes Act II, scene 3, Artemidorus's monologue. Act II, scene 4 (Portia, Lucius, and the soothsayer) was omitted.

In his review of 1874 Frenzel remarked on the success with which excessively frequent scene changes had been avoided, particularly in the difficult battle scenes of Act V. In the nine (later eight) scenes which remained the attempt was made to alternate between those scenes (acts I, III, and V) which made use of the full depth of the stage for the crowd scenes and in which an illusion of still greater depth was created in the backcloth, and those scenes (acts II and IV) which were set in more confined spaces with simpler decorations. In Act III, however, two important scenes, involving large numbers of performers and elaborate sets, were juxtaposed, necessitating the use of the scene-curtain and a long, mid-act pause.[31]

These two scenes, which include the murder of Caesar and the speeches of

9–10   Georg II, sketches for Shakespeare, *Julius Caesar*, Act I, Forum with view of
       the Capitol, 1881.

11   Ferdinand Lindner, Scenes from Shakespeare, *Julius Caesar*, in a production
by the Meininger, Act II, scene 1, Brutus's garden.

12   Johannes Kleinmichel, after a sketch by Georg II of Meiningen, Shakespeare,
Julius Caesar, Act III, scene 3, Antony with the body of Caesar, *Die Gartenlaube*,
27 (1879).

Brutus and Antony, were, together with the spectacular first act, the most important for the success of the production; 'I believe that these decorations are a greater attraction than the whole of *Caesar*', observed the Duke in 1881.[32] The Duke himself had begun work on them almost as soon as a production of *Julius Caesar* was envisaged; in his correspondence with von Stein early in 1867 he wrote:

First decoration: Capitol viewed from the Forum. The foundations of the central section still stand today; the tower also. Top right the temple of Zeus Capitolinus. The Via Sacra passes below the steps in an arc up to the left and leads to the left side of the central part of the Capitol. – The second decoration: the Curia of Pompey, where the Senate met in the year of Caesar's death, because the Senatorial curia on the Forum had

13   Georg II, sketch for *Julius Caesar*, Act v, Plains of Philippi.

been burnt down during the preceding Civil Wars. – In the foreground an open square, in the middle-ground the Curia, opening onto this square. The meetings of the Senate take place in public in the presence of the people. – Caesar's throne between the Curule Chairs, beneath the statue of Pompey re-erected by Caesar. This statue to be a copy of the one in Rome which was excavated at the site of the Curia of Pompey and is therefore definitely the one which stood in the Curia. The original is marble and is three metres high . . . Third decoration Forum Romanum . . . The Rostra facing towards the Curia, with its narrow side towards the people . . . fourth and fifth acts: the *pila* [javelins], the weapon discovered in the war against Pyrrhus, with which the Romans won their victories, as the Prussians did with the needle-gun.[33]

Sketches and correspondence relating to these decorations and their renewal for the London production are the subject of detailed discussion in an article by Inge Krengel-Strudthoff.[34] This confirms the scrupulous concern of the Duke of Meiningen to achieve accuracy in accordance with the most recent archaeological scholarship, but it also shows that – as in the matter of textual authenticity – he was quite prepared to compromise and breach the principle for the sake of a visually impressive effect: for instance by including in the painted backcloth for Act III, scene 3 the temple of Venus and Roma, which was not erected until the time of the Emperor Hadrian. The desire for accuracy sometimes led to that apparently gratuitous display of historical knowledge which offended a number of critics, as, for instance, in the placing of a heap of building rubble in front of the Basilica Julia, which was under construction at the time (although there were other reasons for this); and it leads to the pedantic 'correction' of Shakespeare where he wrongly locates the murder in the Capitol rather than, as in Plutarch's account, the Curia of Pompey. Such additions and amendments serve, of course, to draw attention to the use of external authorities as guarantees of the authenticity of the production and its setting, and they provide that very special pleasure of recognition which is still more widely available in the numerous less esoteric allusions to a 'truth' outside the text of the play.

The technique can also be used to achieve that specifically non-antiquarian effect which was in the Duke's mind as he made the comparison between the Roman *pila* and the Prussian needle-gun. The visible reminder that the Forum was being rebuilt after the Civil War contributes further to the actualisation of Roman history for the benefit of post-war Germany; so too does the placing in the centre of the Forum of an equestrian statue which – the Duke specified in a note on his sketch – should bear a strong resemblance to one of Berlin's most prominent monuments, Schlüter's equestrian statue of the Great Elector in Roman dress, which then stood on the bridge (the Kurfürstenbrücke) behind the Royal Palace in Berlin.

Another important feature of these decorations is the manner in which they exemplify the transition between painted and plastic scenery. The letters of the Duke to the Brückners in the winter of 1880–81 show his desire to overcome certain of the limitations of painted sets, and create a solid

14 Georg II, sketch for *Julius Caesar*, Act III,
scene 3, equestrian statue.

15 Andreas Schlüter, The Great Elector, 1700–09.

environment for the action of the drama. The art of perspective in the painting of backcloths, at which the Brückners were masters, was to be supplemented by the liberal use of three-dimensional decorations and practicable stage furnishings: pillars, the building rubble extending out from the painted backcloth, a bench around the *fica sacra*, the rostra, placed well to the rear of the stage so as to leave room for the crowd *in front of* Antony, and allowing him to move downstage to the corpse of Caesar. Certain constraints still remain, however. The nineteenth-century stage lacked the cyclorama, which was not used in Meiningen until the production of Shaw's *Caesar and Cleopatra* in 1912.[35] And even in 1881 Georg was still restricted by his awareness of the need for financial restraint; on 8 March he wrote to Max Brückner: 'At 2,000 M. the statue of Pompey is much too expensive. I shall manage with a painted one.'[36]

The problem of the statue of Pompey provides a good illustration of the various concerns which informed the work of the Duke of Meiningen as a stage-designer and director, for the compromise solution of 1881 did not satisfy him. In 1884 he wrote to Chronegk from Italy, saying that the large statue in the Palazzo Spada, which he had evidently seen recently, was now firmly believed to be the statue beneath which Caesar was actually murdered. Because of Pompey's expression of unrelenting severity it would, the Duke felt, fit well into his production; authenticity, however, required that its proportions be preserved, and it was a very large statue which, when mounted on a pedestal, might reach up into the flies; before asking Lenbach to have a copy made (in papier mâché) he therefore needed to have the stage measurements. Despite the conflicting demands of aesthetic, realistic, and practical considerations, Georg very clearly wanted to use the statue; he wanted it to stand firmly on the floor of the stage on its own pedestal, and, as the sketch which accompanied his letter shows, he wanted the participants in the murder scene to be so grouped around the statue that it was no longer part of a background decoration, but was fully integrated into the action.[37]

Togas, sandals, weapons, and armour were designed from sketches by the Duke in accordance with the same principle of authenticity as the scenery. In addition to the Musée de Saint Germain, the work of Hermann Weiß provided the major source. Equal attention was paid to the wearing of costume, and this gave rise to a well-known anecdote about the tribulations of the visiting actors, Friedmann and Dessoir, as they struggled into the heavy Meiningen togas.[38] More significantly, the policy of rehearsing throughout in full costume paid dividends in the greater naturalness with which costumes were worn; 'the principal gain is in the manner in which the supernumeraries wear the costumes of a bygone age, and take intelligent part in actions and movements of which they can have had no experience in real life', wrote the drama critic of *The Athenaeum* (4 June 1881). It was praise such as this which provoked the envy and resentment of the *Königliches*

16 Georg II, sketch for *Julius Caesar*, Act III, scene I, statue
of Pompey, 17 May 1884.

17 Roman, Statue of Pompey, Rome, Palazzo Spada.

18 Georg II, costume sketch for *Julius Caesar*, Roman soldier.

Schauspielhaus, and its director joined those who took pleasure in pointing out minor inaccuracies in the Meiningen costumes and the way they were worn.[39] Georg himself, however, was no less careful in his observation, or severe in his judgment, of his own company; writing from Paris shortly before the opening of *Julius Caesar* in Berlin, he instructed Chronegk: 'the citizens in *Caesar* must not, as wrongly happened in the last performance, wear gold bands on their heads; these bands were not in use until the Middle Ages and are not appropriate to the Roman *plebs*'.[40]

Julius Caesar is a play which requires a variety of special lighting and sound effects: the storm of Act I, the night-time conspiracy scene of Act II, the appearance of the ghost of Caesar in Act IV, and the battle scenes of Act V. Even so hostile a critic as Claretie was prepared to praise at great length the technical skill in the production of lightning, rain, and thunder in Act I. The conspiracy scene of Act II in Brutus's garden began in moonlight, and the audience witnessed an impressive, though possibly melodramatic, change in the lighting as day broke.[41] The final scenes on the plains of Philippi were also played on a darkened stage, illuminated by simulated moonlight and torches carried by the attendants of Antony and Octavius. In the gas-lit theatres in which the Meininger performed, effects such as these were created by battery-operated electric lamps, constructed for the company by the firm of Hugo Bähr, and then at a fairly early stage of development. The instructions to the stage-manager and lighting-technicians have not been preserved, though it is clear that the same discipline was maintained as for actors, and the same fines imposed for inadequate performance.[42] Certain changes in lighting were probably effected – as in *Wilhelm Tell*, where the process has been impressively re-created with the surviving sets – by illuminating the backcloth from the rear while masking, and progressively unmasking, parts of it; or else by leaving gauze-covered openings through which beams of 'moonlight' could shine onto specific features of the set.[43] The appearance of the ghost in Brutus's tent in Act IV was effected by fairly simple means: the tent was made of dark red velvet material and a passageway was made in its rear wall with an opening at chest height. Caesar, dressed in a toga of the same red velvet material, was picked out by a light from the front as he appeared in the opening, so that he seemed to be hovering in mid air. Both Archer in London and Ostrovskij in Moscow praised the simplicity and effectiveness of the scene; expectations, however, clearly varied, and Fontane's critical account rings no less true, especially when one considers the means by which the illusion was created: 'the ghost of Julius Caesar in Brutus's tent looks like an alarmed secondary-school teacher, suddenly appearing at a moonlit window wrapped in his dressing-gown'.[44]

The success of the production of *Julius Caesar* clearly did not, and was never intended to, depend on the individual skill of distinguished actors. As we have noted, the Duke of Meiningen was well aware of the relative weakness of the forces at his disposal, and their inexperience when judged by the standards of the capital. The particular weakness on the female side, mitigated somewhat after the engagement of Marie Schanzer and the emergence of Amanda Lindner in the 1880s, but never entirely eliminated, may have

19 Paul Richard as Julius Caesar.

been a further reason for the choice of *Julius Caesar* as the first touring production, and the decision not to follow it up with *Coriolanus*.[45]

In 1874 he was able to fill the rôles of Brutus and Cassius from within the ranks of his own permanent company, with Wilhelm Hellmuth-Bräm and Leopold Teller, who were to serve him for many years and assume many important rôles. Over the 330 performances of *Julius Caesar* the rôle of

Cassius was shared exclusively between Teller and Max Grube. In 1874 Caesar was played by another Meiningen stalwart, Josef Nesper, who, before his departure for the *Königliches Schauspielhaus* in 1884, took on more major rôles than any other member of the company. In the next few years he was to create the rôles of Hermann (*Die Hermannsschlacht*), Graf Wetter vom Strahl (*Das Käthchen von Heilbronn*), Fiesko, and Karl Moor in important touring productions. In *Fach* terms the young heroic or romantic rôle would have been his speciality, although the Duke seems to have had some reservations about his talents in this area.[46] To cast Nesper as Caesar therefore, rather than an older character-actor such as Weilenbeck, was an imaginative move, made, according to Grube, for symbolic purposes; Nesper, through his imposing physical presence, was able to embody the particular conception of Caesar and Rome that was current in Germany in the 1870s.[47] Beyond this symbolic significance, however, the Duke seems to have been aspiring to a visual realisation of the person of Caesar by reference to pictorial authority: Nesper was cast for his actual or potential similarity to the received image of Caesar, and this similarity, brought out in make-up and costume, remained a feature of this production in later performances when the rôle was taken over by Paul Richard. In Moscow, Ostrovskij was to observe:

The first entry of Caesar before the crowd in the Forum was most striking . . . the likeness was amazing; it was as if a picture of Caesar had come to life . . . Chronegk . . . said . . . they did not want to choose an actor who did not resemble him, because the appearance of Caesar was so well-known to everybody from illustrations.[48]

In London Archer had drawn attention to the same practice, showing how central it was to the casting in this particular production:

Caesar (Herr Richard) is a perfect embodiment of the great Dictator, and as he stands there gaunt and stately in his red robe and with a gilded wreath on his close-shorn head, . . . one cannot help feeling that this is a realisation of an actual scene from the life of old Rome . . . In appearance [Brutus and Cassius] are perfect. Brutus (Herr Nesper) is the stately patrician to the life, and Herr Teller, as the 'lean and hungry' Cassius, is a figure to be remembered for its grim picturesqueness.[49]

The other significant feature in the casting is the importance given to the rôle of Antony. Up to 1873 the part had been taken by Weilenbeck. This original choice does not imply any idealisation of the character – quite the contrary, if one bears in mind the parts which Weilenbeck was actually given during the first tour: Shylock, Argan, Sixtus. However, Weilenbeck's age and deteriorating sight caused the Duke to reconsider the casting. What he was looking for is evident from the letter he wrote to Chronegk rejecting the suggestion that an actor called Kreutzkamp be auditioned for the part:

in my opinion he is lacking everything that is necessary in an Antony. He is wooden, pedantic, awkward, clumsy, whereas Antony must be suave, elegant, witty, a man of the world. The only thing in his favour is the strength of his voice; but of course I find that that has a very unpleasant timbre.[50]

The solution, as we have noted, was to invite Ludwig Barnay from Frank-furt; other guests who assumed the rôle were Fritz Dettmer, borrowed from the Dresden Court Theatre for the Viennese tour of 1875, and Emerich Robert in the autumn tour of 1878. Barnay was widely praised for his performance, though a number of critics found his interpretation of the rôle rather restrained.[51] As a well-known actor, however, he inevitably drew a disproportionate amount of attention to himself; whether this brought about any shift in the balance of sympathy away from the republican party is difficult to establish. Comments on the performances without Barnay are contradictory: writing of the performances in Berlin in 1882, Brahm noted the clarity with which *both* the unworldly idealism of Brutus *and* the demonic rabble-rousing of the demagogue Antony are made evident; whereas in Moscow in 1885 Nemirovic-Dancenko severely criticises Willy Felix for his rendering of Antony as a 'noble-minded youth'.[52]

With the exception of Barnay, no actor is singled out consistently for any special praise, though there are, as we have observed, a number of fairly damning accounts of the acting, the most forthright being those written for Viennese readers by Hopfen and Speidel. The most positive comments suggest an even level of performance, with no actors falling below the minimum standard necessary to secure the success of the production as a whole; 'a happy medium of average excellence' is the phrase used by Clement Scott.[53]

The high points of the production, the opening, the murder of Caesar, and the speech of Antony at the end of Act III, depended for their effectiveness on crowd scenes such as – if contemporary responses are a guide – had not previously been witnessed in the German theatre, and which were still sufficiently novel to make a significant impression on London critics and directors in 1881. The numerous extras, recruited locally but led by mem-bers of the company, were costumed and equipped with the same attention to detail and historical accuracy as the principals. The range of these costumes and the precise differentiations, indicating social standing or military rank, produced a new degree of individualisation in the crowd. To a considerable extent this individualisation of members of the crowd was supported by stage-direction; the division into sub-groups, relatively independent of each other in their actions, permitted freer movement and the formation of those more natural groupings advocated by Diderot. This produced crowd scenes which, according to Archer, 'Shakespeare did not intend . . . to be played in this fashion . . . His crowd is the conventional crowd, unanimous as Mr Puff's, an embodiment of the people in the abstract.' Archer, however, does not appear to be entirely consistent, for, although he differs from the more hostile critics of the German 'drillmaster', in insisting that the company's 'splendid drill produces the effect of absolute freedom from drill', he nevertheless observes a uniformity of attentiveness when groups of actors respond simultaneously to the same event, and a uniformity of gesture when a crowd responds as a whole: 'there was a superabundance of arms in the crowd . . . I have not noticed that in modern mass-meetings the arm is such an overwhelmingly prominent limb.'[54] What this suggests is that the Duke of Meiningen's view of *Julius Caesar*, while leaving room for distinctions of social status and personal psychology, did not permit any political differentiation in the presentation of the crowd.[55] The emphasis may have stopped short of the caricature which the Duke thought would have been necessary in *Coriolanus*, but the tendency of the *mise-en-scène* to create the impression of a revolutionary uprising is evident in those classic outstretched arms, reminiscent of David's *Oath of the Horatii* and *Oath of the Tennis Court*.

The major contemporary criticisms of the crowd scenes do not, of course, relate to this particular emphasis, which, as we have had occasion to note, very largely corresponded to current German preconceptions about the characteristic behaviour of the Latin peoples. Concern was expressed, rather, about the upstaging of the principals by the crowd, and the muffling of the dialogue by the background noise.[56] This is a risk of which the Duke was well aware, and which he sought to avoid, even if doing so occasionally involved a certain artificiality. He instructed Chronegk that the battle-noise in the last act should, from the moment of Cassius's entry with the standard in scene 3, be 'discreet', and that it should cease entirely for the first part of scene 5, the scene of Brutus's death.[57] Elsewhere he tried to reduce the potentially melodramatic quality of such an unmotivated pause by providing a recognisable cause in the dialogue (as in the announcement of Octavius's arrival at the end of Act III); or by integrating crowd noise and dialogue.

This interplay between crowd and principals was a feature of the opening scene where, in contrast to traditional practice, 'the crowd does not remain *au deuxième plan*, acting as a background to the tribunes. On the contrary, Flavius and Marullus mix with it and elbow with it, sometimes almost hidden in its midst. It has all the uncertain fluctuations of an actual crowd.' This recognition of the merging of figure and ground occurs in the review by William Archer, who had begun with a declaration that 'the form of theatrical art which [the Meiningen Company] presents is novel to our stage'.[58] As the typical scene of this 'novel' production he identifies the second Forum scene (Act III, scene 3 in the Meiningen version), with the rostra placed upstage and the crowd, as in Act I, milling around in the foreground. The imaginative exploitation of the situation thereby created, in order to freshen up the best-known, most hackneyed line of the play, is described approvingly by Clement Scott: 'there is . . . a dramatic purpose in the crowd . . . Take, for instance, the clever but natural idea of the first words of Mark Antony's speech being drowned in the murmur and confusion. What old-fashioned actor, accustomed to ladle out the well-known "Friends, Romans, countrymen, lend me your ears", would have tolerated the innovation? Yet the triple appeal justifies the interruption, and warrants that shrug of the shoulders from Herr Barnay when, in spite of all effort, he cannot get a hearing.'[59] A rhetorical flourish thus becomes a fully motivated, realistic appeal to the mass of persons assembled on stage, such as will be commended by Antoine:

Dans les tableaux d'ensemble, le protagoniste tenant la scène peut rendre les silences vrais par un geste, un cri, un mouvement. Et si la foule écoute et voit l'acteur, au lieu de regarder dans la salle . . . on trouvera naturel qu'elle écoute et que deux cents personnes se taisent ensemble, dominées, pour entendre un personnage qui intéresse chacun.[60]

Archer's comments here represent an important insight into the changes in style being brought about in the theatre by methods such as those adopted by the Meininger; he expressed himself with great care:

It must have been evident to all that Herr Barnay, while he delivered Antony's address with absolute mastery, did not extract from it such a great *personal* effect as some actors might have obtained. The reason was that he did not address himself to the imagination of the audience, but to the living and moving populace before him. As the scene would be presented under ordinary circumstances in England, with a conventional crowd merely to give the orator his cues as it were, we should be obliged, as far as possible, to put ourselves in the place of the crowd, and to consider Antony's appeals as addressed to us personally. The force of his oratory would reach us, not through the stage crowd but directly. We should feel his strokes of invective and pathos in our own imagination, and not through our senses. The elements of the scene would be two only – the actor and the audience – and the immediate effect of the former upon the latter would be greater. In developing the third element, as an intermediary between actor and audience, the Meiningers sacrifice something of this directness of appeal. It is rather by inference than by personal sensation or intuition that we recognise the power of Mark Antony's oratory. We see how it moves the crowd, and by an act must so move it.

Such effects, it must be said, were not perceived by all observers of this performance; there were those who felt less detachment, and felt that the scene made the 'audience want to leave [its] place to make one with the howling, passionate crowd'.[61] Moreover Barnay's performance in London was clearly a very inconsistent one, for – in contravention of all Meiningen rules – he allowed himself to bow to the audience across the corpse of Caesar, in order to acknowledge the applause in mid scene at the end of Antony's oration.[62] But however imperfectly realised, Archer recognised in this production a further significant development of the realistic tendency in which the actor is *absorbed* rather than *theatrical*, and in which the footlights serve as a barrier between audience and stage. The tendency, which goes back to Diderot, points forward to naturalism; for in a few years time Gerhart Hauptmann will lament the failure of an actor to apply precisely the method described by Archer to his interpretation of the rôle of Alfred Loth in *Vor Sonnenaufgang*.[63] Its implementation depends on overall control of the production by an off-stage authority, such as was clearly the case in this first major production to come out of Meiningen.[64]

(ii) *Prinz Friedrich von Homburg*

This drama, which will be performed, at most, once or twice a year by the leading German theatre, has been presented successfully by the Meininger on ten consecutive nights before large audiences.
                  Karl Frenzel, Berlin, May 1878

After omitting Berlin from their itinerary in 1877 the Meininger returned to the capital in May 1878 with a programme consisting of four new productions. One of these, *The Winter's Tale*, was to be a major success and was to be performed almost as widely as *Julius Caesar*, being seen in all the cities which hosted a full-length tour. Two of the three other productions, Schiller's *Die Räuber* and Grillparzer's *Die Ahnfrau*, were also to remain in the repertoire, and each received a substantial number of performances throughout Europe. Only *Prinz Friedrich von Homburg*, the play now recognised as Kleist's finest, in a production on which a great deal of care was expended, failed to establish itself. The position of Kleist in the Meiningen repertoire was to rest on the two earlier productions, *Die Hermannsschlacht* (1875) and *Das Käthchen von Heilbronn* (1876).

In Imperial Germany the subject matter of *Prinz Friedrich von Homburg* had a similar appeal to that of *Julius Caesar*. A characteristic comparison was made by the historian, Ernst Curtius, writing in the *Deutsche Rundschau* in 1880: 'Just as Themistocles, many years ago, by an irresistible exertion of will-power, suddenly transformed the minor city on the Saronian gulf [Athens] into a great power, so did the House of Brandenburg become a European power through the victory at Fehrbellin.'[65] The famous victory of the Prussian army in 1675 under the command of the Great Elector, Friedrich Wilhelm, provides the historical background of Kleist's play, whose central conflict is derived from Frederick the Great's *Mémoires pour servir à l'histoire de la maison de Brandebourg*. It concerns the conduct of the Prince of Homburg, the officer in command of the Prussian cavalry, whose rash intervention in the battle, in contravention of orders, helped to secure the victory over the Swedes, but, in the view of the Elector, prevented that victory from being as complete as it might otherwise have been. It scarcely needs emphasising that such a reminder of past military triumphs would have had a very considerable resonance in Prussia only seven years after the conclusion of a war which had brought about German unity under Prussian leadership. The analogy had been made officially and very publicly in the victory celebrations of 1871 in Berlin; these had concluded on 18 June, the anniversary of the battle of Fehrbellin. In particular the bold – or rash – use of the cavalry to turn the battle must have struck a very special chord in an audience for whom von Bredow's 'death-ride' in the battle of Vionville-Mars-la-Tour was a recent memory, kept fresh in verse, painting, and panorama.

In 1878 Kleist, whose status as the third canonical German dramatist, after Schiller and Lessing, was of relatively recent date, was unambiguously regarded as a Prussian national poet in a rather narrow sense.[66] His reputation as such had been partially secured by the first of his plays to be performed by the Meiningen Theatre, *Die Hermannsschlacht*, whose subject matter was also receiving the same actualisation as that of *Julius Caesar*. To take two examples: in 1873, in the German section of the World Exhibition in Vienna pride of place was given to Piloty's huge canvas, *Thusnelda im Triumphzug des Germanicus*, where it was flanked by Camphausen's portraits of two Prussian rulers, Frederick the Great and the (equestrian) Great Elector; and the account of the victory of Arminius over Varus and his legions in the fifth volume of Mommsen's *Römische Geschichte* was particularly appreciated by Julius Rodenberg for its exemplary quality in the contemporary context.[67]

Die Hermannsschlacht was (and remains) a problematic and controversial work. Certain scenes, such as the one in which the German leaders fight for the privilege of killing the captured Varus, and the one in which Thusnelda brings about the death of the young Roman officer, Ventidius, by luring him into the cage of a fearsome bear, revealed the Germans as particularly barbaric, and provoked both criticism and apologies from several commentators. That the Duke of Meiningen was able – in at least some cities – to restore some of the violence to this play without creating undue hostility, suggests that, whatever reservations were felt, the German public of the 1870s was fairly easily able to come to terms with the imputation of barbarism to its ancestors, by justifying this passionate expression of hatred in historical (that is to say anti-Napoleonic) terms.[68]

The shortcomings of *Prinz Friedrich von Homburg* proved less easy to excuse. The scene in which the hero, condemned to death for failing to follow orders in battle, collapses utterly at the prospect of his execution and pleads abjectly for his life, had proved unacceptable to the Prussian court when the play was first written, and it had been banned from the *Königliches Schauspielhaus* during the 1820s. Despite its patriotic subject, it had not secured a firm place in the repertoire of the German theatre. Between 1860 and 1870 it was given only ten performances at the *Königliches Schauspielhaus*; in October 1876 it had opened in a new production, but, although Fontane praised it, and noted the justice now being done by the German theatre to the neglected dramatist, it was not a great success with the public.[69] Between 1828 and 1879 *Prinz Friedrich von Homburg* was performed only forty-seven times at the *Königliches Schauspielhaus*.[70]

In the first full-length scholarly study of Kleist, which appeared in 1863 and is referred to by several critics of the Meiningen production, Adolf Wilbrandt gives a representative account of the virtues and shortcomings of the play as seen at the time. He identifies the virtues in Kleist's idealisation of the martial state of Brandenburg, which the dramatist had previously rejected; and he sees these virtues concentrated unambiguously in the person of the Great Elector, the perfect embodiment of the state, a born ruler, wise, sovereign in his understanding of events and individuals, but a stern guardian of the law.[71] The problems arise for Wilbrandt from the character of the Prince of Homburg. Kleist, departing from historical truth, has made the Prince not just into a young man, but into an unstable, romantic young man, with dreams of glory on the battlefield, which he hopes will be rewarded by the hand of Princess Natalie (the Elector's niece). For the Prince the dreams take precedence over the reality of his duties, as expressed in the orders of the day, which give him an important, but restrained, tactical rôle in the battle. Carried away by the dreams, he intervenes prematurely; and, after the victory, he continues to act with the same romantic excess when, in response to the false news of the Elector's death on the battlefield, he assumes the rôle of protector to Natalie and executor of the national mission of the fallen leader. The reappearance of the Elector and the sentence of death passed on Homburg reduce him, once he begins to see that the latter is intended seriously, from the heights of enthusiasm to the depths of despair. He abandons his dreams, renounces Natalie, and asks only for bare survival.

So long as he views the play in biographical, aesthetic, or psychological terms Wilbrandt is able to accept and even to praise the extremity and intensity of Kleist's presentation of the action and the principal character:

The Prince of Homburg, as the author shows him, can, after his aspirations have reached up to the stars, do no other than fall equally far beneath himself; only then do we understand him completely and, however profoundly it shakes us, his fall does not make us despair of him; for a soul such as this only recovers when it reaches the bottom of the abyss. And in this it is a reflection of the author's image, for in this scene he is casting off a pathological element from himself.

For Wilbrandt, however, the external 'truth' evoked by the historical setting and costume is so compelling that it excludes this particular view of the play; the presentation of *this* character in *this* uniform is a contradiction:

We can tolerate any peculiarity in the Prince, any eccentric outburst of enthusiasm, so long as it does not contradict the primary and inescapable demands of the costume; but we utterly reject this monstrous negation of the qualities of a Prussian officer of that period; it seems to us to be quite impossible.   (pp. 376–77)

Wilbrandt's recognition of an almost pathological dimension to the Prince's character is an important idea, and it will be further developed by Otto Brahm in his book on Kleist;[72] but Wilbrandt himself is not ready to place this at the centre of his interpretation. No more is Meiningen's chief apologist, Karl Frenzel, who, anticipating his cool response to Ibsen's *Ghosts*, which the Duke of Meiningen was to produce in 1886, wrote in his review of the Berlin performance of *Prinz Friedrich von Homburg* that the weakness of the play lay not so much in the fact of the Prince's fear of death, as in the complexity with which the question of guilt and causation is treated: 'Not until the beginning of the fifth act, with the intervention of the officers, do we escape from the oppressive atmosphere of the psychological problem, and emerge again into the fresh, invigorating atmosphere of history.'[73] It is important for the understanding of this production to note that the Freifrau von Heldburg, who was closely involved in the preparation of Josef Kainz for the title-rôle, was of a quite different opinion from her correspondent and regular literary adviser, Frenzel. In a letter to Chronegk, written shortly before the opening of the production in Berlin, she wrote: 'Prinz Friedrich von Homburg is a very difficult play because it depends so much on points of detail. For the most part the action unfolds on the psychological level, and this has to be spelt out.'[74]

Viewed in the way Frenzel – and possibly the majority of his contemporaries – preferred, as an uncomplicated historical spectacle and a tribute to the Prussian state, *Prinz Friedrich von Homburg* had almost as much to offer contemporary theatrical taste and Meiningen methods as *Julius Caesar*. Its night-time opening scene in the garden of the palace at Fehrbellin required the same effects of lighting and atmosphere, the same movement of a number of actors between different levels as in Act II (the conspiracy scene in Brutus's garden) and Act V (Philippi, with Antony and Octavius looking down at Brutus) of the earlier production. The battle scenes of Act II, with shells exploding both in the distance and close at hand, provided an opportunity to demonstrate those special effects of sound and lighting for which Meiningen productions were renowned. Moreover, to judge by Frenzel's

20   Georg II, sketch for Kleist, *Prinz Friedrich von Homburg*, Act II, scene 1, Battlefield of Fehrbellin, 1878.

description of the scene, it must have borne a certain resemblance to contemporary depictions of Kaiser Wilhelm I, Moltke, the General Staff, and their retinue observing the battle of Sedan from the heights of Donchéry and Fresnois, or Paris from the German siege positions:

It is not possible to see anything more splendid or characteristic than the groups of officers and the arrangement of the battlefield in the second act. A landscape of the Mark [Brandenburg] with gently undulating terrain, a distant horizon, a grey-blue sky, birches and alders, a windmill in the background. From the hilltop old Kottwitz and the Prince, with their retinue, are following the course of the battle being waged in the distance.[75]

The scene in Berlin, before the royal chapel, in which the body of Froben is carried past (Act II, scene 9) required the combination of a large and varied crowd with an architectural setting which anticipated the Meiningen rendering of the coronation scene in *Die Jungfrau von Orléans*. It had the additional advantage of being set in a familiar location, which permitted the very special pleasure of recognition, and a more immediate sense of identification than was afforded by the indirect references or parallels to this very same location (just beneath the Kurfürstenbrücke and, in 1878, overlooked by Schlüter's equestrian statue of the Great Elector) in the Roman setting of *Julius Caesar*.

The production was given its first performance in Meiningen on 28 March 1878, just over a month after the marriage of Crown Prince Bernhard of Meiningen to Princess Charlotte, a granddaughter of Kaiser Wilhelm I.[76] This performance was part of the celebrations welcoming the couple back to Meiningen, and its presentation on such an occasion is further confirmation of the patriotic qualities of the play in the eyes of the Duke of Meiningen. These were to be even more in evidence when the production opened six weeks later in Berlin, for earlier on that day, 11 May 1878, an unsuccessful attempt had been made on the life of the Kaiser by Hödel, and the audience was in a great state of excitement. In Berlin *Prinz Friedrich von Homburg* ran for ten performances, compared with thirteen of *Die Räuber* and nineteen of *The Winter's Tale*; for Frenzel this constituted another success.[77] From Berlin it was taken straight to Frankfurt where, in a tour that had to be curtailed because of a fire in the theatre, it received three performances. It was dropped for the first two stages of the autumn tour of that year (Prague and Leipzig), but brought back into the programme for Breslau, where it was performed four times. In the spring tour of 1879 it was performed four times in Cologne, three times in Hamburg (once on the occasion of the Kaiser's golden wedding),[78] and in the autumn it was taken outside the *Reich* for two performances in Prague and Vienna respectively. In the spring tour of 1880 it was not performed in Amsterdam, but was presented three times in Düsseldorf; in the autumn it was presented three times in Leipzig, but not in Graz. It was omitted from the spring tour of 1881, when the company visited

Bremen and London; but in the autumn it was brought back to be performed twice in Budapest and, finally, twice in Graz, making thirty-eight perform-ances in all. The limited life of the production may have had something to do with the departure of Kainz for Munich in 1880, although Heine, Kraus-neck, and Arndt all took turns as the Prince in the later performances. However, the total number of performances indicates no more than moder-ate success, and the pattern outlined above suggests a certain hesitation about taking what was felt to be a very Prussian play to parts of Europe where it might not have been immediately appreciated – or, for that matter, to parts of Germany, for Kainz (not a man to underestimate the response to his own performances) noted a certain coolness in recently annexed Frankfurt, both with himself and Robert in the title-rôle; and Wedde notes, with regret, poor attendances in Hamburg.[79]

An edition of *Prinz Friedrich von Homburg* published by Reclam of Leip-zig, which was used as a prompt-book, is in the possession of the Theatre Museum in Meiningen. In it are noted the dates of the performances in Berlin (1878), Cologne, Hamburg, Prague, and Vienna (1879), and it con-tains the seal of the Prague censor, with the date 28 September 1879. The editing of the text is much less extensive than in the case of *Julius Caesar*, though there are a number of cuts of up to nine lines at a time, marked in pencil; further minor amendments are indicated in two sets of written instructions sent by the Duke of Meiningen to Chronegk.[80] The official Meiningen edition of this play was published by Grumbkow of Dresden in 1879. This published text is not identical to the prompt-book, some of the material cut having been restored in the printed edition; moreover, contem-porary reviews suggest that not all of the cuts indicated in the prompt-book were, in fact, made in all performances. Here, too, it is difficult to reach firm conclusions about important aspects of the production.

The amendments indicated fall into three categories: historical, dramatur-gical, and substantive. The historical corrections are slight and concern only names: in Act I, scene 5 (l. 233) the name of the *Kurfürstin*, mentioned once by her husband, the Elector, is changed from Elisa to the historically correct Luise; the name of the Prussian field marshal is improved from Dörfling to Derfling (not, however, to the historically correct Derflinger, for the extra syllable would have disrupted the verse where the name is mentioned in the dialogue (l. 417)). More serious discrepancies with the historical record are not susceptible of correction; in fact the whole of the central conflict in the play is fictitious, and in Frederick the Great's account it figures only as a hypothesis; at the time of the battle of Fehrbellin the Prince of Homburg was a married man of over forty, with an artificial leg;[81] and the palace at Fehrbellin, the setting for much of the action, existed only in Kleist's imagination. The dramaturgical amendments are also fairly slight, and serve to concentrate the action around Homburg, the Elector, and Natalie (for instance the cutting of the lines which Natalie addresses to her lady-in-waiting in Act IV, scene 4 (ll. 1,319–21), when Homburg has received the crucial letter from the Elector with the conditional offer of pardon), or else to heighten the dramatic effect by speeding up the action towards the end of a scene or act (the cutting of Hohenzollern's last moment of hesitation (ll. 494–95) before he follows Homburg and Kottwitz into battle).[82]

Of more importance for the substance of the drama is the omission of two lines from Hohenzollern's speech to Homburg in Act III, scene 3 (ll. 920–21) and three lines from Homburg's speech in Act III, scene 5 (1,027–29). Both speeches refer to the possibility of marriage between Natalie and Karl Gustav of Sweden as a means of sealing the peace between the two states. The aspirations of Homburg to the hand of Natalie, and any consequent unwillingness on her part to co-operate in a dynastic marriage, would undermine the political calculations of the Elector, and this introduces an ambiguous element into the motivation of his treatment of Homburg, to which Hohenzollern draws the latter's attention. The omission of the five lines referred to does not eliminate this factor entirely, but it goes some way to mitigating its critical implications for the character and conduct of the Elector, and so contributes to the idealisation of him as a wise, responsible, and understanding sovereign.

More important still is the omission of six lines from the speech in which Natalie appeals to the Elector on Homburg's behalf in Act IV, scene 1, where she asks him to balance the severity of the Prussian military code by acknowledging also the claims of human feeling. The climax of this appeal in the two lines: 'Das Kriegsgesetz, das weiß ich wohl, soll herrschen, / Jedoch die lieblichen Gefühle auch' (ll. 1,125–30), occupies a central rôle in modern interpretations of the play, which see the Elector, the stern embodiment of the letter of the law, undergoing an educational process comparable and parallel to that experienced by Homburg, the exponent of unfettered individualism.[83] The omission of these lines would very seriously distort the tendency of Kleist's play by shifting the balance in favour of the Elector; it would, however, be entirely characteristic of the 1870s, when such idealisation was the order of the day, and criticism of the Prussian state and its rulers was alien to the German mentality.

However, in his review of the Berlin performance, Lindau actually quotes the important lines of Natalie, though he does so without, it seems, recognising any of their critical implications; nor is it clear from his review that he is in fact referring to the play as performed.[84] Wedde, on the other hand, who takes a simple, unidealised view of the Elector's aims: 'To crush headstrongness and assert the claims of discipline!', and a very critical view of his character: 'one of the most hideously distasteful tyrants of world literature', and who emphasises the significance of the relationship of Homburg and Natalie as a possible motivating factor for the Elector's severity, does not

base his appraisal on an interpretation of Natalie's lines, with their implications of inflexibility and inhumanity.[85]

If the implications of this particular omission are clear enough, its causes
are not. Performing in public theatres, the Meiningen company was subject
to control by the censor, and occasionally suffered at his hands.[86] If cuts were
not made directly at his behest, they may well have been made in anticipation. In this particular case it seems unlikely that the text was consciously
being given a more unambiguously pro-Prussian tendency, for the lines of
Natalie are restored in the official printed text; and, in any case, such an
intention is not easily reconciled with other important aspects of this production.

To accommodate the text to the realistic stage required slightly less ingenuity
than had been the case with *Julius Caesar*, since the second half of the play
calls for sets that have already been used in the first part. Furthermore,
Kleist's own act and scene divisions produce an alternation between exterior
and interior locations, between deep and shallow sets, reducing scene
changes, or else permitting them to be effected smoothly with the aid of the
scene-curtain. The scenes and settings were as follows:[87]

Act I	scene 1	Fehrbellin; garden of the palace	(scenes 1–4)
	scene 2	Fehrbellin; room of the Elector	(scenes 5–6)
Act II	scene 1	Fehrbellin; battlefield	(scenes 1–2)
	scene 2	Village inn	(scenes 3–8)
	scene 3	Berlin; outside the chapel of the royal palace	(scenes 9–10)
Act III	scene 1	Fehrbellin; prison cell	(scenes 1–2)
	scene 2	Fehrbellin; room of the Kurfürstin	(scenes 3–5)
Act IV	scene 1	as in I, 2	(scenes 1–2)
	scene 2	as in III, 1	(scenes 3–4)
Act V	scene 1	as in I, 2	(scenes 1–9)
	scene 2	as in I, 1	(scene 10)

The real basis for the designs was, as we have indicated, largely provided
by familiar locations in and around Berlin. Documents, descriptions, and
sketches were, as usual, sent to the Brückners by the Duke, who, as for the
Caesar decorations, specified those esoteric details which historical accuracy
required. The sketch of the scene outside the royal chapel (Act II, scene 3)
was annotated as follows:

Prince of Homburg. Scene before the royal chapel in Berlin. Setting: looking from the
Kurfürstenbrücke, on the right the Spree, on the left the arcade which used to stand in
front of the main wing of the palace, and which resembles the gallery which used to be
in the *Stechbahn* [A street in Berlin in which, since the eighteenth century, a number of
publishers had their offices] in the 1850s. The higher this arcade can be, the better.
Instead of the two chapel windows in the chapel door, which must be wide enough to
allow Froben's coffin to be placed there, surrounded by clergy and soldiers [*sic*]. On the
right the square is bounded by a balustrade and statues. The wings on the right

represent the Elector's ship, which can be seen in the photolithograph of the Elector's palace in Cöln on the Spree. The ship should be so arranged that people can stand on it.

The flies: festoons of foliage and flowers which hang from the windows of the palace across to the ship and are wrapped round with flags in parts. Brandenburg flags: either white and red, or white with the eagle of Brandenburg; and flags of the House of Orange, in honour of the *Kurfürstin* Luise, née Princess of Orange, who appears in the play. The colours are, I believe!!! orange and blue. Look into this. At present there are high trees growing in this square; would it be a good idea to put one in?

Below:

It must be possible for Froben's coffin to be carried past behind this pillar.

Moon and torchlight.[88]

For the imaginary palace at Fehrbellin he proposed local models, the French wing of his own castle at Heldburg, and his palace at Liebenstein; he specified a building in the renaissance style of the seventeenth century, because that was the style the Elector loved.[89]

The practice of breaking up the stage area and creating a number of different levels by the introduction of steps and other practicable units was continued, and their use for expressive rather than merely decorative purposes was further developed; Wedde, for instance, found this aspect of the production more satisfying than in *Julius Caesar*.[90] In the opening scene in particular the space thereby created was used with great care and deliberation to render visible the contrast between the world of the Elector and his court, and the world inhabited by Homburg, the romantic dreamer. The Elector and his party came out by a door in the rear of the set from the artificially lit and animated renaissance palace, entering the stage at an elevated level. From there they were able to observe the Prince, in the quiet, moonlit garden below, before descending the steps and advancing downstage to approach him, seated under a tree in line with the second wing. Frenzel describes the scene as follows:

The garden, wonderfully illuminated by the silver moonlight, with the castle, behind the windows of which lights were moving to and fro, and from which a staircase led downwards; the Prince sitting dreaming on the bench, weaving a laurel wreath, when suddenly the palace door was opened and the Elector, followed by ladies and gentlemen, in the gleam of the lights and torches, came down the steps to listen to the strange hero.[91]

The crucial action takes place at the dividing line between the two parts of the set: downstage right and upstage left; and as the Elector and his party hastily retreat it is at the foot of the steps that Homburg snatches Natalie's glove, only to be left, outside and below, as the palace door is firmly shut (see the Duke's sketches, figs. 21 and 22).

The isolation and confusion of Homburg in his position between dream and reality, established in this first scene, are recalled and reinforced by the arrangement of the final part of the act. Here, in the Elector's room, the court party, including Natalie, form a group, again on the left; and, following

21–2   Georg II, sketches for *Prinz Friedrich von Homburg*, Act I, scene I, 1878.

23 Georg II, sketch for *Prinz Friedrich von Homburg*, Act I, scene 5, 1878.

Kleist's own stage-direction, the officers gather around Dörfling for the briefing on the opposite side of the stage. The Duke's instructions specify that the Prince is left very much on the fringe of the group of officers, on the side nearer the court party:

During the Elector's speech to the gentlemen of the court and the princesses the officers and Derfling move together in such a way that the Prince stands on the left, at the edge of the group, with Hohenzollern next to him, and Golz behind. Before Derfling begins to dictate he speaks quietly with Truchß and Hennings. [See the sketch, fig. 23.]

Another characteristic feature of Brückner-Meiningen sets, the implication that the space of the action continues beyond the visible area of the stage, is evident in the prominent openings leading off from the set: the door to the palace referred to above (acts I and V); the entrance to the Elector's room (Act I, scene 2); and the *aperçu* through the open doorway of the royal chapel (Act II, scene 3). In this last scene the effect was intensified by another typical Meiningen technique. The stage, whose useful space was already reduced by the hall projecting from the main wing of the palace on the left, and the river Spree, with boats, on the right, was filled with a large crowd, which was allowed to spill over into the wings. Not all observers found this effect pleasing or appropriate, for this is the scene of the first peripeteia, when the

24   Georg II, sketch for *Prinz Friedrich von Homburg*, Act II, scene 10, scene before the royal chapel in Berlin, 1878.

Elector has Homburg placed under arrest, and, Frenzel argued, it was the principals who needed to be the focus of attention:

Because the stage is over-filled with groups of actors and extras, the action is not made as fully visible as it should be. The Elector, the Prince, the officers, need more room for free movement than they have; from the real heroes the spectators take space, air, and light, as it were.[92]

The implication of action close by, but off-stage, is essential to the battle scene in the first part of Act II, but this follows directly from Kleist's clear intentions. The development of the battle is conveyed through the reaction and comments of the officers; and the dramatic action of this scene reaches its climax in the conflict as Homburg gives the order to signal the advance of the cavalry. The actual fighting is not realised on stage, as it was in *Julius Caesar* within a few paces of the commanding officers, but in the distance and it is concealed by a hillock where the officers stand in order to observe (in the classical manner). Rather than simply leaving his actors to peer vaguely over the horizon, however, the Duke extrapolates from Kleist's dialogue and supplements the stage-directions with very precise indications of how the off-stage action is shaping, and how the action on the stage is related to it. Special effects, in particular battle-noise, including fireworks attached to the scenery to create the impression of shells bursting near to or among the actors, were used to integrate the action in the foreground with the general situation of which it was part.

Authentic models for costumes and equipment for use in this Prussian play were, of course, even more readily available than for *Julius Caesar*, as the

25–6 Georg II, costume sketches for *Prinz Friedrich von Homburg*: Prince of Homburg, General of Cavalry; Colonel in the Regiment of the Kurfürstin.

Hohenzollern Museum had only recently been opened in the Monbijou palace in Berlin. The tapestries on display there, illustrating the exploits of the Great Elector (*Die Kriegstaten des Großen Kurfürsten*), were named by the Duke as the principal source, and these were supplemented by material from the *Zeughaus*, the museum of military history, and by contemporary wood-cuts. As in *Julius Caesar*, there was a high degree of particularisation as to military rank and function in the costuming. Women's costumes were based on contemporary illustrations, but the Duke did not specify which; the eight ladies of the court who appeared in Act II, scene 3, all had new costumes, which the Duke particularly wanted to be seen.[93]

He is most precise in the instructions he gives for the appearance of the Elector. As with Julius Caesar, the correspondence to an image firmly established in the visual arts as the accurate one is an important consideration; the Duke had in mind a very particular portrait, with the highest claims to authenticity:

In Act I the Great Elector appears as he is shown in a painting by a Dutch artist; the portrait is the one which hangs in the Gothic House in Wörlitz. This painting was a gift from the Great Elector to the Prince of Anhalt-Dessau, Commandant of Berlin at the time of the campaign of 1675 against the Swedes.[94]

Clearly he was aiming for that same pleasure of recognition as he had achieved in the earlier production and which, in this particular play, would have provided an even greater degree of satisfaction for a Prussian audience. Fontane evinced this very satisfaction in 1863 in his response to a painting by Hermann Kretzschmer, *The Landing of the Great Elector on the Island of Rügen*: 'the freshness and the well-known figure of the Great Elector, which invariably gives us pleasure whenever we encounter it, will (quite rightly) secure success for this painting'. But Fontane continues with a qualification of his praise which recalls the response of Ostrovskij to the Julius Caesar of Paul Richard in 1885, namely that the success achieved and the satisfaction given by this identity will remain superficial and ephemeral if they are not supported by the substance of the action in which the figure is participating, as was, alas, the case in the painting described by Fontane:

The interest that is aroused here derives solely from the figures of the Great Elector and old Derflinger, but it is an interest such as we normally feel towards the portraits of well-known people, and it is not at all to be confused with the interest in an event that is being depicted: the whole thing is predominantly a *tableau*.[95]

This brings us to the important question of casting, for the resemblance of the actor to a pre-conceived visual image of the character was clearly an important consideration in this production. The actors who took the most characteristically Prussian rôles, Teller as Dörfling, Hellmuth-Bräm as Kottwitz, and, most of all, Josef Nesper as the Elector, seem to have been

27 Adriaen Hannemann, The Great Elector.

particularly successful in this respect. The critic of the *Berliner Gerichts-Zeitung* (14 May 1878) speaks for many in his praise of Nesper's interpretation of the rôle: 'Herr Nesper as the Great Elector corresponded in tone, appearance, and bearing entirely to the image of the creator of Prussian power which lives in the grateful heart of the Prussian people.'

When looking for a possible alternative to Nesper, in case the need should suddenly arise, the Duke reflected: 'Who could replace Nesper? I think Richard would be best, and then Nissen would have to learn the part of Hohenzollern immediately, and Richard that of the Elector, *whom he would also resemble very closely*' [my emphasis].[96] The reference to Paul Richard,

28 Georg II, costume sketch for *Prinz Friedrich von Homburg*, the Great
    Elector, 1878.

who was already playing Caesar on the strength of his close personal resemblance to a received image, is an indication of the nature of the image of the
Great Elector that was being re-created and propagated in the Meiningen
production of *Prinz Friedrich von Homburg*; it is also a reminder that Nesper

did, in fact, have more to bring to the rôle than his imposing physical presence. As the Julius Caesar of the 1874 Meiningen tour he had acquired a special aura; to cast him in 1878 as the Great Elector was to confirm a parallel that had been made implicitly in the earlier production, and to renew that flattery of Prussian national pride which had informed it.

Even more important in its consequences for this production than the casting of Nesper as the Great Elector, indeed, perhaps the most significant aspect of the whole production, was the bold casting of the leading rôle. In order to strengthen the company in the way he had previously done by the engagement of Ludwig Barnay, the Duke of Meiningen had engaged Emerich Robert (currently working in St Petersburg), a well-known actor with a strong public following, whom he knew from his visit to Meiningen in December 1875, when he had played Hamlet and Romeo. In February contractual arrangements had been finalised for Robert to take part in the spring tour, and he had been guaranteed a fee based on a certain number of rôles, including that of Leontes in *The Winter's Tale*.[97] In the previous autumn Chronegk had also engaged the promising young Josef Kainz, after he had given a trial performance as Ferdinand in *Kabale und Liebe* in the course of the summer season at Bad Liebenstein. When preparations began in the New Year for the spring tour Kainz, then in his twentieth year, was given the rôles of Kosinsky (*Die Räuber*), Florizel (*The Winter's Tale*), and – before the engagement of Robert – the Prince of Homburg. It was Kainz who took part in the extensive rehearsals in Meiningen, playing the part of the Prince without the substantial cuts to which Robert was accustomed.[98] He developed his interpretation of the rôle working closely with the Freifrau von Heldburg, and she followed his progress with great interest.

As the time for the spring tour approached, the engagement of Robert began to be experienced as something of an embarrassment; on 24 April the Baroness wrote to Chronegk of the difficulty of making sufficient use of him to provide the agreed honorarium, but she notes (in advance of the Grunert affair, which was to break during this very tour) that she is afraid of trouble with von Hülsen, as chairman of the *Bühnenverein*, if this should not be done.[99] In Berlin Robert was, in fact, given the rôles of Leontes, Karl Moor, and the Prince of Homburg, but he shared this last rôle with Kainz who, after his success as Kosinsky in *Die Räuber*, was chosen by Chronegk to open in *Prinz Friedrich von Homburg* on 11 May, before Robert's expected date of arrival. Kainz played the part three times before being replaced by Robert. On 15 May (after the first reviews, which appeared in the Berlin papers on 13 and 14 May) the Duke wrote to Chronegk that he doubted whether Kainz would be able to play the Prince of Homburg to full houses for twelve consecutive nights, and telling him to make use of Robert; but immediately after the first performance Chronegk had already decided to do so; in a letter to his parents dated 12 May, Kainz describes the precise arrangements for the alternation of the two actors in the rôle. Kainz played the Prince for seven of the ten performances.[100]

The sharing of the leading rôle had interesting results, almost making for two contrasting interpretations of the play. This anticipates curiously the confrontation in Berlin, almost a century later, of the productions of the same play by Hans Lietzau and Peter Stein, the one an accomplished production on traditional lines (but with unorthodox decorations and a significant degree of actualisation in the dramaturgical interventions), the other a radically new reading of the play, by a young ensemble which was in the process of establishing itself as the leading German theatre of the decade.[101] Robert's influence on the production, and his interpretation of the title-rôle, which, like the performances of Nesper and Hellmuth-Bräm, conformed to expectations, were praised by a substantial section of the press and were compared favourably with the interpretation of Kainz. Gottschalk's judgment is characteristic:

In comparison with Herr Kainz, his youthful predecessor in this rôle, who is still a novice . . . the performance of Herr Robert stood out so strikingly that the physiognomy of the hero of Fehrbellin, and at the same time that of the whole play, became quite different.[102]

It seems probable, however, that Robert relied for his success on a traditional, rhetorical style of acting, and on his personal rapport with the public, as a well-known matinée-idol. This departure from Meiningen principles was also noted by contemporary reviewers, a number of whom observed that he was not properly integrated into the ensemble. Albert Lindner (author of the drama *Bluthochzeit*) wrote about this problem:

The part was first played . . . by Herr Kainz – inadequately, everybody said, then he was replaced by Herr Robert – much too well, say I. This example is a very instructive one as far as the merits of the Meiningen productions are concerned. Herr Robert has gradually developed into a virtuoso; he travels around making guest appearances, and has long since forgotten the meaning of the term ensemble; he is accustomed to regard a drama as having been written exclusively for himself, and the other actors as a necessary evil . . . Herr Robert performed too well, and in doing so stepped out of the frame . . . Indeed, the inadequate Herr Kainz was preferable, because at rehearsals in Meiningen he had been schooled in the correct relationship of the parts to the whole.[103]

Kainz, performing in the Prussian capital with an unorthodox interpretation, was handled very much more roughly by the majority of the critics, especially for his rendering of the scene in which Homburg is overcome by his fear of death:

how indescribable was his failure in the celebrated scene in which he expresses the fear of death! . . . It must be played throughout in a tone of horror; not as an outpouring of pitiful cowardice, but as a cry of terror, which must also seize us, move us, and shake us to the core. Instead, Herr Kainz so whined and wailed that there cannot have been anyone in the theatre who did not scornfully reject this prince.[104]

Like his mentor, the Freifrau von Heldburg, Kainz had no illusions about the difficulty of the rôle, but precisely because of its difficulty he saw it as an opportunity to be grasped with both hands: 'Once I have been applauded as the Prince of Homburg in Berlin, I shall be able to deal much more confidently with Dingelstedt, for some of the greatest actors have come to grief over this rôle, and even for Sonnenthal it was a tough nut.'[105] It says a great deal for the courage of Kainz, and for that of the Baroness and Chronegk, who supported him, that he did so in such an uncompromising fashion, for criticism did not only come from hostile Berlin critics.

Among those who attended the first Berlin performance was Professor Karl Werder, dramaturgical adviser to the Duke and his wife, who had been present at rehearsals and had assisted in preparations for the production. From Berlin he wrote enthusiastically about every aspect except the performance of Kainz:

Yet another great success! Kleist's glorious work has been seen for the first time in the theatre . . . and if Kainz were able to accomplish more than he has done so far and than he showed yesterday, one would also have to say that it had been *heard* for the first time . . . Sc. 1: a wonderful impression, acted well by everybody – *until* Kainz began; then I became anxious and was relieved when he left the stage. In both of the rehearsals he had been holding something back – now I *heard* him in the part for the first time – he got everything wrong . . . Act III: Kainz a little better, and when he is overcome by fear quite good . . . Here he brought out the essential point in the character, which is the reason for the instability and the collapse, and which explains the following scene . . . Sc. 2: Kainz tried his best here . . . but he will have to learn to do it differently. Through what happens to him the Prince *becomes* a man. Kainz remains too much of a youth . . . As soon as he has to express anything other than extreme excitement he does so in a manner which enrages me.[106]

With hindsight, it is possible to see that Werder's criticisms are focussed on those very features of Kainz's acting which were to become characteristic of his art, and were to secure him the reputation of the representative actor of his generation, the modern actor *par excellence*. Three critical points are made: firstly, Werder, himself praised by the Duke as a model for his 'delightful' recitation of one of the Elector's speeches ('Wenn ich der Dei von Tunis wäre', ll. 1,414–24) is critical of Kainz's declamation, which makes many of his lines inaudible; secondly, he praises the extreme, emphatic end of Kainz's expressive register, but is critical of the rest; and he sums up his impression with criticism of the excessively youthful quality of the interpretation.

The mature Kainz was particularly known for the speed of his delivery, which was achieved by disregard of the rational structure indicated by punctuation, and a hasty passing-over of the trivial or banal in order to bring out most clearly the line of the essential emotional or psychological development. A well-known example is, in fact, a speech from the opening of this very play, where he so displeased Werder, the speech in which Homburg explains to Hohenzollern how he came to be in possession of Natalie's glove: 'Hoch auf, gleich einem Genius des Ruhms, / Hebt sie den Kranz' (ll. 172–91). Kainz is said to have delivered this speech in half the normal time, because he treated the first eighteen lines as a preparation for the last two, the dream as a contrast to reality.[107] Such a contrast would have been very much in keeping with the character of the opening of the drama in the Meiningen production. Interestingly, the instructions sent by the Duke to Chronegk after rehearsal refer explicitly to this speech. Although he makes no mention of speed, the Duke's comments do seem to indicate his assent to the division created by Kainz in his recitation of the lines: 'The great speech: "Hoch auf etc." must be spoken with an undertone of real astonishment, of incomprehension, but not too loudly, and rising only at the end.' Moreover, there is, at the end of this act, a counterpart to Homburg's glove speech, beginning when Natalie discovers that she has lost the glove (l. 286), continuing throughout Homburg's inattentive participation in the vital briefing before the battle of Fehrbellin, and reaching its climax in the Prince's concluding monologue (ll. 355–65). Here the Duke's rehearsal notes specify that the final sentence be spoken slowly and emphasis be concentrated on the crucial word 'Glück' ('fortune'); the director seems intent on bringing out the parallel between the two episodes.[108]

The more intense outbursts of Kainz, which are the only thing about his performance which Werder can find to praise, seem not to have impressed the Duke to quite the same extent, at least not when they are allowed to become too dominant. The rehearsal notes contain four warnings to Kainz not to be too loud (and one to speak really *mezzo voce*), and one instruction not to be too angry; he also makes the general observation that there is 'too much shouting'. What this suggests is that the Duke was not interested in excitement for its own sake, but that he was seeking a differentiated expression of the full range of Homburg's emotions, from elation to sudden and unexpected despair, from resistance to the total abandonment of resistance. It may well be that he had caught a glimpse in Kainz of the actor who was to win the admiration of Hofmannsthal and his generation for the completeness and rapidity of his transformations, for his portrayal of instability and nervous tension; *angespannt* (tense and excited) is the word the Duke uses to describe how Kainz should appear in the battle scene of Act II.[109]

It was, to come to Werder's third point, precisely in youthful rôles that Kainz was to secure his reputation, in particular in youthful rôles which brought him into confrontation with much stronger or older figures: Ferdinand in *Kabale und Liebe*, Mortimer in *Maria Stuart*, Don Karlos, Romeo, and, above all, Hamlet.[110] In the ideal cast proposed by Otto Brahm for Ibsen's *Ghosts*, before it had yet been performed in Germany, in 1884, it was 'self-evidently' Kainz whom he proposed for the part of Oswald.[111] It was with even greater prescience that the Freifrau von Heldburg wrote to

Chronegk after the bad press which Kainz had received in Berlin in 1878, urging him to support and encourage the young actor:

Tell him that no one is better aware of his faults and short-comings than I am – for the rôle of the Prince his worst fault is his youth, but he must not let it annoy him, he must press on regardless. He really is a great talent and he will get on – he has his failings, but justice has not been done to his performance as the Prince.[112]

As it happened Kainz scarcely needed such encouragement. His own letters speak enthusiastically and proudly of his success as Homburg, above all in comparison with Robert. It may, of course, be that, in writing to his parents, he was simply putting on a brave face; but it may equally well be a reflection of the actor's confidence in a carefully considered and thoroughly rehearsed approach to the part, and a determination to stand by a new interpretation until it secured the recognition it deserved. This recognition was not to be long coming. Otto Brahm, whose influence was growing rapidly, was to write in 1885 of the inspired naturalness of Kainz's performance in this scene which decided him in favour of the actor; and his close associate in the emergent naturalist theatre, Paul Schlenther, was to observe in 1892 that it was Kainz who first opened people's eyes to the way this rôle should be played.[113]

On only one other occasion was the Meiningen directorial team able to work with a very gifted, but still young and inexperienced performer as the star of a new production. In 1887 Amanda Lindner, then only seventeen, was cast as Johanna in Schiller's *Die Jungfrau von Orléans*. The consequence, if we follow Brahm's account, was a production not unlike that of *Prinz Friedrich von Homburg*, full of extreme contrasts between the ideal, the historical, and the psychological, between dream and reality.[114] With Amanda Lindner's portrayal of the protagonist as innocent, childlike, naive, and enthusiastic, these contrasts could be emphasised and given their full theatrical value; whereas the Amazonian figure of an actress such as Klara Ziegler made nonsense of the suggestion that the delicate maid might have taken on an unsuitable job: 'Was will die zarte Jungfrau unter Waffen?' Unlike *Prinz Friedrich von Homburg* this production was an almost unquestioned public success; its path was smoother because it did not contradict national preconceptions in the way that Kainz's interpretation of Homburg did. Indeed, the reduction in the heroic scale of Johanna, and the shift of emphasis to the realistic aspects of Schiller's complex portrayal of her character, would most probably have proved congenial to German audiences, for this was a time when the qualities of Joan of Arc as resistance heroine were being celebrated by the recently defeated enemy, France.[115]

In both of these productions the Freifrau von Heldburg played an important part in the preparation of the leading performer; and both bear, in the very special care applied to their visual and historical aspects, the strong and unmistakable imprint of her husband. They are equally balanced productions, which show a readiness to exploit the potential of a particular individual talent within a coherently conceived production, and to do so in an original way. There is no firm evidence, in the form of explicit statements, that the Duke or his wife understood the full implications of Kainz's performance: the modern, existential anxiety expressed in his total collapse after the sight of his open grave. However, the priority they gave to aesthetic criteria, the search for an original and consistent production, enabled them to transcend the ideological limitations which restricted their more traditionalist advisers and critics in their understanding of this important play.

For the production of *Prinz Friedrich von Homburg* there is a complete set of *Inszenierungsvorschriften* (the Duke's notes and instructions, set down by the Baroness after rehearsal). They have already been referred to extensively, but because of their considerable documentary value, they are printed here in full.[116]

Act 1

scene 1

1. Kainz looks too dressed – the Duke does not want him to be wearing a sash; however, this will have to be fitted with hooks so that it can be put on quickly during the interval before the next scene.

2. Kainz must take a lot more trouble with the wreath – it would also be better if there were some more leaves near him on the bench – there need not be much.

3. Pay attention to Richard's [Hohenzollern] pronunciation of the sounds 'eu' and 'au', especially in these first lines, in the words: 'Und sich erst *heute* wieder atemlos', 'Der ganze Flecken könnt in *Feuer* aufgehn', 'Wie eine florne *Haube auf*probieren'.

4. When Richard wakes him Kainz gets up too quickly and is awake too soon. He must still be rubbing his eyes and be half-asleep when he says the words: 'Ah, my friend' [94], and: 'What cavalry?' [98]; and he must still be sleepy during the next three speeches: 'Quick, my helmet, my armour' [101]; 'On the right, Heinz' [102]; and 'Yes, there I think I put . . .' [103]; otherwise he would notice that he is not in his own room. Then with great excitement and anger: 'Come here, Franz, that scoundrel who was supposed to wake me up' [109]. The action is *very* difficult here, and the longer Kainz appears disorientated, not entirely lucid, not fully awake, the easier it will be for him. I have not yet been entirely satisfied with this part of the scene; Kainz must rub his eyes and hold his hand to his brow as if he does not fully comprehend his situation; he must look now at Richard, now at the garden, and, as I have said, not be awake too soon.

5. Then, as if looking for an excuse: 'Forgive me! I remember. It was the heat you know' [117]; at least as far as here.

6. After Richard's words, 'Go on!' [164], Kainz does not pause – but it must be made clear that he is thinking to himself: 'No, it is better not to tell him', before he says drily and ironically: 'It probably was Fräulein von Platen' [165].

7. The great speech: 'High, like an angel of Glory etc.' [172], must be spoken with an undertone of real astonishment, of incomprehension; but not too loudly, and rising only at the end.

8. The words: 'What! Me? Upon my soul –!' [199] must be more emphatic.

9. As he leads the Prince off stage, Richard must place his arm around his shoulder; the Prince, of course, must be on the side nearer the audience.

scene 2

1. The notebooks provided here are poor; at least a few larger and better ones could perhaps be provided, for instance for the Prince, who tears a sheet out of his notebook in Act II and writes down an order on it – here his notebook has always seemed ridiculously small to me. I also noticed the officers smiling at it during the first performance.

2. I have already told Frau Berg [*Kurfürstin*] that she must not be too tearful here – solemn, concerned, but composed. The Elector always took his wife on campaigns, and so she was already accustomed to battles; but there must, of course, be no suggestion of indifference. At the end of the scene, in the actual leave-taking, she can shed a tear, but she must not overdo it. Here I should also like to add that I find the small lace handkerchiefs of the two leading ladies, which they roll up in their hands like dumplings, quite dreadful. Such little rags did not become fashionable until recent times, and even now only at balls or with formal dress, never on a journey. Frau Berg and Fräulein Pauli [Natalie] should have simple linen handkerchiefs – they can surely afford them out of their salary. In Act II, with all the weeping, the little lace dumplings are just too silly.

3. Nesper [the Elector] must say: 'Ramin will take my dear *Luise*' [233]. *Not* Elisa. The Elector's first wife, whom Kleist wrongly allows to be still alive (his second wife was called Dorothea), was called Luise, as every Prussian knows nowadays.

4. One of Teller's [Dörfling] main faults in this scene is that he speaks all his lines as if dictating, and not just the actual plan of the battle. Please watch out for this, dear Director, and if you have not first drawn his attention to it, you will see what I mean. In the *prompt-book* (which I am enclosing, but which I would like you to have yourself because of all the comments I have made during the rehearsals) I have underlined the passages *to be dictated* in red. Take care that Teller does not speak too *quickly*, and pay attention to his 'a', which always sounds like an 'ä'.

5. At the end of the scene Nesper must be more forceful, although he is quite right to avoid all pathos in his characterisation of the Elector.

6. From the moment when Natalie recognises the glove as hers, Kainz must look blissful, his face must be *radiant*, it must be radiant when he says: 'Then he will have the fanfare sounded' [322], radiant while the orders are being dictated, radiant when the Elector gives his warning, in short, radiant throughout. But he must not speak the last sentence too quickly, and must give more emphasis to the word 'Fortune' [358]. However, he has always spoken the lines beautifully. But, if the other gentlemen do not also look forward to the battle with excitement and enthusiasm, the scene does not achieve any effect. Just let *everyone* stand still for a moment before the final exit, so that there is absolute silence. It is only a matter of a minute.

7. Nissen [an officer] should, of course, participate in the action here, in Berlin [Act II, scene 10], and in Act V.

Act II

scene 1

Who can replace Hellmuth [-Bräm] [Kottwitz] on the day of a performance? Kober? Speak to him some time, for as soon as the weather turns damp Hellmuth might get rheumatism. Have you given him my book? The remedy is a well-tried one. Who could replace Nesper? I think Richard would be best, and then Nissen would have to learn the part of Hohenzollern immediately, and Richard that of the Elector, whom he would also resemble closely. Foresight is the mother . . . as you know.

1. In the battle scene the gentlemen express the various sensations too monotonously – I have made the appropriate comments in the text.

2. There is also too much shouting.

scene 2

1. Heine [Mörner] ought to tie a white cloth around his head, the black one does not stand out against his hair. He speaks too softly. It must sound as if it is meant to be quiet, but it must be more than a whisper.

2. The *Kurfürstin* must prepare her swoon well, in the way we agreed – for instance, at Heine's final words: 'Then there would have been no one' [560], she must, while she is standing, indicate with her hands that she feels faint. The sentence: 'A victory too dearly bought; I like it not; pay me back the price it cost' [563–64], must be spoken *without expression, staccato* – not with resonance and pathos, but feebly.

3. In this scene, especially at the beginning, Kainz must make more pauses, and speak quietly and with restraint of the misfortune; for instance, he should make a pause immediately after his entrance, before he begins to speak; he enters, and looks not only at Natalie but, with sympathy, at the *Kurfürstin, silently* takes Natalie's hand, presses it to his heart and speaks really *mezzo voce*.

4. 'I will be the executor of this last will' [585–86], should be spoken in a really firm and manly way; I have always found it too muffled.

5. During Kober's [Sparren] report Frau Berg should not forget for a single instant to indicate her joy that the Elector is alive. Even when she shudders at the description of the battle she must not appear *anxious* any longer, for she now knows that he has come to no harm. At Froben's death: sad but thankful; a few tears, but no sobbing; it must not look like a repetition of the reaction to Heine's report, for the situation is quite different. In the two scenes the difference in the acting of Frau Berg has never been clear enough for me.

6. In her moment of embarrassment towards the end of the scene Fräulein Pauli assumes too grim an expression – she must appear *graciously* embarrassed.

7. Kainz's concluding words, 'O Caesar Divus! etc.' must be no less fiery than hitherto, but not too loud.

scene 3, Berlin

1. The eight ladies-in-waiting with the new costumes must be so placed that they can be properly seen and they must not hide themselves. The most beautiful outfits are those of Frau Bittner and Fräulein Brückmüller; in the foreground the two principal ladies near Schwenke look very attractive.

2. The Director must look from the side boxes at the scene when the Elector is outside [the circle of officers] and, if necessary, move everything back a little so that *something* can be seen from there. The present groupings must, of course, be preserved.

3. Tell all the officers firmly to participate with actions and gestures, both when the Elector gives the order relating to the Prince, and when the latter permits himself to inveigh against it. They must glance cautiously at the Elector to see what he is going to say, and look anxiously at the Prince – Richard and Prasch [Golz] could try, by discreet signs and looks, to prevent him from talking himself more deeply into trouble. In the speech: 'Perhaps you will be free again tomorrow' [776], Prasch must be more distinct; I have not yet understood it.

4. The crowd must also show more interest: joy and enthusiasm in welcoming the Elector when he enters; surprise and astonishment at the arrival of the Prince; and

sympathy when he is arrested; but for heaven's sake let us not see any bored or even indifferent faces, either among the officers or among the groups in the crowd.

Act III

scene 1
Warn Kainz *very firmly* not to make a particular habitual gesture with his hand splayed and raised in the air.
    1. At the beginning Kainz innocently relaxed, not downcast, quite confident; Richard, on the other hand, indicating his depressed state all the more evidently. He should look sideways at the Prince, shaking his head, should make pauses, etc.
    2. Here already Kainz is often speaking too loudly, for instance in the words: 'Because I did so' [843], and several others. Please read my comments in the prompt-book, as I do not have time to write at length.

scene 2
    1. The *Kurfürstin* must not forget to go to the window when she says: 'In the study . . . light' [955].
    2. When the *Kurfürstin* puts the scarf on Natalie she should put it *underneath* her hair – in the circumstances Natalie herself must not bother with it, but it does not look good if, as was the case here, her hair is flattened by the scarf.
    3. Fräulein Krause [second lady-in-waiting] should participate *only* by means of facial expression, in a very considered and attentive way.
    4. Kainz is too *loud* throughout this scene. Look at the comments in the prompt-book. Kainz also sweats a great deal – could you not tell him gently and tactfully that, *if it is possible*, he should discreetly wipe away the sweat.
    5. Frau Berg performs least well in this scene; the tone she adopts is too detached; it is a question of the Prince's *life*; nor is she sufficiently shaken by his sudden – for her surprising – display of cowardice.

Act IV

scene 1
    1. Nesper must take care to avoid the mannerisms and tone of a romantic lead.
    2. Fräulein Pauli must make a pause before she kneels down, and another after kneeling, but before she speaks.
    3. At *all* rehearsals the sealing, the writing with ink, and the use of sand must be decently rehearsed with all the props. Nothing looks worse than when all of this, especially the sealing, is not done properly, but is awkward and hurried. For instance, a tiny drop of sealing wax, which is then smeared around, looks effeminate – the wax should be held properly to the flame and then allowed to drop down onto the paper.
    4. Make sure that Fräulein Pauli carries out all the dramatist's stage-directions, when reading etc.

scene 2
    1. 'Bring up a chair' [1,320]; little Grevenberg [Fräulein von Bork] must not forget to go across the stage to the chair, which, however, is not then used.
    2. In this scene, too, take full note of the dramatist's stage-directions; in the last performance this was forgotten.
    3. In the speech: 'Since he stands so worthily before me [The Duke misquotes 'gegenüber' instead of 'vor'; the suggestion of confrontation might well be a reflection

of a particular emphasis in Kainz's performance.], I will etc.' [1,380], Kainz must be noble, dignified, calm, determined, but not rude or angry towards the Elector. The speech must evoke respect for the Prince.

4. Tell Pauli to begin the words: 'Take this kiss' [1,386] in a deep voice; she must not, for heaven's sake, as in the last performance, pause after 'Take'.

5. At the end of the scene a farewell gesture towards the Prince, but she leaves willingly.

Act v

scene I

1. Nesper ought some time to listen to Werder reciting his little monologue: 'If I were the Dey of Tunis' [1,412]; he is present at the rehearsals and speaks it delightfully.

2. Teller must be more excited in tone and manner.

3. In this scene particularly, Nesper ought to take care with his upper register, which does not match the person of the Elector, nor his own imposing appearance.

4. The Duke has written to you about the silent playing of the officers.

Several important characteristic features emerge from these notes, and they illustrate further the principles which underlie the Meiningen production style: the visual realisation of details which explain and reinforce what is implicit in the dialogue (Homburg's waking from his dream, Act I, scene 4); the complete absorption of all the participants in the action taking place on the stage (the briefing of the officers, Act I, scenes 5 and 6; the arrest of Homburg, Act II, scene 10); the scrupulous attention to the slightest detail of costume, requisites, and procedures, so as to ensure both authenticity according to historical or social criteria and appropriateness in terms of aesthetic criteria (the ladies' handkerchiefs and the officers' note-pads, Act I, scene 5); the desire for ease and naturalness in carrying out stage-business, to be achieved by constant practice with the actual properties to be used in the performance (the sealing of the letter, Act IV, scene 2), an insistence on naturalness in speech, combined, where appropriate, with the dignity required by rank (Nesper, Act v); the avoidance of excessive shouting; the preservation of the distinction between normal conversation and dictation (Teller, Act I, scene 5); the avoidance of stereotyped mannerisms (Nesper, Act IV, scene 1) and stereotyped gestures (Kainz, Act III, scene 1); a very careful attention to positioning, grouping and physical contact between actors, both to achieve pleasing visual effects and to bring out clearly the relationship of the participants to each other at a particular stage in the action (Homburg and Hohenzollern, end of Act I, scene 3).

Running through these instructions is a suspicion of theatricality, that is to say effect of a meretricious kind; this is combined with the clear desire to create an attractive visual spectacle. The paradox inherent in this combination is resolved by transforming *effect* into *situation*, that is to say by providing motivation. This procedure is exemplified in the instruction relating to the exit of the officers at the end of Act I, namely that they should all

stand silent and still for just a moment before leaving the stage. The situation
is that of tense expectation in anticipation of the forthcoming battle; the
effect is that of the *tableau* of the conventional act-ending.

The Duke's instructions to Chronegk prescribe that same indirect relationship between actor and public as was noted in the production of *Julius
Caesar*. The speeches are to be delivered to the other characters on the stage,
and these other characters are required to signal their attentiveness by visible
reactions. This may well have been one of the aspects of the scene of the
arrest of Homburg which Frenzel found disturbing. The Duke, on the other
hand, was disturbed by the indifference of the bystanders, and he severely
criticises his actors if their attention flags, for instance with reference to Act
v, scene 5, when Kottwitz surprises the Elector by his arrival at the head of
his regiment with a petition on behalf of the Prince of Homburg:

> Throughout their entire scene the officers must make it a matter of pride to concentrate
> on the action with the greatest attention. If just one of them thinks of anything else even
> for a moment, the scene will be spoilt. Will you therefore take Herr Rüdiger aside and
> tell him that during the last performance I noticed that he was distracted for a moment
> and looked in a direction that had nothing to do with the action, and that that ruined
> the whole scene for me. Such inattentiveness is worse than if an actor in the leading-rôle
> gets his lines wrong.[117]

Kainz was evidently very committed to this manner of performing. Shortly
before he opened as the Prince of Homburg, and after he had been widely
praised as Kosinsky in *Die Räuber*, he wrote self-critically to his parents of
his performance in this latter rôle: 'In this part I am still playing too much for
applause'; and he was scornful of what he regarded as the mannered acting of
Emerich Robert, implying that it was intended to appeal directly to the
female members of the audience.[118]

The special circumstances under which the opening performance of *Prinz
Friedrich von Homburg* took place in 1878, however, conspired against such a
clear separation between stage and auditorium. The attempt on the life of the
Kaiser earlier in the day had created a situation very like that at the beginning
of the third act of Kleist's play: false rumours of the death of the Prussian
ruler had been in circulation for some time, and, to general relief, had then
been corrected. Chronegk responded to the state of excitement which prevailed by prefacing the performance with the Prussian anthem, 'Heil dir im
Siegerkranz', to which the audience responded with wild applause. The
same direct response was evoked by the concluding line of the play, which, in
the circumstances, must have assumed a distinctly threatening character
towards the enemies of the contemporary state: 'In Staub mit allen Feinden
Brandenburgs!'[119]

The critics, as we have seen, were divided about this production, traditionally patriotic elements being widely praised, and Emerich Robert

being played off against Kainz (as Barnay had been played off against the permanent members of the company in the production of *Julius Caesar*) by a number of reviewers. It was felt in Meiningen that the general response of the Berlin critics was, on this occasion, particularly hostile. The Baroness wrote to Chronegk:

I do believe that this will be the last time the theatre visits Berlin, for the tone [of the criticism] there is almost insupportable; not only must it undermine the pleasure derived by our members from their work, as it does for the three of us, but it will also significantly lessen the attractiveness elsewhere of those productions which have been criticised in Berlin. Frenzel would like us to have some opposition! Well, I think he can be satisfied after Homburg!! Disregarding the quite contemptible articles in the [*Berliner*] Tageblatt [Blumenthal] and the *Börsenzeitung*, which run each other very close in terms of baseness, both the Duke and I find that there is less informed comment than before, whether this be well-disposed and favourable, or carefully considered, but critical.

She wonders whether some steps might not be taken to counter the attacks, for instance by asking Julius Rodenberg to write something, which might at least give the members of the company a taste of revenge.[120] Clearly, then, the bitterness was very deep and genuine; which suggests a profound commitment to the production of *Prinz Friedrich von Homburg*, the most censured production of the 1878 tour, and one of the most challenging and provocative productions mounted by the Meiningen Court Theatre during the whole touring period.

The following notices are by Fontane's colleague on the *Vossische Zeitung*, Max Remy. He was a respected drama critic, and was largely sympathetic to the work of the Meininger, although the Baroness was not happy about even his reports in 1878.[121]

Last Saturday, as the second offering in this year's touring programme, the Meiningen Court Theatre Company presented Heinrich von Kleist's play, *Prinz Friedrich von Homburg*. As has already been reported elsewhere in the Sunday edition of this newspaper, the universal joy at the rescue of our beloved Emperor from threatening danger was given happily improvised and heartfelt expression in the singing of the national hymn by the orchestra behind the curtain and the enthusiastic applause of those present, who had stood up from their seats. Then the curtain rose, and in an atmosphere of solemnity the public followed the changing scenes of this patriotic work. In this, the finest and most beautiful drama of the unhappy writer who was prompted by dissatisfaction with his personal fate and the hopeless state of the fatherland to take his own life, those dubious and misconceived elements which are very prominent at the opening, recede even further into the shade behind more positive qualities; from the last scene of the second act there is nothing further to impair our enjoyment of the work; from here onwards the spectator remains enthralled by the overwhelming force which is manifest in the vigour of the style, in the significance of the characterisation, in the intensification and resolution of the conflict. The introduction of visionary elements into the historical action and the consequences which follow from the somnambulistic character of the hero for his development and the way he is judged must unquestionably damage the impression and confuse the spectator in the initial stages. An amorous 'Hamlet in uniform', a dreaming sleepwalker, does not make a good soldier, and it is difficult to understand the enthusiasm of the war heroes of Brandenburg for a comrade whose wilfulness and irresponsibility have already cost the Elector two of the finest victories; who is found at the beginning of the play sleeping on a bench in the gardens of the palace at Fehrbellin while the squadrons are ready to march and are vainly awaiting their commanding officer; who is sweetly dreaming while the plan of battle is being dictated and pays no heed to the instructions which are meant for him; and who finally, on the day of the Battle of Fehrbellin, is once again impelled by a pathological rapture to make the premature attack which secures victory, but which costs him his head. In this, his last play, the dramatist has again paid tribute to the errors of romanticism. Not until the moment when the decision over the life or death of the Prince is placed in his own hands does his image emerge from romantic obscurity, and then we see in his character a ripening of that ability, lucidity and resolution from which the problem of the play derives its ethical significance and its dramatic *raison d'être*. Almost seventy years have passed since Heinrich von Kleist wrote the *Prince of Homburg*, and until a few years ago it was one of the plays most rarely seen on the German stage. The author had invested his final hopes in this work; at the very least, he had ventured to hope, the treatment of the patriotic subject ought to bring him public support, but he was to be bitterly disappointed. If only he could have foreseen with what love and devotion, with what careful preparation and what profusion of spectacular means his play has now achieved scenic realisation, and how much it has been able to inspire and elevate a large public! Kleist's *Hermannsschlacht* and his *Käthchen von Heilbronn*, the production of which has perhaps been the finest and in its way the most perfect among the achievements of our guests, have for some time been among the special glories of the Meiningen Court Theatre; the *Prince of Homburg* has now most worthily taken its place alongside them. Once again the secret of the success is to be explained by the harmonious and artistically beautiful overall impression of the performance; again one is inclined to suppress criticism of details because of the praise which the whole demands; again the attraction does not reside in one or other of the external aspects, in the splendid scenery, in the historically accurate costumes, in the beautiful groupings or the effective scenic arrangements, but in the fact that all the means serve the purpose of faithfully revealing the spirit of the work in a vivid and stylish manner. The dream scenes at the beginning and end of the play, the scenes in the Palace of Fehrbellin, the battlefield at Fehrbellin, the scene with the body of Froben in the old Berlin *Lustgarten* are, at times, spendidly effective. The principal participants in the performance were Herr Nesper and Herr Kainz, and, among the ladies, Frau Berg and Fräulein Pauli. Herr Kainz in the title-rôle left much to be desired. It would be wrong to seek to deny that this artist possesses a fresh talent that is capable of development, but he seems, as yet, to be completely lacking in artistic maturity. In itself his performance was guided by the right intentions, but the artist permitted himself to be too carried away by fiery enthusiasm: all sense of proportion, all moderation in expression and change of mood was absent. Still worse was his declamation; the drawing-out and fragmentation of words often made it positively unpleasant and – remarkable enough in an actor of the Meiningen school – unnatural. Herr Kainz did not speak Kleist's verses, he sang tenor. Herr Nesper, in the rôle of the Elector, was able successfully to combine gravity, authority and understanding, and to give added life to his performance with a subtle touch of humour. Frau Berg, as the Elector's wife, spoilt things by exaggerations in her movements; Fräulein Pauli, as the Princess, did not get the measure of her task until the subtly played scene in which Natalie begs the Elector to have mercy on the Prince, and, indeed, as far as acting is concerned, this was the best scene of the evening. Herr

Hellmuth-Bräm's Kottwitz was a splendid character, and his fiery speech in the fifth act was delivered excellently. Along with him the Field Marshal Derfling of Herr Teller stood out from the ranks of the Elector's loyal comrades-in-arms for the originality of his appearance and characterisation. Herr Kober (Graf von Sparren) delivered the report of the rescue of the Elector and the death of Froben warmly and movingly. Graf Hohenzollern was also fittingly represented by Herr Richard. Among the crowd in the scene before the Palace in Berlin every spectator will have noticed the most charming pair of children, a boy and a girl, who followed events with the liveliest attention: two amusing little figures in the costume of the time, the girl with the peculiar hairstyle which was then usual and in a long light-green dress which reached to the ground. In the ensemble scene there were occasional excesses. The roar of the cannon in the battle scene of the second act made understanding of the text difficult. In the final act the officers must restrain themselves considerably in their excitement; they are in the Elector's palace, in the presence of their lord and master, and must not forget themselves so far as to abandon all semblance of military bearing.

Vossische Zeitung, 14 May 1878

Since last Thursday Herr Emerich Robert has been taking part in the tour of the Meiningen Court actors and, in the first instance, he appeared as *Prinz Friedrich von Homburg* in Heinrich von Kleist's play. The interpretation of this rôle by the member of the Meiningen Company, Herr Kainz, provoked, in many respects, critical observations, but he does possess one quality: youthful freshness and warmth of sentiment, and this was not the strength of the achievement of the much-celebrated Herr Robert, at whose feet half a dozen obligatory laurel wreaths were thrown from the auditorium as soon as the curtain rose. Herr Robert performed with that histrionic virtuosity which functions with absolute reliability. Every scene is designed to reach an effective climax, every word is weighed, every nuance calculated. The musicality of the voice shares the same virtuosity as the acting: now it permits the artist to sink to a scarcely audible whisper, now to surge back to a powerful roar. But in all this virtuosity the spontaneous freshness is lost, the performance becomes stilted and calculated, the interest with which one follows the performance remains superficial, just as the means by which the effect is created remain superficial. It is not possible to reach that state of illusion, which, at least for a few moments, makes one forget that one is in the theatre; one does not think one is seeing the Prince of Homburg, one sees only the virtuoso who is representing him. The departure of the Prince for the battle was enacted with lively pathos, the monologue before his arrest ('My cousin Friedrich intends to play the part of Brutus' (l. 777)) was adorned with the greatest rhetorical finesse, the difficult scene in which the Prince's fear of death finds expression, was decorated with the subtlest nuances, but even so one could not warm to it. In the conception of the rôle, and without prejudice to the dreamlike aspect, to which justice must be done, the heroic quality could have been more powerfully presented. All things considered, we want to see the Brandenburg cavalry general and not a pining Amynthus of the theatre. The artist's penchant for the sentimental comes to the fore here. Moreover, his voice sounds strained and this makes it seem even more advisable than ever that prudent use be made of it. Herr Robert was called back after every scene. Among the others Herr Nesper (Elector) in particular and Herr Hellmuth-Bräm, together with Fräulein Pauli, received deserved recognition for their excellent achievements.

Vossische Zeitung, 18 May 1878

6   Policy and principles

Concentration on externals would find in me the most determined opponent.
Duke Georg II of Meiningen, 25 October 1879

L IKE ALL THE MAJOR FIGURES in the history of the theatre, the
Duke of Meiningen and his close collaborator, Ludwig Chronegk,
have been the subject of a large number of anecdotes to be found in the
recollections of actors and other contemporaries. Some of these are informa-
tive, some are amusing, many are lacking in credibility. However, the image
of the two men which emerges from such anecdotes is one which deserves
credence because of its consistency. It is an image of firm and unwavering
authoritarianism. For the members of the Meiningen company, and for
others who worked with them, Georg II was not just the director, he
remained the ruling prince.

Bjørn Bjørnson, one of a select band of important theatre directors who
witnessed the performance of the Meininger, and whose later work was
decisively influenced by what they experienced, was for a short time a
member of the company. In 1881 he took part in the tours to Budapest and
London, where he played Casca in *Julius Caesar*. He was, of course, the son
of the Norwegian dramatist, Bjørnstjerne Bjørnson, a personal friend of the
Duke, who included a number of his plays in the programmes in Meiningen,
and one, *Between the battles*, in the touring repertoire. In his autobiography
the younger Bjørnson explains that he left Meiningen in protest at the Duke's
policy of insisting that the actors themselves paid for the replacement of
requisites which were accidentally broken in performance or rehearsal. Since
the requisites were often genuine articles of great value, this could prove
costly; in Bjørnson's case it was antique glassware, used in the production of
the *Wallenstein* trilogy. When Bjørnson discussed the incident with his
father, the latter expressed his approval of the step taken by his son, observing that what the Duke was doing to his actors smacked of despotism.[1]

The same authoritarianism was evident in the disputes between the Duke
and Chronegk, on the one hand, and performers such as Therese Grunert,
Hildegard Werner, and Marie Schanzer, on the other. In a performance of
The Winter's Tale in Berlin on 6 June 1878, Therese Grunert was due to play
the rôle of Time in the tableau at the opening of Act IV, and refused to do so.

This was probably the consequence of a growing reluctance on the part of the actress to assume secondary, especially non-speaking, rôles; such a reluctance was not confined to Fräulein Grunert, for, earlier in the year, the Duke had written to Chronegk of Hildegard Werner: 'She is not a Meininger if she does not regard it as a matter of honour to take walk-on parts, for the battle-cry of our members must be: "All for one and one for all".'[2] The *Dienstregeln* (1868, §22) did, in fact, state that members of the company who regularly took leading rôles should generally be excused from walk-on parts, and Fräulein Grunert's rôles in this tour included Amalie (*Die Räuber*), Natalie (*Prinz Friedrich von Homburg*), Perdita (*The Winter's Tale*), and Bertha (*Die Ahnfrau*). However, Fräulein Grunert, who had played the part of Time on previous occasions and had been praised for her performance on the opening night, chose to make her point during the interval between acts III and IV, and was dismissed by Chronegk.[3]

On the basis of the available evidence it is difficult not to be more sympathetic to Marie Schanzer. Here again, however, the actress may not have been sorry to leave the company at this particular moment. For some time she had been reluctant to take non-speaking rôles, and the Duke had insisted that she do so in order not to create precedents for other actors; she had previously been fined for failure to attend rehearsals and scheduled performances. Finally she was dismissed for being absent overnight without permission while she was on tour, having taken advantage of an opportunity to spend some time with her husband. She missed a rehearsal for a play in which she did not have a main rôle, but this was clearly less disruptive than Fräulein Grunert's behaviour; and in a letter (which reads very persuasively) she drew the Duke's attention to the mitigating factor of her dual responsibilities to her husband and her profession: 'I must beg Your Grace's pardon if my duties as a housewife caused me to forget for a moment my duties according to my . . . contract. I have always been painfully aware how little the terms of the latter permit me to fulfil my *twofold duties equally*.'[4]

The husband of Marie Schanzer was, in fact, the Director of the Meiningen Court Orchestra, no less a person than Hans von Bülow (who most certainly shared the authoritarian views of the Duke where his orchestra was concerned). But the Duke backed up Chronegk: Marie Schanzer was dismissed, and soon afterwards von Bülow asked to be released from his post. Not only was a principle upheld, it was upheld very publicly; the case is referred to for its exemplary quality in Antoine's account of the methods of the Meiningen Theatre in 1888.[5]

Stanislavskij responded with the same admiration and approval of the methods of Chronegk, whom he observed closely at rehearsals. The consequence was the unity achieved in his own early productions, praised in turn by Diaghilev: 'The Moscow actors were able to put on a classic, and produce it in a most finished manner, such as befits a modern, a most modern spectator

... The Moscow actors ... know what discipline is, and that ... is what combines all colours into one single picture.'[6] With hindsight, however, Stanislavskij modified his views, and conceded the harmful effect of such despotism when it was not combined with the talents of Chronegk and the Duke of Meiningen: '[the] directors of the new type became mere producers, who made of the actor a stage property on the same level with stage furniture, a pawn that was moved about in their *mises-en-scène*'.[7] An earlier example of misplaced despotism can be found in the treatment of Richard Wagner and Josef Kainz by Ludwig II of Bavaria. In both cases an already crumbling relationship was finally brought to an end by the King's insensitive attempt to exert authority where his wishes came into conflict with the convictions of the artist.[8]

We have already seen the opposite side of this coin. It is illustrated by the comparative weakness of so apparently powerful a theatre director as Botho von Hülsen in his relationship with his actors. In the theatre of the nineteenth century *this* was the more immediate problem.

The foregoing examples serve only to illustrate the intensity of the control exercised over production by Georg II of Meiningen, or, at least, by the production team of which he was the leading member. The extent to which this approximates to the artistic control of the modern stage director, in the commercial or the subsidised theatre, or contributes to the emergence of such a figure, is one of the questions which will be considered in this concluding examination of the central Meiningen principles. At the level of conception, the Duke, who was first and foremost a visual artist, did not document his productions for posterity with the care of Max Reinhardt; nor did he theorise with the proselytizing zeal of Brecht. At the level of execution, Chronegk remained exclusively a practical man of the theatre, with no evident ambition to do more than serve the immediate needs of the company and its productions. The relevance of the available material to our question – and it is, of course, a historian's question, which was not being asked at the time – is therefore rather indirect. This is not to say, of course, that the Meiningen Court Theatre was lacking a consistent direction or a consistent artistic policy; that much should by now be clear. To assess that direction and that policy it is necessary now to look in more general terms at those matters which have already been considered with reference to the history of the tours, and to two specific productions: repertoire and textual editing, *mise-en-scène* and acting.

The major principles which governed the touring repertoire of the Meiningen Theatre are threefold: political, stylistic, and commercial. The political tendency was national-liberal in the broadest sense; beyond this, plays were chosen which would respond to the decorative style and ensemble playing at which the company excelled; and their continued presence in the repertoire depended on their financial viability (even productions in which a lot had been invested, such as *Papst Sixtus V* and *Marino Faliero*, were rapidly dropped when they proved unsuccessful).

In 1857 the Duke of Meiningen visited the exhibition of paintings in Manchester. There, as we have already noted, his interest seems to have been concentrated exclusively on the works of the great masters of the past; and it was such works, in so far as they were available, which provided the central focus for the exhibition which he himself mounted in Meiningen in the same year. Identical principles, and they are moral and educational rather than narrowly aesthetic principles, underlie the choice of authors whose works form the basis of the touring repertoire of the Duke's theatre. Two authors are clearly dominant: nine plays by Schiller and six by Shakespeare account for over 2,000 of the 2,877 performances. The only other significant contribution to the repertoire was made by Kleist, whose stock was rising, and whose status was enhanced by the Meiningen performances. Grillparzer was represented by two non-canonical works, one of which, the fragment, *Esther*, formed half of a double-bill with Molière's *Le Malade imaginaire*. Surprisingly neglected is Lessing, but *Minna von Barnhelm* had, for some time, been a speciality of the *Königliches Schauspielhaus*, where it was von Hülsen's favourite patriotic play for occasions of national significance.[9] Apart from *Miß Sara Sampson*, the genre domestic tragedy is completely absent from the touring repertoire, although *Minna von Barnhelm*, *Emilia Galotti*, and *Kabale und Liebe* were all performed at home in Meiningen. The stylistic austerity, which the Duke gave as a reason for not performing *Maria Magdalena* in Berlin, was probably a contributory factor to the neglect of the genre, together with – in the case of Hebbel in particular – the company's shortage of strong actresses. This latter weakness is probably the explanation for the total absence of Hebbel from the repertoire, for, although his historical dramas had a lot to offer the Meiningen style, contemporaries were accustomed to seeing his heroines embodied by actresses of the style and (physical) stature of Klara Ziegler.

The more adventurous choices of works by the lesser-known dramatists, Minding and Lindner, do not reveal a great sureness of touch in the assessment of contemporary literature, but they do make clear the political factor in the choice. The same is also true of what would seem, after *Ghosts*, to be the boldest and most far-sighted choice of all: namely a play by Ibsen as early as 1876. *The Pretenders* did, however, have a very topical theme. The translator, Adolf Strodtmann, who was, like Frenzel, a regular contributor to the *Feuilleton* of the *National-Zeitung*, wrote: 'the political idea on which this play is based, the unification of the long-divided members of an empire into a great and mighty nation, should . . . above all in present-day Germany, enjoy the widest sympathy and universal understanding'.[10]

The choice of plays from among the works of the three major dramatists reflects the same national tendency, most evidently in *Julius Caesar*, *Die Hermannsschlacht*, and *Wilhelm Tell*; but it also shows an awareness of the company's reliance on *mise-en-scène* rather than gifted performers. The avoidance of Shakespeare's Tragedies (apart from *Macbeth*) probably stems from the same reason, as does the absence of Kleist's *Der zerbrochene Krug*, and *Penthesilea*, and Schiller's *Don Karlos*. The absence of Shakespeare's Histories (*Königsdramen*) requires a word of explanation, for their visual qualities had been spectacularly exploited by Charles Kean, as the Duke of Meiningen was well aware, and they clearly had a great deal to offer to his style of production. However, the Histories were regarded as problematic plays in mid-nineteenth-century Germany, particularly to the national-liberal mentality, because of their lack of immediately recognisable dramatic unity, and the generic impurity. Only by radical adaptation could they be made to yield up that sense of a comprehensive and stable historical process so valued by the liberal critics: 'These Histories of Shakespeare are not so very different from the sibylline books of Roman legend. It requires an extraordinarily great effort and application to rescue these plays in their entirety for the stage, but the reward is all the greater . . . if one wants to secure only parts of the whole', wrote Alfred Klaar.[11] This was the thinking behind the work of Dingelstedt in preparing a version of the six plays from *Richard II* to *Richard III*, which he had produced in Weimar (1864) and Vienna (1875) as a continuous cycle; another version had been produced by Wilhelm Oechelhäuser, which had entered the repertoire of the *Königliches Schauspielhaus* in 1873. Radical adaptation of this kind, of course, infringed a basic Meiningen principle; and, furthermore, it would have been very risky, because of the inflexibility and the expense, for the Meiningen Theatre to perform a six-play cycle within the course of a six-week tour.

A further point to emerge from an examination of the repertoire, its development, and the details of its presentation in the theatre, is that the Meiningen tours were an efficiently run business operation. The plays were carefully prepared and the season carefully planned, but only in outline. As the man on the spot, Chronegk had the discretion to present the programme in the most profitable and advantageous way, although he regularly consulted the Duke. In Berlin he adopted a policy of long runs; in 1874 *Julius Caesar* and in 1887 *Die Jungfrau von Orléans* were played continuously (and this included Sundays) as long as the theatre could be filled. During the touring period the theatre, unlike the Meiningen Orchestra, was almost entirely self-financing; however, after the end of the tours its financial position deteriorated significantly.[12] There were, of course, variations; even the artistic success and public acclaim achieved in London did not offset the disappointment or mitigate the concern at the poor financial results. This was probably one reason for the element of caution which was a factor in preventing the finalisation of the planned tours to Italy and the United

States. Theatre could be a moderately profitable activity in Imperial Germany; but it should be noted that the Duke of Meiningen achieved his results from a much less secure base than von Hülsen at the *Königliches Schauspielhaus*, without the star actors on whom his chief rival could rely, and without making the same artistic compromises with boulevard theatre.

The Duke of Meiningen began his involvement with the theatre at a time when there was a lively debate in progress about the use of adapted rather than authentic texts in theatrical productions. It is consistent with his historicist convictions that he should have supported the case for authenticity and signalled his standpoint by the appointment of Bodenstedt as *Intendant* in 1867. The Duke came to be widely acknowledged as a champion of the unadapted word of the dramatist, and high, not to say extravagant, claims were made for his fidelity to authorial intention. After the end of the tours he continued to adhere to the same views; when, in 1901, he was offered for performance a new adaptation of *Das Käthchen von Heilbronn* by Kleist's editor, Karl Siegen, he scornfully rejected it, declaring that Siegen's adaptation was designed to ingratiate him with the Kaiser and secure him a medal, and that 'adaptors always do too much. I . . . prefer . . . to see the dramatist's text performed without alterations.'[13]

Such unambiguous statements of principle were not, in fact, put into practice in the performance texts which carried the *imprimatur* of the Meiningen company itself. On the contrary, this series, published initially by R. von Grumbkow in Dresden, and subsequently by Friedrich Conrad in Leipzig, was advertised as follows: 'This authorised edition of the repertoire is the one which accurately reproduces the text of the performance, in the adaptation which often departs significantly from the original text.'[14]

In our discussion of *Julius Caesar* and *Prinz Friedrich von Homburg* we noted amendments of varying significance in three broad categories: those designed to improve the historical accuracy of the drama according to external criteria; dramaturgical amendments which serve, directly or indirectly, the predominantly visual style of the production; and changes which affect the substance or tendency of the drama. Examples of such amendments could be multiplied by the examination of other plays from the repertoire, although *The Merchant of Venice* is the only other play for which such consideration has been seriously attempted. Here Wolfgang Iser has undertaken a detailed comparison of the published Meiningen performance-text with a modern English edition; he does not, however, take much account of the actual production, which, in its first version, antedated the publication of the authorised text by several years.[15] Iser's findings confirm that, even with the scene-curtain, the elaborate realistic staging of the Meininger necessitated the omission of whole scenes and the transposition of others in order to reduce the number of the changes and the length of the intervals to acceptable proportions; and that lines, particularly those which seem to have a retarding character, were eliminated in order to make the action tauter and offset the reduction of pace caused by the more static, visual character of the *mise-en-scène*. More importantly, and more critically, Iser notes a regrouping of scenes in acts II and III to produce a much stronger contrast between the ideal world of Belmont and the real world of Venice than that which emerges from Shakespeare's more extended and more subtle scene-by-scene comparison. He very plausibly attributes this to the desire to render the contrast between the two environments in a manner that makes it immediately accessible to the eye; but even Iser's critical account makes it clear that the restructuring was carried out intelligently, not so as to emphasise the decorative component for its own sake, but so as to ensure that it was employed in such a way as to bring out the leading idea of the production. The visual realisation of strong contrasts such as this was, in fact, a recurrent stylistic feature of Meiningen productions.

As a contrast to his own very critical approach to the employment of the techniques of the nineteenth-century theatre of illusion in the production of Shakespeare, Iser cites Albert Lindner's defence of Meiningen principles:

Shakespeare composed his drama and stopped at that. He did not prescribe decorations because he knew nothing about decoration . . . What more could he do than provide the action and convincing human agents, the characters? Anything more than this is a matter for each particular period and the level of its culture. The author defines a problem – for the theatre, not for the imagination of his reader. It is up to each age to solve this problem in terms of the means at its disposal.

The desire for the fullest possible realisation of the dramatic text, with the use of all the means available to the contemporary theatre, is characteristic of artist and public during the period of the Meiningen tours. The minimalist style of the Elizabethan stage, with its reliance on the imagination of the audience and, in consequence, its amenability to rapid changes of scene, would, no doubt, have permitted a greater degree of fidelity to the Shakespearean text. A few experiments were indeed made in the nineteenth century with this different – but no less – historicist style of production, but effectively such an alternative was not available to someone so deeply integrated in the visual culture of his own day as was Georg II.

The authenticity of his performance texts is, in fact, a relative matter, and it has to be considered in context; that context is provided by the practices of adaptors such as Dingelstedt, who cut, revised, and invented pseudo-Shakespearean lines in his version of *The Winter's Tale*; Deinhardstein, who transformed *Twelfth Night* into *Viola*, in a way which permitted a single actress to assume the rôles of both Sebastian and Viola; Holbein, who had romanticised Kleist's *Das Käthchen von Heilbronn*; and Genée, who had removed the bear scene from *Die Hermannsschlacht* and substituted a *récit*. When he came to Meiningen in 1867 as an exponent of textual integrity,

Bodenstedt was advancing a policy which had only begun in England in the 1840s, when Planché, Webster, and Phelps had led the movement away from the corrupted texts of the eighteenth century. Even here the development was far from unidirectional; the productions of Kean in the 1850s mark a distinct step backwards in this area.[16] Against such a background the reputation of the Meiningen editors for purism seems not undeserved.

During the period after the end of the tours, when Paul Lindau, one-time scourge of the Meininger in Berlin, was serving as artistic director in Meiningen, it was the Duke's practice, as it had been with Chronegk, to send him written comments after rehearsals. Lindau assembled a selection of the more general observations from the letters he received, and published them in 1909. Lindau's document is not a complete or programmatic account of the Duke of Meiningen's methods of stage-direction, but it has considerable value as the most comprehensive and general statement that is available. Despite its late date, it is not a retrospective document, for the Duke continued his active involvement in production and stage-direction almost up to the end of his life. It needs to be supplemented by other documents, the most important of which are the instructions to Chronegk relating to individual productions, the sketches of the Duke, the correspondence of the Duke with his scene-painters, the Brückner brothers, and the correspondence of both the Duke and the Baroness with Frenzel and Werder. However, it provides a good basis for a discussion of the Meiningen principles, and is therefore printed in full below.[17]

In the composition of the set care must be taken to ensure that its centre is not identical with the centre of the stage.

   If the composition is organised around the geometrical centre two equal halves will be produced, and then there is always the danger that in the disposition of the groups and their incorporation in the whole a more or less symmetrical balance between right and left will be created, which will be wooden, inflexible, and uninteresting in its effect.

   (The charm of Japanese art resides to a not inconsiderable extent in the avoidance of all symmetry; 'l'ennui naquit un jour de l'uniformité', said Boileau about works of art in general. In the visual arts the uniformity which the French aesthetician described as the mother of tedium goes by the name of symmetry.)

   The exception proves the rule: a composition in which the main figure – or main group – is in the real centre, and the subordinate figures – or groups – stand more or less equidistantly to the side, can be artistically justified even on the stage in the special case where a solemn, severe, so to speak ascetic effect is intended (think, for instance, of the Sistine Madonna). In such a case the composition will invariably have the quality of serene repose. The main function of the theatre, however, is to present movement, the relentless forward progress of the action; and so this arrangement is generally to be avoided, since it has a static effect and holds up movement.

   It rarely looks good if anything stands exactly in the middle of the stage. Set pieces or other items of scenery should, whenever possible, be placed to one side, at some distance from the wings, of course, so as to increase the possibility of their being seen by all those seated in the auditorium.

The actor, too, must never stand in the middle of the stage, directly in line with the prompter's box, but always slightly to the right or left.

The middle section of the stage, approximately the width of the prompter's box and stretching from the footlights to the backdrop, should be used by the actor only when crossing from right to left, or vice versa; otherwise he has no business there.

Equally to be avoided, as far as possible, is the situation where two people stand at the same distance from the centre of the prompter's box.

Special care must be taken to establish a pleasing relationship between the actors and the decorations; it is particularly important that this should be a correct relationship.

One widespread shortcoming in stage-direction is that insufficient care is taken over the position of the actor in relation to the architecture, to the scenographically painted trees, buildings, etc. All discrepancies cannot, of course, be eliminated, because, with every step backwards, the living figure of the actor, with its unchangeable proportions, becomes, relatively speaking, too big in comparison with the painted set. The discrepancies can, however, be reduced and disturbing nonsense can be eliminated.

For instance, the actor must not go so close to the decorations of the upstage wings and the backdrop that the impossibility of the proportions becomes noticeable. He must not – as is so often seen – stand directly in front of a painted house whose door only reaches up to his waist and where, without stretching, he could look into the first-floor windows and, if he raised his hand, touch the chimney.

Those decorations which the actor has to approach closely must always be at least in approximately correct proportion to the size of the human figure: for example the temple in *Iphigenie auf Tauris*, which for this very reason is best erected downstage in the front wings, so that the columns, which can reach up almost into the flies, tower over the human figure. It is not important that the whole of the temple, from top to

29   Max Brückner, *Romeo and Juliet*, Act II, scene 2, Capulet's garden.

bottom, should be seen from the auditorium. It must rather suffice if part of the entablature, the cornice, and part of the roof are visible; the rest, the pediment, can be concealed in the flies.

(The balcony in *Romeo and Juliet* is also usually placed much too low. The rather elevated position in which Juliet would be standing with a balcony of approximately the correct height, is not a serious disadvantage compared with the disturbing feeling created by a balcony of the conventional, very modest, height: namely that without having to be a particularly good gymnast, Romeo would only need to take a jump in order to reach the unattainable beloved and take her in his arms.)

Actors must never lean against painted scenery (pillars and suchlike). If the actor moves freely in doing so it is inevitable that the painted decorations will shake when touched, and the illusion will be destroyed; if the actor takes the care which is necessary to avoid shaking the canvas, his movements acquire a certain constraint, which is disturbing because of the evident intention behind it.

Pieces of scenery against which the actor can lean or on which he can support himself (such as doorposts, tree-trunks etc.) must be made out of solid material, they must be three-dimensional. (This, at any rate in recent times, has been the practice in the better theatres.)

When both painted and three-dimensional scenery are used together on the stage care must be taken to ensure that the difference in the materials employed is not noticeable and does not disturb the desired uniformity of effect. The transitions, for instance from real or artificial flowers and leaves to those which are painted, must be effected with particular finesse, so that the one can scarcely be distinguished from the other.

(A quite inartistic – indeed a ridiculous – effect is produced if, for instance, on a rose bush the one rose which is to be picked is the only three-dimensional one among the painted ones; or if, in the workshop of the 'Violin-Maker of Cremona', there are half a dozen painted violins with painted shadows on the backcloth, and one can see among them, in all its reality, solid and with a real shadow, the one and only violin which is going to be used, and which, moreover, appears to be unreal in comparison with the painted ones, because of its apparently excessive size, approximately that of a viola.)

The attempt to match the human figure to the scenographically reduced proportions of the architectural features of the upstage area – for instance in the scene showing the construction of Zwing-Uri in *Wilhelm Tell*, by employing youths and boys, suitably costumed and made-up, as building-workers, so that they would look like adults in the distance – cannot be considered successful. The whole deportment of boys is completely different from that of adults. Besides, the blurring of outlines and the modulation of colouring which, in nature, is caused by the distance and is reproduced in painting, cannot be achieved with figures who are physically present on stage. The living forms preserve a much more distinct outline than the painted surroundings, and the eye of the spectator does not see adults who appear smaller because of the distance, but diminutive, gnome-like creatures, pygmies with faces made up to look old.

Aerial flies, those straight-edged strips of blue-painted canvas which run across the top of the stage and are supposed to represent the cloudless sky – known in the trade as ozone rags – must never be used. In rural scenes the top of the set must always be masked by trees with widely spreading branches. These arcades can normally be used also for town scenes, streets, and market-places. Sometimes the action permits the decoration of streets and squares with floral garlands or pennants, flags and streamers. If this is not possible and there has to be open sky above the scene, then clouds are always preferable to the blue strips. These tedious and unpleasant blue rags have no place in any self-respecting stock-room.

In the first rehearsals for a new play with crowd scenes and a large cast the director's hair usually stands on end. One almost despairs of ever bringing life and responsiveness to this awkward and recalcitrant mass. It is a great help in overcoming this problem if the decorations are firmly in position from the outset. The alteration of the decorations, rehanging or relocation of set-pieces and furniture during the rehearsals, causes terrible delays; it also irritates, wearies, and bores the members of the company.*

In costume dramas, rehearsals with weapons, helmets, armour, swords etc. must take place at as early a stage as possible, so that in the actual performance the actors are not hindered by the unfamiliarity and the heavy weight of the equipment.

In such plays it is essential that even before the dress-rehearsal, which should be distinguished from the first public performance only by the exclusion of the public, the actors should rehearse in costume – either in the actual one or, if this is not yet ready or has to be treated with special care, one of a similar cut. Before the dress-rehearsal they must, in several rehearsals, wear head-gear, cloaks, trains etc. exactly, or at least approximately, as in public performance. In the performance the artist must not be confronted with anything unforeseen or anything surprising. The actor must be given the opportunity to familiarise himself with the unaccustomed clothing of the past. It must not be evident from his actions and movements that he is wearing a 'costume' in which the wardrobe-master has just dressed him; nor should we be reminded of a fancy-dress parade or a masked ball.

Posture and movement have not remained uninfluenced by the development of costumes and changes of fashion. What we regard as the normal position of the feet, with heels together, as in a soldier standing to attention, a position also adopted by civilians (for instance when dealing with superiors and people in positions of respect, or when exchanging greetings), looks dreadful in the costume of earlier periods from antiquity to the Renaissance and later; it is, moreover, incorrect. This position of the feet, heel to heel, seems not to have been widely adopted until it was introduced in the steps of the minuet. However, a leader of the *Landsknechte* should not stand with his feet together, like an *abbé galant* of the eighteenth century, or a lieutenant in a present-day salon.

In costume up to the eighteenth century it is natural, correct and also visually most pleasing to stand with legs apart, or else with one foot in front of the other.

As a general rule all parallel lines are, as far as possible, to be avoided on the stage. This rule has special implications for plays in historical costume.

Pikes, halberds, lances, and spears etc. must never be held pointing in one direction, like the weapons of our modern infantry and cavalry. When older weapons are carried this must be done with a certain pleasing arbitrariness; they must not be equidistant, nor should they all point in the same direction. In some places they should be close together, in others they should be spread out; they should not be held vertically, but diagonally, and they should cross over each other.

Whenever an actor wears a helmet of the non-classical style it must be pulled down so far over his forehead that no more than the muscle over the eyebrows is visible. The favourite way of wearing the helmet, on the back of the head and over the neck is tenor's style and is not appropriate in drama. When they are performing in historical costume our romantic heroes are probably afraid they might spoil their coiffure if they push their helmets down properly. In our view that does not matter.

In the positioning of actors in relation to each other, parallels are particularly bad. The placing of a single actor in the full *en face* position, parallel to the footlights, does

---

* The Duke came to this view only in later years, after the acquisition of practical experience in the theatre.

not look at all pleasing; it is positively ugly when two or more actors of approximately the same shoulder height stand parallel to the footlights.

Lines parallel to the footlights are also undesirable in the movement of the actors. If, for instance, an actor has to cross from downstage right to downstage left, then he should avoid the straight path, which, on the stage, is never the best, and instead try discreetly and unobtrusively to give the line of his path an angle.

When there are three or more actors in a scene the straight line should be avoided absolutely in their positioning in relation to each other. They should always stand so as to form an angle. The distances between the individual actors must always be unequal. If the distances are identical this has a dull and deadening effect, reminiscent of the figures on a chess-board.

It is always advantageous if an actor can, in an unforced way, establish a relationship to a piece of furniture or some other object on the stage. This increases the impression of reality and naturalness.

If the stage has different levels – steps, hilly ground with rocks and suchlike – the actor should not neglect the opportunity this provides of giving his pose a pleasing and harmonious appearance. For instance, he must never stand with both feet on the same step. If he stands on a rock or something similar he should place one foot on it. If he is coming down from an elevation and has to pause on the way, to speak or to look at something, then he should place one foot lower than the other. In this way his whole posture becomes more natural and more pleasing. 'One leg up!' should be the director's standard instruction in such cases.

The treatment of crowds on the stage requires especially careful preparation. There is hardly a single theatre company that is in a position to supply all the extras needed for a large crowd scene from its own ranks. Apart from the members of the chorus and the so-called house-supers, to whom the quite skilful stage-hands, who already feel at home in the theatre, can often be added, it is always necessary to make up the numbers by recruiting a considerable number of extras for whom such employment is only casual work and who are paid for each rehearsal and each performance at a specified rate. Occasionally, of course, some of these people, who are always changing and whom the director cannot know personally, are quite utilisable, can be well trained, understand what they are told, and are not unskilled in carrying out instructions; there are also, however, many rather dubious elements, who can be taught nothing, who are clumsy, who look ridiculous, who sometimes even want to go their own way, pursue their own ideas and perform independently, and who can do great damage. It is the job of the director and his stage-manager to discover as quickly as possible among this great mass those who are particularly suitable and those who are particularly unsuitable, and to separate the sheep from the goats, so that the unreliable elements be employed only to fill in, in places where they can do no harm.

The whole body of extras is divided into a number of smaller groups, each of which has to be drilled independently and separately.

All of these groups are led by an experienced actor from the company or a skilled member of the chorus who 'covers' the others – that is to say stands prominently in the foreground. This leader has, to some extent, the responsibility for ensuring that those who have been placed under him follow their instructions. He himself is responsible to the director for ensuring that positions are taken up and movements carried out correctly and on cue.

The leaders are given written parts with cues in which those very general terms normally used by the dramatist, such as 'noise', 'uproar', 'murmuring', 'shouts', 'screams', and suchlike are expanded by the director into words, which must then be memorised by the appropriate extras. There must, of course, be several distinct versions of the interpolations, and they must not be recited uniformly and simultaneously.

These leaders of groups of extras do not have an easy task, and it is a regrettable error, which often has artistically damaging consequences, that the members of a company who are employed as 'actors' have little esteem for such rôles, or regard them as unworthy of a genuine artist; and that, whenever possible, they try to avoid such rôles, or else, if they can be forced to perform them, make their reluctance all too apparent.

In Meiningen all the artists, without exception, are required to assume such non-speaking parts. This accounts for the quite startling effect created at the first appearance of the Meininger, which was achieved by the liveliness of the involvement of the masses, by the real participation of the crowd, which contrasted so starkly with the woodenness, awkwardness, and lack of interest which we had previously had to accept in non-speaking parts.

The faults and errors in the positioning of the individual actors in relation to each other are particularly disturbing in crowd scenes. The principal attraction in the grouping derives from the pleasing line formed by the heads of the actors. Just as uniformity of posture is to be avoided as far as possible, so too is equality of height among actors who stand next to each other. If it can be so arranged, the individual actors should stand on different levels; if the situation permits it, some might kneel while others take up standing positions nearby, some leaning forward, others erect. A good effect is created if an irregular semicircle can be formed around the person or object on which the attention of this group is focussed.

Care must be taken to ensure that those persons who stand closest to the public, and so are most exposed to the scrutiny of the audience, position and comport themselves in such a way that their shoulders are not all at the same angle to the footlights. It must be impressed upon every extra that he should change his posture as soon as he notices that he is standing in the same way as his neighbour. In a good picture you will never find many figures in the same pose, with shoulders aligned in the same way, standing next to each other. Actors and extras should be told this at almost every rehearsal of crowd scenes, because it is always being forgotten.

Extras should be forbidden particularly emphatically from staring out at the public. The instinct to do so is perfectly natural because, for very many of them, theatrical performance is something novel and unusual, and this stimulates their curiosity to look around in the darker auditorium.

Actions which have a displeasing effect, such as carrying off the dead and wounded, must be 'covered', that is to say concealed, as far as possible, from the view of the audience. But this must not be done by forming a tight and impenetrable wall of people around the action; this looks deliberate and therefore ridiculous. The covering should be fairly loose, so that not too much of the action can be seen, and yet just enough to permit some sense of what is going on.

If the impression of a great crowd of people is to be created on the stage the groups must be so arranged that those who stand at the sides extend deep into the wings. From no seats in the auditorium should it be possible to see that the group is finite. On the contrary, the arrangement should permit the audience to have the illusion that there is an even greater mass of people behind the scenes.

The emphatic insistence on the need to avoid symmetrical composition, with which the foregoing document begins, is visibly reflected in many of the sets executed by the Brückners. It is achieved both by the displacement of the centre in the manner prescribed by the Duke, and by the use of angled flats in the construction of box sets. The court scene in *The Merchant of Venice* provides a good example.[18]

Underlying this insistence is a reluctance to allow the space within which the action of the drama appears to take place to be determined by the geometrically regular and therefore – from a realist point of view – arbitrary shape of the stage area; lines, patterns, and arrangements of actors which reflect the actual (vertical or horizontal) boundaries of the stage, and so remind the audience of the limitations imposed upon the movement of the actors within those boundaries, are to be avoided; the composition of the picture must not be determined by the size of the canvas or the shape of the frame; on the contrary, every effort is made to break up and reshape the stage for expressive purposes. This represents a radical departure from the classicising tradition which had a significant following until the mid nineteenth century, and which had favoured that harmony and equilibrium which Winckelmann had recognised in the art of the Greeks, and in Raphael's Sistine Madonna; and it corresponds to the renewal of those baroque principles of composition which inform the work of the historical painters of the Belgian school, and Piloty and his followers in Germany. This new tendency will, in due course, be challenged by the theatre and stage-designers of the *Jugendstil* period, Peter Behrens and Georg Fuchs, advocates of a shallow, relief-stage, although Reinhardt will be rather scornful of their experiments.[19]

In dramatic theory and criticism there had long been a corresponding advocacy of regular classical form and a rejection of generically impure works; along with Shakespeare's Histories, this had meant the rejection of the fragmentary and allusive dramas of a *Sturm-und-Drang* writer such as Lenz, and the total neglect of the work of Büchner, whose dramas did not reach the stage until the naturalists began to take an interest in him in the 1890s. In his highly regarded treatise on dramatic form, *Die Technik des Dramas* (Technique of the drama), Freytag emphasised the static qualities of concentration, simplicity, and completeness, and he explicitly warned against those qualities and effects which were to become the hallmark of Meiningen *mise-en-scène*:

full development of the material in scenic terms is to be avoided; the subject of the drama should be treated concisely, simply, plainly; the best, most concentrated aspects should be presented in word and action; the scenes, with their indispensable links, should be arranged in a closely knit group vibrating with life; so long as the action is in progress new or difficult stage-effects, especially crowd scenes, should be avoided.[20]

It is not surprising that Freytag should have been critical of the Meiningen productions; he wrote to Duke Ernst of Saxe-Coburg that their success was evidence of a general decline in acting and the theatre.[21]

Those dynamic qualities which Freytag condemns in drama are, as we have already noted, present in abundance in the works of Büchner and Lenz, who come together in the *Novelle* by Büchner. The comparison made there by the fictitious Lenz further illustrates the difference between the openness and irregularity of the kind of design favoured by the Duke of Meiningen, and the self-contained, enclosed quality of designs in the classical tradition. Büchner's Lenz rejects the Winckelmann canon, the Apollo Belvedere and the Sistine Madonna, and, in praising the realism of a Dutch genre scene, he explicitly emphasises the openness of the composition to a world beyond the interior depicted in the foreground:

The woman has not been able to go to church and she is worshipping at home, the window is open, she is sitting facing it, and it is as if the sounds of the church bells are coming across the flat, open landscape from the village and in through the window, and the singing of the congregation can be heard coming from the church, and the woman is following the service in her book.[22]

The scene on which attention is focussed is presented as part of a greater whole that is so rich and varied that it resists containment within the narrow frame of the picture or the shallow foreground; the painting derives its vitality from the relationship between foreground and background, between what is seen clearly and what is implied, between the individual figure and her environment.

A recurrent feature of the Meiningen sets was the presence of openings, such as windows, arches, doorways, and gateways, which afford a (complete or partial) view into the depths beyond: the open doorways to the Sistine Chapel (*Papst Sixtus V*) and the Cathedral of Reims (*Die Jungfrau von Orléans*), the view of the Rialto (*The Merchant of Venice*) and the Bay of Genoa (*Fiesko*).[23] This was not just a means of permitting the Brückners to demonstrate their virtuosity in the use of perspective and the creation of the illusion of depth, it was also a means of establishing a sense of continuity and communication between the stage and the world outside.[24] The Duke of Meiningen's sketch for the set of Ibsen's *Ghosts* shows a room with a large window in the rear wall, and through this window one sees the oppressive mountain landscape of Norway (actually borrowed from the decorations for the mountain landscape of *Wilhelm Tell*), which provides the isolated environment that is crucial to the action of Ibsen's drama.

A more dramatic variant of this can be achieved by the use of practicable doors, precisely because they conceal what lies beyond until the moment when they are opened. They are therefore particularly effective in expressing the strong contrasts between different kinds of environment which often figured in Meiningen productions. The work of Schiller, rich as it is in visual contrast and the tensions between different worlds, lends itself readily to the creation of powerful and immediate scenic effects of this kind. Two similar

30–1 Georg II, sketch and ground plan for Schiller, *Maria Stuart*, acts I and V.

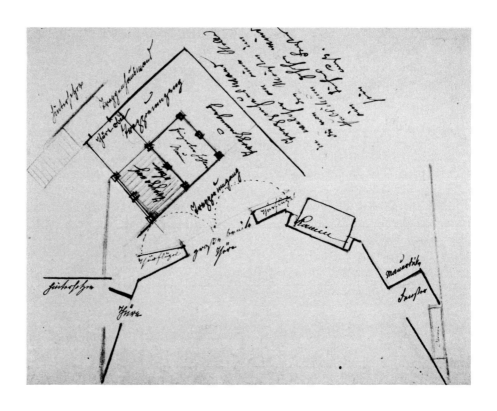

32 Georg II, sketch for Ibsen, *Ghosts*, 1886.

examples are to be found in *Maria Stuart* and *Die Jungfrau von Orléans*. In the former (Act II, scene 2) the French ambassadors arrive for an audience with Elisabeth, bringing with them as they enter all the visible signs of the lighter, more frivolous world of the French court, in contrast to the restrained sobriety of the English. In *Die Jungfrau von Orléans* (Act I, scene II) the situation is reversed, as the contemptuous English herald enters to deal with the pathetic Dauphin and the defeated French court.[25] These scenes depend almost equally for their effect on contrasts of costume, but in *Fiesko* the use of the stage space for dramaturgical purposes, and the powerful implication of the existence of a world behind the scenes which can influence the visible action, is achieved almost entirely by set design. In the design for the fifth act, which includes the storming of the *Thomastor*, the gateway into Genoa, the city wall and gate were constructed diagonally across the stage, taking up one quarter of the depth on the left-hand side and leaving in the foreground a relatively shallow space into which the action, among the defenders of the city, was compressed. Outside the gateway, and at first invisible to the audience, were the attackers; in the course of the scene of the assault, their noise and their impact on the action in the foreground increases as they threaten to burst through the gateway, suddenly and radically altering the entire scenic arrangement.[26]

The implication of such designs, and their potential for development by the naturalist directors, can be further illustrated by the contrast with the response of nineteenth-century interior decorators to the modern window. It was felt to be a problem because, by admitting more light, it deprives the

33 Georg II, sketch for Schiller, *Fiesko*, Act V, scene 2, storming of the Thomastor, 1875.

room of its self-contained tranquillity, and creates a relationship between the interior and the world of the the street outside. This, of course, is precisely what the naturalist dramatists will wish to see in the productions of their plays.[27]

The same primary concern for the creation of the illusion of a continuous natural space, inhabited by living and moving people, is also evident in the Duke's observations on the relationship between the actors and the decorations and requisites: it should not just be aesthetically pleasing, it should also be correct. This meant that particular care had to be exercised in the design of the more distant parts of the stage, where the illusion could suddenly be disturbed by the approach of an actor to the scenery. It is further reflected in the preference for solid and stable stage furnishings rather than painted ones, whose artificial character could be all too evident (as when, in a rare lapse, a pair of stockings was seen to hang flat over a bush which was supposed to be three-dimensional);[28] and in the very frequent and extensive use of practicable elements and set pieces, such as steps, rocks, trees, and, in the production of *Die Jungfrau von Orléans*, even a large stuffed horse, all of which re-create the irregularity of a natural space, and require the actors to consider their response to them in terms of movements and groupings.[29] The sketches of the Duke, and contemporary illustrations of the productions show how seriously these principles were put into practice, and the more friendly critics noted here, too, a welcome corrective to the deficiencies of other German theatres.

Warning voices were, however, also raised to point out what is apparent from the sketches and illustrations of *Die Hermannsschlacht*, namely that the stage was sometimes overfilled with scenery and furnishings, or that the combination of practicable and painted scenery in outdoor settings was not always a happy one. The production of *Die Räuber* provoked the following criticism in London.

the landscape scenes are very bad. A dais of three steps covered with green baize in a forest scene is absurd enough . . . but no tradition can warrant the scattering about the stage of a number of ridiculous boulders, supposed to represent either rocks or tufty hillocks, but which look like so many lumps of suet pudding with plums in them.[30]

The desire to blur or mask the perimeter of the stage in open-air scenes is reflected in several proposals. The aerial flies, conventionally used to represent a cloudless sky, and to which the Duke seems to have taken grave exception, are firmly banished; in the Meiningen sets the upper opening was concealed by irregularly shaped decorations representing trees and foliage, flags and bunting; there are several examples in the surviving decorations (the tournament scene in *Das Käthchen von Heilbronn*, the scene before the royal chapel in *Prinz Friedrich von Homburg*), and the practice can be seen illustrated in the sketches for the first forum scene of *Julius Caesar*.[31] Archer, whose overall response to the Meininger was positive, is critical of this:

The scenery of *Preciosa* exemplified one defect which I have often noted in the Meiningen mounting, namely a tendency to exclude all air and distance from exterior scenes. This is a fatal error of many landscape painters who give their canvases a stifling effect by shutting them in with foliage, buildings, etc., to the exclusion of every glimpse of blue sky. The error is equally unpleasant on stage. The scenes in *Preciosa*, and several other landscape scenes in other productions, seem to lack ventilation – I believe 'aerial perspective' is the technical term.[32]

This seems to suggest a failure of execution, for the intention to imply space beyond seems unambiguous enough in the Duke's writings, and it is evident also in his recommendation that certain decorations be set up in such a way that only part be visible, while the remainder seems to extend up into the flies or out into the wings. In crowd scenes a similar effect was achieved by not confining the crowd to the visible area of the stage, where its actual size could be ascertained by the audience, but by allowing it to spread beyond. A relatively limited number of extras, used with care, could thus produce a more impressive and apparently larger crowd than could be obtained by the unconsidered deployment of sheer numbers, as the Baroness remarked in her criticism of the production of *Die Hermannsschlacht* at the *Königliches Schauspielhaus*. Her simple proposal, that the actors forming the Roman army need only disappear behind the backcloth and reappear on the other side, was refined and implemented in the Meiningen production; executed on the smaller stage of the *Friederich-Wilhelmstädtisches Theater*, its effect was such as to secure the praise of the otherwise critical Hopfen:

The marchpast of the Roman army did not hold up the drama for a moment and did not at all resemble a balletic display; the weary men came pouring out of the first wing on the left, only to disappear, apparently behind a hill, into the second wing on the same side. It was, of course, always the same extras; but since they were only seen from the rear and no faces could be distinguished, the illusion was complete.[33]

The emphasis on correctness in the relationship of the actor to the set, which reflects the Duke's fundamental concern with the movement of the human figure in the stage space, is matched by his concern for another kind of correctness which depends very much on reference to external guarantees of authenticity, provided by works of historical scholarship, by consideration of the real localities in which the fictitious events of the drama are purported to have taken place, by specialist knowledge of matters such as court ceremony and etiquette which a ruling Duke would have at his fingertips, and by works of the visual arts, especially those which have contributed to the creation of a particular expectation in the mind of the public. The apparent pedantry of this was criticised even by contemporaries, and it does seem, on occasion, to have had curious consequences. A characteristic example is the repainting of the backcloth for *Wallensteins Lager*, when the Duke learned that the action took place in December (the snow-covered version now hangs on permanent display in the Meiningen Museum). *Maria Stuart* was also given a winter setting, because the execution took place in February; illustrations of the castle at Fotheringhay and the surrounding landscape were obtained from England, and were faithfully followed by the Brückners in their painted backcloth; for the interior the Duke acquired a detailed drawing of a fireplace that had been removed from Fotheringhay and installed in a house in Oundle; for the appearance of Paulet a copy of a miniature of Sir Amyas Paulet was acquired from the family.[34] For the opening of *Die Jungfrau von Orléans* the Duke made a number of sketches for the set for the prologue in order to place the tree and the chapel in the most effective position, but at the same time to adhere to the real situation, as he had observed it at Domrémy.[35] In late summer, 1875, Max Brückner travelled in Switzerland making sketches of the Rütli and the Vierwaldstätter See which were to serve as a basis for the sets of *Wilhelm Tell* in the following spring.[36] The setting of the trial scene in *The Merchant of Venice* was modelled on the College in the Doge's Palace, and the interior of the final act on an authentic Italian renaissance villa, the Duke's own Villa Carlotta on Lake Como. For the production of *Ghosts* Ibsen was consulted personally, and he replied in a letter giving precise details of a characteristic interior in a middle-class Norwegian home; on the reverse of Ibsen's letter Georg drew his first sketch for the set. The sketches which accompany his own letters show his constant work in recording visual impressions even before he thought of using them for his own productions; but once he became actively involved in the theatre his way of looking at his surroundings became more functional, he became more interested in the potential value of a scene as a theatre set, or an object as a stage property. Occasionally one even gets a glimpse of that tendency to confuse historical event and historical drama which is more usually associated with Ludwig II of Bavaria: in 1885 he wrote to his mother of a visit to Genoa, saying that he had seen there the river where Fiesko was drowned, near to the Church of St Thomas, 'which is depicted in our sets for the fifth act of *Fiesko*', and remarking that it was indeed very favourably placed for such a murder.[37]

This concern for historical accuracy equally informs the design of costume in the Meiningen productions, and it is impressively documented in the Duke's own costume sketches. We have already noted that advances had been made in the study of historical costume before the Duke's time, and that there were works of reference which he could consult, as well as paintings and drawings. In this matter, too, there was no lack of criticism of the practices of the Meiningen Theatre from those who thought that the elaborate and splendid costumes drew a disproportionate amount of attention to themselves and away from the performers. There is also evidence that, as with the scenery, the Duke was well aware of the attractiveness of his costumes and (not unreasonably) was prepared to exploit it.

This aspect of the production style of the Meininger, however, also needs to be considered in context, for there was still a widespread practice of guest-artists providing their own costume and displaying themselves to advantage against the company with which they were performing. Klara Ziegler, who made guest appearances at the *Königliches Schauspielhaus* as Johanna in *Die Jungfrau von Orléans*, wore a costume consisting of 'a red velvet robe embroidered with golden fleurs de lys, decorated with golden fringes, and on top of it, not just a breast-plate, but arm and leg pieces which formed a brilliant contrast with her hose of purple velvet. The armour is richly decorated.'[38] It is quite probable that this costume was inspired by the painting of Joan of Arc by Ingres. If so, the richness of the model was evidently increased, whereas in the Meiningen version it was considerably toned down. Amanda Lindner also wore a breast-plate, but above leggings of chain mail and a plain white skirt. The real difference, however, was that her whole costume, though clearly prepared with great attention to detail, was not such as to make her stand out from an ensemble of performers whose costumes had been designed to match.

Over and above his concern for accuracy in costume design, the Duke of Meiningen also applied his historian's concern for the way costume was worn, and his stage-director's concern for the expressive implications of this. The requirement that full costume be worn from the first rehearsals of a new production, that equipment should be carried, and that stage business be practised, was designed to contribute to the establishment of an easy and natural relationship between the actor and the most immediate elements in his environment;[39] it was intended to remove the sense of strangeness inherent in the process of 'dressing up', and to eliminate that theatricality

34 Klara Ziegler as Johanna
in Schiller, *Die Jungfrau
von Orléans*.

35 C. W. Allers, Amanda
Lindner as Johanna in
*Die Jungfrau von
Orléans*.

which prompted actors to wear their helmets on the back of their heads rather than well down over their eyes, where they might conceal their faces from the audience.

Along with their costumes the Duke made a practice of giving his performers illustrations, with written instructions, telling them how their costumes were to be worn. In such sketches the character was not normally shown at rest, but carrying out some movement or gesture in the way the Duke required. The rehearsal notes to *Prinz Friedrich von Homburg* show how attentive he was to such details. While the anecdote of Ludwig Barnay's leather boots illustrates very tellingly the way in which, by control of costume, the Duke, as director, secured greater control over interpretation; it further emphasises the fact that his passion for historical accuracy was informed by a greater intelligence and seriousness of purpose than the literal-mindedness which prompted Ludwig II of Bavaria to send his Melchtal, Josef Kainz, on a long and exhausting walk through the Alps in order to prepare himself for one scene in the production of *Wilhelm Tell*.[40]

In 1873, when Barnay first went to perform in Meiningen, one of his rôles was to be that of Petruchio in *The Taming of the Shrew*. He therefore took with him a pair of new, thigh-length leather boots, even though he was well aware that the production was to be performed in renaissance costume. Despite all his prior knowledge of Meiningen rules, he expected to be able to wear his own boots (and spurs) because it was customary to express the masculinity which this rôle required with the aid of the military dress of the Thirty Years War. Despite Barnay's protests at the skimpy, seemingly effeminate costume he was given, the Duke insisted on maintaining the stylistic integrity of his production, and the visiting actor had to comply. Only slowly did he begin to perceive that the costume issued to him required a much more subtle and intellectualised conception of male superiority than the conventional aggressiveness of his original understanding of the rôle: 'Thanks to this purely external element the style of my interpretation imperceptibly underwent a transformation, and came, perhaps, to correspond more closely to the dramatist's intentions.'[41]

There are contemporary criticisms of some of the Meiningen costumes which resemble Barnay's initially contemptuous response to his costume as Petruchio. These need to be considered with caution, for there is ample evidence of the careful use of costume for specific interpretative purposes. We have already noted the contrast between the English and French courtiers in *Maria Stuart*; there are similar strong contrasts of costume between Weislingen and Götz, and between their respective environments, in the (non-touring) production of *Götz von Berlichingen*; and in *Die Hermannsschlacht*, to bring out the extreme differences between the barbaric but loyal Germans and the decadent Latins. More precise use is made of costume in *Die Jungfrau von Orléans*, where the Dauphin is initially made to look

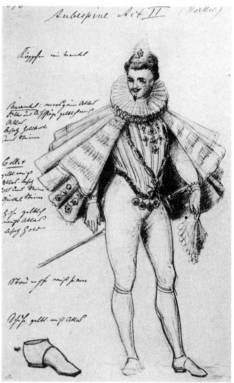

36 Georg II, costume sketch for
Shakespeare, *The Taming of the
Shrew*, Petruchio.

37–8 Georg II, costume sketches for
Maria Stuart, Burleigh,
d'Aubespine.

insignificant and pathetic in a costume which dwarfs him, but, after his self-confidence has grown under the influence of Johanna, he is clad in a dignified manner for the coronation.

On the art of acting in the sense of the emotional and intellectual penetration of a rôle and its interpretation, the Duke of Meiningen has little to say. Nor does he have a great deal to say about the rhetorical aspect of the actor's art, the declamation, consistently criticised as stilted and old-fashioned, the weakest feature of the Meiningen style. There are, it is true, some remarks in the rehearsal notes to *Prinz Friedrich von Homburg* which indicate a preference for restrained and natural speech, but to judge solely by the comments to Lindau the Duke was concerned with the actions of the performer and – above all – with choreography. The actor appears to have been seen primarily as the movable element in a static set, someone who wore costumes, carried

39–40   Georg II, costume sketches for *Die Jungfrau von Orléans*: the Dauphin, Act III; Charles VII, coronation scene.

spears, or participated – perhaps as the leader of a group of extras – in carefully organised and rehearsed crowd scenes. The excellence of these external aspects of the Meiningen productions was widely acknowledged, and perceptive critics, such as Fontane, recognised that it was not really possible to make the firm distinctions which others made, for the quality of the external elements could not but have an effect on the quality of the acting (particularly in theatre with realist aspirations); of a post-Meiningen production of *Wallensteins Tod*, with new decorations, at the *Königliches Schauspielhaus* in 1887, Fontane writes:

It has often been feared, and equally often stated, that *Meiningerei* would kill art; there was not the slightest evidence of this. On the contrary, it brought about its triumph. The senses and the spirit of the spectator are attracted, but not distracted. And as for the actors! Like people who, through no fault of their own, have been living in straitened circumstances, and because of their lack of gloves or hats have not moved around freely, and who, at the prospect of a well-paid position or even the distant possibility of marrying into money, totally cast off all constraint, look around in quite a different way and seem to say in every expression: 'Yes, here I am', our Court Players have regained their pleasure in life and in their profession. And since they now carry out their tasks with this pleasure a rocket has suddenly appeared on the dead stick of their artistic existence, and it has shot into the sky throwing out sprays of light. The proposition that people are made by their clothes [Kleider machen Leute] has never been more thoroughly demonstrated than in the new production of the *Wallenstein* trilogy.[42]

There were, however, those who felt that the price paid for the particular excellence of the Meiningen productions was indeed a neglect of acting skills in the more traditional sense. It was the established critics of an older generation who tended to put this view most forcefully: Speidel in Vienna, Scott in London, Ostrovskij in Moscow, and Sarcey in Paris. For these men, adherents of an individualist conception of theatre, the personal contribution of the actor of genius remained the decisive factor, rather than the collective achievement of a whole company, even when, as in the case of the Meininger, the company was subject to a fairly authoritarian individual will. Their praise of the crowd direction and ensemble playing is never unqualified, for they feel they recognise here the inhibition of the individual acting talent by a restraining discipline, a mechanical rather than a spontaneous effect.

Reservations about the quality of the Meiningen performers were also expressed by younger critics and aspiring directors who were themselves committed to the notion of the ensemble, and who were to contribute to the movement away from the actor-dominated theatre of the earlier nineteenth century. Of the three most important, Otto Brahm remarked on a distinct falling-off in the second part of *Julius Caesar*: 'what [the Meininger] cannot do is adequately present a scene which depends purely on effective acting and strongly developed artistic personalities and not on extras'. Antoine seeks an explanation for this, stating that the principal criteria in the recruitment of actors seemed to be physical and visual, in particular the ability of the actor to display the Meiningen costumes to the best advantage.[43] There is some evidence that Antoine was right up to a point; in 1869 Bodenstedt replied to a letter recommending an actor to him, saying that he would be interested if the actor (Bauer) measured up to the demands which the Duke made of a romantic lead by being 'well built and of pleasing appearance'. In 1890 the Duke rejected Anna Haverland as a second Joan of Arc, alongside Amanda Lindner, because he felt she was too fat.[44] It seems probable that Josef Nesper owed his prominence in the company to his physique rather than his voice or his manner; imposing but insignificant, is how Fontane described him in one of a number of reviews (dating from after he had left Meiningen and joined the *Königliches Schauspielhaus*) which draw attention to the discrepancy between his commanding appearance and his limited abilities; while Kainz, a colleague (but for that reason a rival for public acclaim) describes Nesper's acting as beneath criticism.[45] The Duke seems, in fact, to have been aware of Nesper's limitations, but the positive response he elicited from the public and from some of the critics, in numerous rôles, suggests that Georg was also aware that such an actor could be employed to considerable advantage in his visually oriented productions, notably in those parts where authority could be expressed through physical presence.[46] Stanislavskij also remarks on the discrepancy between the quality of the acting and that of the stage-direction, with particular reference to the production of *Die Jungfrau von Orléans*, which he saw in Moscow in 1890:

The stage-director thickened the atmosphere of the defeated court so that the spectator waits impatiently for the coming of the Maid, and he is so glad when she does come that he does not notice the cheap acting of the woman who uses the worst stage methods . . . rolling her eyes and giving vent to vocal fireworks. The talent of the stage director hid the faults of the actress.[47]

The probability that the Meiningen methods were, to some degree, a way of making a virtue out of necessity, is clear enough. We have noted the difficulty of this provincially based touring company in attracting major actors and keeping them; the traffic tended to flow in the other direction as actors such as Kainz, Nesper, and Hellmuth-Bräm established a reputation with the Meininger and moved on to advance their careers elsewhere. This does not, of course, amount to a principle, but it is not unreasonable to assume on the part of the Duke and the Baroness some preference for actors of limited ambition or limited experience, for such actors could well have proved more pliable, more responsive to the wishes and intentions of a director, than the great virtuosi of the nineteenth century. In fact, in the last few touring years and in the 1890s the Meiningen Theatre became something of an actors' school. A number of talented actors and actresses worked, as Kainz had done, for a few seasons in Meiningen before moving on and

making their reputations elsewhere; they included Artur Krausneck, Adele
Sandrock, Gertrud Eysoldt, Albert Bassermann, and Helene and Hermann
Thimig.[48]

To the charge that the policy of the company was to neglect essentials in
order to concentrate on externals Chronegk could reasonably reply, as he did
in Moscow, that if the externals attracted the greater interest, then this
reflected only on the public: 'I brought them Shakespeare, Schiller, and
Molière and they are interested in the furniture. What kind of a taste have
they anyway?'[49] The realistic principles of the Meiningen style of production
directed attention to the relationship between the externals and the actors, to
the influence of scenery, furnishings, and costume on grouping, movement,
and gesture; the Duke was interested in the function of the several elements
in theatrical art and their harmonious fusion in the creation of a unified
production.

A further advantageous consequence of the absence of established or star
performers was that it gave to the director a greater freedom in casting. By
the 1870s the *Fach* system was in decline; and in Meiningen the right of any
actor to a particular category of rôle was expressly excluded. Even so,
individualised or unorthodox casting was much easier with actors who had
not yet acquired particular habits or expectations, or who did not still have
contractual rights of an earlier date. There were, in Meiningen, no obstacles
to the immediate employment of promising newcomers as soon as they had
joined the company. While Paula Conrad was languishing frustratedly at the
Königliches Schauspielhaus, her contemporary, Kainz, was acquiring valu-
able experience in the rôles in which he was to become famous; six years later
Amanda Lindner, seventeen years old and probably a less gifted actress than
Paula Conrad, was playing Johanna in *Die Jungfrau von Orléans* in Berlin.

It also seems reasonable to assume that less established actors would have
been more ready to participate, as they were required to do, in the crowd
scenes; and, of course, Sarcey had a perfectly valid point when he remarked
that the presence of a particularly well-known star would, by his or her very
presence, disrupt the unity of a stage crowd from the point of view of the
audience. The presence of trained actors was clearly essential to the Meiningen crowd scenes; without them the fundamental tenet, that the theatrical art
is concerned with the representation of movement, could scarcely have been
implemented in such scenes. Contemporary critics are, moreover, almost
unanimous in noting how thoroughly this principle was implemented,
although they are far from unanimous in praising this. 'Something is always
going on', observes Clement Scott of the opening scene of *Julius Caesar*,
'men and women change places; they converse in dumb show; one leaps
upon the pediment of a statue to see the procession of the advancing Caesar,
another strains his eyes to catch the first glimpse of the coming procession';
Lindau confirms the impression in his review of *Papst Sixtus V*:

This dynamism: if someone walks past, five people point . . . at him, the others, at the very least, nudge each other; they display the most incomprehensible interest in every occurrence; things that are far from being remarkable set them in a state of the most extreme astonishment; and if one of them should make an observation that an indulgent observer might describe as moderately amusing, they fall about with hilarity. To judge by these people's state of mind, a Caesar might be being murdered every day.[50]

What is clear from these descriptions, apart from the apparent excesses, is that the extras taking part in the crowd scenes were given fairly precise instructions and guidance as to their actions. Instead of staring out at the audience, a practice which the Duke quite explicitly condemns, the crowd is actively involved in the events being enacted on the stage. However melodramatic the gestures and movements described here appear to be, they are manifestly conceived as responses, which draw the attention of the audience to the *effects* of the principal action, rather than claiming that attention directly for themselves. The intention of the Duke, as expressed in his instructions, is that the arrangements of actors and crowds should not produce frozen *tableaux*, which halt the action of the drama, and which are clearly posed for the benefit of the audience; they are designed to support the dialogue by completing it, by realising what is implicit in it, or, if they do appear to distract from it, to emphasise the changes brought about by the dialogue in the relationship between the characters on the stage.

The evidence of contemporary criticism suggests that, here too, the realistic intention may not always have been perfectly realised. Writing of the London performance of *The Winter's Tale* Clement Scott remarked on the predominance of *tableau* effects which fail precisely to contribute to the forward progress of the action:

As set, grouped, banked up and posed for the stage, this mass of colour, life and movement is the best possible example of the effect, and we may add, the defect of the Meininger school. Granted that every stage picture is to be what we call a 'tableau vivant', nothing could well be more admirable. The light is skilfully managed; the colours are most carefully blended. But we feel all the time that it is a *tableau vivant*. Up goes the curtain, and the scene presented is startling. It has all been arranged by a photographer in colour: nothing is out of place, and every one appears to be posed for a picture in a group. All idea of the injured Hermione and the jealous Leontes is for the moment gone. It is a picture designed to court applause.[51]

Such applause, as the curtain rose on the landscape scene in Act II of *Esther*, was noted by a reviewer in Metz; and in Berlin it was reported that the curtain was raised several times at the end of Act II of *Wilhelm Tell*, over the *tableau vivant* of the oath-taking, a clear concession to contemporary taste, since this is a scene with a strong tradition in the visual arts.[52]

Such an inconsistency, like many of the other inconsistencies pointed out (often rather malevolently) by critics of the Meininger, and noted in the course of this investigation, indicates that the Meiningen style was still evolving: the realistic principles were not yet so far developed as to inform every aspect of every performance. The *mise-en-scène* continues to rely on conventional effects, and to include aesthetically pleasing pictures; and the audiences continue to expect them, and continue to respond. But lapses such as the *tableau* at the end of the Rütli scene in *Wilhelm Tell*, or Barnay's manner of acknowledging the audience in *Julius Caesar* at Drury Lane, are not characteristic. The place of the Meiningen Theatre in the development of realistic staging is more accurately indicated by the ambiguity of the Duke's instructions for the conclusion to Act I of *Prinz Friedrich von Homburg*; or by his proposals for the deployment of the crowd in Act III, scene 2 of *Julius Caesar*: when Caesar enters the Curia the populace should not withdraw, but should form 'picturesque groups' (the aesthetic principle), 'with their backs to the audience in order to listen to the proceedings' (the realistic principle).[53] Conventional effects are here given a *raison d'être* that is consistent with contemporary standards of realism.

Conclusion

The Meiningen Court Theatre had its devoted admirers and its fierce critics. It also elicited directly contradictory responses from some of those who witnessed its productions. One of these was the leading German dramatist of the decade which followed the end of the Meiningen tours, Gerhart Hauptmann. In a single volume of his autobiography he both acknowledged the fruitful stimulus he received from the Meininger, and, no less firmly, consigned them without regret to a nineteenth-century past transcended by his own naturalistic dramas.[54]

The reasons for this paradox lie in the ambiguities of the Meiningen Theatre itself, and the transitional place of the company in theatre history. Known for the spectacular quality of his productions, for *Meiningerei*, Georg II nevertheless energetically repudiated the suggestion that his principal achievement had been merely to provide major dramas with a decorative frame that was entirely worthy of them: 'That . . . is certainly not the purpose of my endeavours . . . I can assure you . . . that the picturesque, the decorative, is never the major factor in my relationship to a work of art.'[55] The problem is that the desire for effect, manifest in carefully staged and visually spectacular productions, tends to detract from the realistic significance of these same effects.

It was for this reason that the majority of the younger naturalists were inclined to reject the methods of Georg II, along with the historical drama which these methods had served. A small number, and this number includes the theatre directors, Antoine, Brahm, and Stanislavskij, recognised what was only barely evident in the touring repertoire (most notably in the two performances of Ibsen's *Ghosts*), but is evident to the careful reader of his instructions to Lindau, and must have been no less evident to the careful observer of his productions: namely that what had evolved here was a style whose potential for development lay not in the historical drama of the past, but in the contemporary social drama, where the relationship between man and his environment was fundamental to the whole conception of the work, and positively invited expression by stage-direction, by the exploitation for expressive purposes of the relationship between the actor and the set.

As if to make good what might be regarded as the one great failure of the Meiningen tours, the great German director of the next decade, Otto Brahm, will, from 1894, in that very same theatre in which these tours had begun, place the social dramas of Ibsen at the centre of his repertoire; and he will produce them in a style which shares all the *anti*-theatrical principles of the Duke of Meiningen, but which is bare of the *theatrical* splendour and colourful decorations of his productions. In a slightly less austere way, Antoine was to do the same in France, and Stanislavskij in Russia. The balance will be restored by Reinhardt, who gave up his career as an actor in Brahm's company in 1903 to begin his own career as a theatre director. His production of *The Merchant of Venice* in 1905 looks back to the second Meiningen production of this play in 1886, and beyond that to Charles Kean. The prominence of *The Merchant of Venice*, together with *Twelfth Night* and *The Winter's Tale*, in Reinhardt's repertoire, confirm him as the renewer and developer of the Meiningen tradition, both in its generally spectacular and dynamic qualities, and in the combination of the realistic and the fantastic.[56]

To argue that the emergence of these first great stage-directors, in the modern sense, was directly dependent on the preparatory work of the Meiningen Theatre and the propagation of its methods in its European tours, would be to attribute too much to a single cause. However, at a time when the theatre in Europe was entering a period of rapid change, and its relationship with neighbouring arts was becoming very fluid, this small provincial theatre, starting virtually from scratch, and operating under very special conditions as a hybrid between a court theatre and a commercial touring company, and, moreover – let us not allow the belief in the determining power of socio-political and institutional factors to obscure the fact – managed by a supremely gifted and ideally balanced collective, carried out a great task of synthesis. Whether, and if so to what extent, the heterogeneous instrument that was thereby created corresponds to, or anticipates, modern directors' theatre, can be judged only on the basis of what the company actually achieved; it has been a major part of the task of this study to analyse that achievement.

The answers to certain important questions tend to confirm the view that the Duke of Meiningen and his collaborators stand at, or fairly near to, the head of the modern development to which we have referred.[57] The repertoire of the company was determined at directorial level and, within the constraints of the commercial theatre, it shows a high degree of coherence, both in its reflection of the artistic strengths and specialities of the company, and in its consistent national and educational orientation. The texts used in the productions were edited and prepared at directorial level, in accordance with principles which also clearly reflect the overall artistic policy. Actors were carefully considered in terms of consistent criteria, before being engaged; they were prepared individually for their parts and required to take part in extensive rehearsal. Casting was not done by *Fach*, but by the director, taking into account the specific aims and requirements of the production and the strongly visual orientation of the style. Scenic design was the responsibility of the principal member of the directorial team, the Duke himself, and he supervised closely the execution of his designs by scene painters who were familiar with, and sympathetic to, the aims of the company, and who served it continuously and personally throughout the touring period and beyond. Costume design was also in the hands of the Duke, and the wearing of costume was controlled with great firmness and attention to its implications for the interpretation of the drama. Arrangements, crowd scenes, and stage business were worked out carefully at directorial level, were carefully rehearsed, and carried out according to plan. Off-stage control of the production was, in short, comprehensive and overwhelming.

This control did not, however, rest with one individual, but with a team of three. It is impossible to be absolutely sure of the precise division of labour, but it can be said with some confidence that it was not very precise at all. In fact, the existence of a collective directorship probably went a long way to mitigating the inherent despotism of the Meiningen methods. In this respect the Meiningen Theatre did not differ significantly from the *Deutsches Theater* under Otto Brahm, who, like Georg II, lacked a background in the practical theatre, did not sign himself as director, and used his assistants, Emil Lessing and Cord Hachmann, to implement his ideas on stage. It is, moreover, clear that designers of the stature of Ernst Stern and Alfred Roller exercised a considerable influence on the productions on which they collaborated with Max Reinhardt; just as Caspar Neher did with Brecht, and, more recently, Karl-Ernst Hermann with Peter Stein.[58] The notion of collaborative work by a directorial team is at odds with some of the more romantic ideas about the rôle of the theatre director, but in other respects it is far from paradoxical. The crucial factor is the degree of off-stage control, and the conscious use of this to produce a consistent interpretation of the drama as a whole.

In her letter to Frenzel, criticising the *Königliches Schauspielhaus* and its production of *Die Hermannsschlacht* in 1875, the Freifrau von Heldburg noted the absence of artistic direction in this sense from the productions of Germany's leading theatre: 'for tragedy they lack . . . a director with the ambition to be a reformer of classical production'.[59] Underlying her criticism is the implication that the activities of the Meiningen Theatre were informed by just such an ambition. The evidence of the Meiningen productions indicates a high degree of success in carrying it out.

Appendix 1

Table 1. *Plays performed, by city*

	Julius Caesar	Papst Sixtus V	Twelfth Night	Bluthochzeit	Between the Battles	Le Malade imaginaire	The Merchant of Venice	Die Hermannsschlacht	Esther	Les Femmes savantes	Fiesko	Das Käthchen von Heilbronn	Der Erbförster	Wilhelm Tell
Berlin	52	4	6	11	6	11	5	15	15	10	29	16	2	21
Vienna	16	–	5	4	1	2	–	17	3	3	7	4	–	8
Budapest	9	–	6	9	1	6	5	4	6	1	5	2	–	10
Dresden	10	–	11	9	2	6	8	10	5	3	9	10	–	7
Breslau	35	–	20	11	5	12	8	10	10	3	18	5	–	19
Cologne	14	–	5	3	–	3	–	–	3	–	12	6	–	12
Frankfurt/Main	8	–	3	2	–	3	–	–	3	–	4	4	–	3
Prague	10	–	5	5	1	3	3	4	3	1	4	7	–	11
Leipzig	19	–	10	8	4	7	6	8	7	2	12	5	–	9
Hamburg	4	–	3	–	–	2	–	4	2	–	3	4	–	5
Amsterdam	6	–	4	3	–	3	–	–	3	–	5	–	–	7
Düsseldorf	11	–	5	3	–	2	3	5	2	–	6	5	–	8
Graz	11	–	6	4	–	2	6	6	2	–	5	4	–	13
Bremen	7	–	3	–	–	2	–	4	2	2	5	2	–	6
London	16	–	2	–	–	1	–	–	–	–	3	3	–	8
Nuremberg	4	–	–	–	–	2	–	–	2	–	3	–	–	4
Barmen	6	–	3	–	–	–	4	–	–	–	3	3	–	5
Magdeburg	4	–	2	–	–	2	–	–	2	–	3	–	–	3
Munich	7	–	1	–	–	–	4	3	–	–	–	–	–	6
Mainz	7	–	3	–	–	2	4	–	–	–	3	3	–	4
Strasburg	6	–	2	–	–	2	4	–	2	1	3	–	–	7
Baden Baden	–	–	1	–	–	1	–	–	–	–	–	–	–	–
Metz	–	–	1	–	–	1	–	–	1	–	–	–	–	–
Basle	10	–	1	–	–	1	3	4	1	–	2	–	–	9
St Petersburg	12	–	1	5	–	1	4	3	–	2	2	–	–	6
Moscow	7	–	3	3	–	1	4	2	–	–	3	–	–	3
Warsaw	4	–	1	–	–	2	–	–	–	–	–	–	–	4
Königsberg	4	–	2	–	–	1	–	–	–	–	–	–	–	4
Trieste	4	–	1	–	–	–	–	–	–	–	–	–	–	4
Antwerp	3	–	1	–	–	–	3	–	–	–	–	–	–	3
Rotterdam	4	–	1	–	–	–	3	–	–	–	–	–	–	4
Brussels	3	–	2	–	–	–	4	–	–	–	–	–	–	3
Gotha	1	–	1	–	–	–	–	–	–	–	–	–	–	–
Stettin	4	–	2	–	–	–	3	–	–	–	–	–	–	3
Copenhagen	3	–	3	–	1	–	3	–	1	–	–	–	–	2
Stockholm	4	–	2	–	–	–	4	–	–	–	–	–	–	2
Kiev	2	–	1	2	–	1	1	–	–	1	1	–	–	–
Odessa	3	–	1	3	–	1	2	2	–	–	2	–	–	–
	330	4	130	85	21	83	94	101	75	29	152	83	2	223

	The Pretenders	Macbeth	Die Jäger	Die Räuber	Prinz Friedrich von Homburg	The Winter's Tale	Die Ahnfrau	Wallensteins Lager	Iphigenie auf Tauris	Preciosa	The Taming of the Shrew	Die Piccolomini	Wallensteins Tod	Die Hexe
Berlin	7	5	–	13	10	27	6	24	1	6	–	24	21	13
Vienna	–	–	–	5	2	10	10	6	–	–	–	6	6	7
Budapest	–	–	–	2	2	9	4	7	–	4	4	3	3	–
Dresden	–	–	–	4	–	10	6	8	–	3	–	8	7	10
Breslau	–	5	–	8	4	17	7	16	4	8	6	12	10	10
Cologne	–	–	2	5	4	7	2	–	–	–	–	–	–	–
Frankfurt/Main	–	–	–	5	3	9	–	–	–	–	–	–	–	–
Prague	–	–	–	6	2	14	6	6	–	3	–	6	6	3
Leipzig	–	–	–	8	3	11	5	8	2	5	2	8	7	4
Hamburg	–	–	–	4	3	5	2	–	–	–	–	–	–	–
Amsterdam	–	–	–	6	–	5	–	–	–	–	–	–	–	–
Düsseldorf	–	–	–	4	3	9	1	3	–	–	2	3	3	–
Graz	–	–	–	3	2	11	6	8	–	3	3	5	4	3
Bremen	–	–	–	2	–	6	3	6	1	2	–	4	3	2
London	–	–	–	3	–	7	1	2	2	8	–	–	–	–
Nuremberg	–	–	–	–	–	5	–	3	2	3	–	3	3	–
Barmen	–	–	–	2	–	6	1	6	–	–	2	6	6	–
Magdeburg	–	–	–	–	–	4	1	4	–	–	–	4	4	–
Munich	–	–	–	2	–	5	3	7	–	–	–	7	7	–
Mainz	–	–	–	–	–	6	2	6	–	–	2	6	5	2
Strasburg	–	–	–	3	–	3	2	6	–	–	–	6	6	–
Baden Baden	–	–	–	–	–	–	1	–	–	–	–	–	–	–
Metz	–	–	–	–	–	–	–	–	–	–	–	–	–	–
Basle	–	–	–	3	–	3	2	7	–	–	–	7	5	–
St Petersburg	–	–	–	3	–	4	2	7	1	4	–	7	6	–
Moscow	–	–	–	2	–	4	1	6	–	2	–	6	5	–
Warsaw	–	–	–	2	–	3	1	3	–	–	–	3	2	–
Königsberg	–	–	–	2	–	4	2	3	–	–	–	3	3	–
Trieste	–	–	–	3	–	3	1	3	–	–	–	3	2	2
Antwerp	–	–	–	–	–	4	–	3	–	–	–	3	2	–
Rotterdam	–	–	–	–	–	4	–	2	–	–	–	2	2	–
Brussels	–	–	–	–	–	3	–	3	–	–	–	3	2	–
Gotha	–	–	–	–	–	–	–	–	–	–	–	–	–	–
Stettin	–	–	–	–	–	4	1	3	–	–	–	3	2	–
Copenhagen	–	–	–	3	–	3	–	–	–	–	–	3	2	–
Stockholm	–	–	–	1	–	3	–	4	–	–	–	4	3	–
Kiev	–	–	–	–	–	2	–	1	–	–	–	1	1	–
Odessa	–	–	–	–	–	3	–	2	1	3	–	2	2	–
	7	10	2	104	38	233	79	176	14	54	21	161	140	56

	Lydia	Der Hergottschnitzer von Ammergau	Maria Stuart	Miss Sara Sampson	Die Braut von Messina	Marino Faliero	Die Jungfrau von Orléans	Galeoto	Alexandra	Ghosts	Die Rosen von Tyburn	Frau Lucrezia	's Nullerl
Berlin	–	–	9	3	–	3	55	–	–	–	–	–	–
Vienna	–	–	–	–	–	–	–	–	–	–	–	–	–
Budapest	–	–	3	–	–	3	5	–	–	–	–	–	–
Dresden	5	3	8	2	–	–	13	3	2	1	–	–	–
Breslau	2	3	10	2	–	2	14	1	3	–	2	–	–
Cologne	–	–	–	–	–	–	–	–	–	–	–	–	–
Frankfurt/Mainz	–	–	–	–	–	–	–	–	–	–	–	–	–
Prague	–	–	3	–	–	3	5	–	–	–	–	–	–
Leipzig	–	–	3	–	–	1	11	–	–	–	3	–	–
Hamburg	–	–	–	–	–	–	–	–	–	–	–	–	–
Amsterdam	–	–	–	–	–	–	–	–	–	–	–	–	–
Düsseldorf	2	–	4	–	2	3	–	–	–	–	–	–	–
Graz	–	–	5	–	2	–	4	–	–	–	–	–	–
Bremen	–	–	–	–	–	–	–	–	–	–	–	–	–
London	–	–	–	–	–	–	–	–	–	–	–	–	–
Nuremberg	–	–	–	–	–	–	–	–	–	–	–	–	–
Barmen	2	–	3	–	–	–	–	–	–	–	–	–	–
Magdeburg	–	–	–	–	–	–	–	–	–	–	–	–	–
Munich	–	–	4	–	–	–	10	–	–	–	–	–	–
Mainz	4	2	2	–	1	2	–	–	–	–	–	–	–
Strasburg	1	1	4	–	–	–	10	–	–	–	–	–	–
Baden Baden	1	–	–	–	–	–	–	–	–	–	–	–	–
Metz	–	–	–	–	–	–	–	–	–	–	–	–	–
Basle	–	2	5	–	–	2	11	3	–	–	–	–	–
St Petersburg	1	–	3	–	2	–	9	–	–	–	–	2	–
Moscow	1	–	4	–	1	–	5	–	–	–	–	–	1
Warsaw	2	–	2	–	–	–	–	–	–	–	–	–	–
Königsberg	1	–	3	–	1	–	–	–	–	–	–	–	–
Trieste	1	–	3	–	2	–	–	–	–	–	–	–	–
Antwerp	–	–	3	–	–	–	7	–	–	–	–	–	–
Rotterdam	–	–	4	–	–	–	6	–	–	–	–	–	–
Brussels	–	–	4	–	–	–	5	–	–	–	–	–	–
Gotha	–	–	–	–	–	–	–	–	–	–	–	–	–
Stettin	–	–	–	–	–	–	5	–	–	–	–	–	–
Copenhagen	–	–	–	–	–	–	6	–	–	1	–	–	–
Stockholm	–	–	–	–	–	–	7	–	–	–	–	–	–
Kiev	–	–	–	–	–	–	2	–	–	–	–	–	–
Odessa	1	–	–	–	–	–	4	–	–	–	–	–	1
	24	11	89	7	11	19	194	7	5	2	5	2	2

Table 2. *Performances given, by city and year*

	1874	1875	1876	1877	1878
Berlin	47	60	48		46
Vienna		37			
Budapest		17			
Dresden			25	26	
Breslau			33	39	32
Cologne				41	
Frankfurt/Main				24	20
Prague					27
Leipzig					32
Hamburg					
Amsterdam					
Düsseldorf					
Graz					
Bremen					
London					
Nuremberg					
Barmen					
Magdeburg					
Munich					
Mainz					
Strasburg					
Baden Baden					
Metz					
Basle					
St Petersburg					
Moscow					
Warsaw					
Königsberg					
Trieste					
Antwerp					
Rotterdam					
Brussels					
Gotha					
Stettin					
Copenhagen					
Stockholm					
Kiev					
Odessa					
Total	47	114	106	130	157

Note: double-bills are counted as one performance.

1879	1880	1881	1882	1883	1884	1885	1886	1887	1888	1889	1890
			78		43			63			
40				35							
23		29							30		
		21	30	29			33				
		31	33		34			35		32	
34											
31				25					27		
	40		21						31	35	
39											
	39										
	48						34				
	32	30				28			18		
		26		28							
		56									
			29								
				26			24				
				27							
				31				28			
					28		28				
					29			31			
					3						
					2						
					28			45			
						39					38
						29					28
						24					
						29					
						29					
									29		
									30		
									29		
										2	
										27	
										30	
										30	
											14
											30
167	159	172	182	202	196	178	86	235	194	156	110

Appendix II

Table 1. *Income and Expenditure*

	1881		1880	Comparative figures 1882	1883
Income		M.			
1. Surplus from previous year	75,633.62[a]		28,749.21		
2. Net income from spring tour	34,130.59[b]		60,000	70,000	75,000
3. Net income from autumn tour	70,988.16		39,250.79	70,000	75,000
4. Sale of tickets in Meiningen	41,572.62		24,000	23,000	19,000
5. Sale of programmes	455.70		556		
6. Miscellaneous	2,239.49		900		
	225,020.18		153,456	173,500[c]	177,000
Expenditure					
1. Salaries	127,453.56		123,400	128,000	140,000
2. Honoraria etc.	2,485.53		1,800		
3. Costumes	33,527.28		4,000	12,000	8,000
4. Decorations and machinery	35,693.47		4,000	9,000	5,000
5. Furnishings	2,347.65				
6. Heating, lighting, cleaning	10,981.23				
7. Costs of performances	6,014.69		5,300		
8. Postage	122.20				
9. Library	53.45				
10. Office and printing costs	370.36				
11. Insurance	3,726.15		3,376		
12. Reserve fund	3,728.58				
	226,504.15				

[a] This figure must refer to 1879 since the accounts for 1880 do not show a surplus.
[b] 25,100 M. from Bremen; 9,030 from London.
[c] Includes a ducal subsidy of 5,100 M.

Table 2. *Daily rentals for the leasing of theatres, 1881–1887*

1881		
Breslau	Stadttheater	800 M.
Graz	Stadttheater	350 Gülden
1882		
Berlin	Friedrich-Wilhelmstädtisches Theater	600 M.
Breslau	Lobetheater	600 M.
Dresden	Residenztheater	600 M.
1883		
Barmen	Stadttheater	300 M.
Bremen	Stadttheater	450 M.
Magdeburg	Stadttheater	300 M.
Munich	Königliches Theater am Gärtnerplatz	500 M.
Dresden	Residenztheater	600 M.
1884		
Mainz	Stadttheater	300 M.
Strasburg	Stadttheater	400 M.[a]
Basel	Stadttheater	350 M.
Berlin	Victoria-Theater	900 M.
Breslau	Lobetheater	550 M.
Dresden	Residenztheater	550 M.
1885		
Königsberg	Stadttheater	500 M.
Trieste	Politeama Rossetti	250 Gülden
1886		
Barmen	Stadttheater	300 M.
Mainz	Stadttheater	350 M.
1887		
Berlin	Victoria-Theater	900 M.
Strasburg	Stadttheater	100 M.[a]
Munich	Königliches Theater am Gärtnerplatz	500 M.
Dresden	Residenztheater	600 M.

[a] In 1883 the Municipal Theatre in Strasburg had been sub-let to the Meiningen Theatre by Ammann. When his lease expired on 31 May 1884 it proved possible to rent the theatre on very favourable terms from the municipality. Correspondence on this subject is in the possession of the Staatliche Museen Meiningen (Inv. No. IVC 1,427–1,430).

The figures in the above table are taken from contracts between the Meiningen Theatre and the respective theatres rented; STAM, Hofmarschallamt, Hoftheater 96.

Notes

The following abbreviations are used in the notes:

COL   Institut für Theater-, Film- und Fernsehwissenschaft der Universität Köln, Sammlung Niessen

GSA   Goethe- und Schiller-Archiv der Nationalen Forschungs- und Gedenkstätten der klassischen Literatur in Weimar
(Rodenberg = Nachlaß Julius Rodenberg; Frenzel = Nachlaß Karl Frenzel)

STAM   Staatsarchiv Meiningen, DDR (HA = Hausarchiv)

StBBH Deutsche Staatsbibliothek Berlin, DDR, Handschriftenabteilung, Nachlaß Georg II von Sachsen-Meiningen (K = carton; M = folder; B = sheet)

Material from the Staatlichen Museen Meiningen, DDR-Meiningen, Theaterhistorisches Archiv is referred to by its archive number.

1 Culture and politics

1 There had also been a major fire in the town on 5 September 1874. See *Meininger Ansichten*, edited by Staatlichen Museen, Meiningen (Meiningen, 1982), pp. 18, 23.

2 See Ernst von Wildenbruch, 'Von Meiningen nach Weimar', *Berliner Tageblatt*, 10 and 21 April 1908.

3 See Robert Prölß, *Das Herzoglich Meiningen'sche Hoftheater und die Bühnenreform* (Erfurt, 1876).

4 Paxton, head gardener to the Duke of Devonshire at Chatsworth, was neither a qualified engineer nor an architect, and yet in the Crystal Palace he produced 'the most advanced and wonderful building of the nineteenth century'; Robert Rhodes James, *Albert, Prince Consort* (London, 1983), pp. 147, 198–99.

5 *Statistik des Herzogthums Sachsen Meiningen*, edited by the Statistischen Bureau im Herzogl. Staatsministerium, Abtheilung des Innern (Meiningen, 1882–85).

6 E. Schocke, *Die deutsche Einheits- und Freiheitsbewegung in Sachsen Meiningen. Ein Beitrag zur Geschichte der ersten deutschen Revolution*, Schriften des Vereins für Sachsen-Meiningensche Geschichte und Landeskunde, 86 (Hildburghausen, 1927), pp. 1–8.

7 A. Erck, H.-J Kertscher, I. Schaefer, *Kunst und Künstler in Meiningen* (vol. 1) *Von den Anfängen bis 1871* (Meiningen, 1984), p. 94. On the development of liberalism in general, see James J. Sheehan, *German Liberalism in the Nineteenth Century* (London, 1982, first published 1978), pp. 13–14.

8 Volker Reißland, 'Herausbildung und Grundzüge der Meininger Theaterreform im letzten Drittel des 19. Jahrhunderts als Wegbereiter für die Weiterentwicklung der Schauspielkunst im beginnenden 20. Jahrhundert' (unpublished dissertation, Karl-Marx University, Leipzig, 1977), hereafter, Reißland, 'Theaterreform', p. 23. A shortened version of this dissertation has been published as 'Die theater-reformatorischen Bestrebungen der "Meininger"', *Südthüringer Forschungen*, 17, hereafter, Reißland, 'Bestrebungen', pp. 85–96. See also Steven DeHart, *The Meininger Theater, 1776–1926*, Theater and Dramatic Studies, 4 (Ann Arbor, 1981), pp. 37–38.

9 *Statistik des Herzogthums*, 1, p. 63; 11 (1885), p. 68. Figures for production in the mining

industry are (in *Reichsmark*): 1880: 5,335,950 M., 1881: 4,986,362 M., 1882: 5,572,102 M., 1883: 4,879,708 M. (*Statistik*, II, pp. 21, 143, 277).

10 Erck *et al.*, *Kunst und Künstler*, I, pp. 95–96.

11 StBBH, K7 M37 B3–4 (10 March 1848).

12 See Reißland, 'Theaterreform', p. 29.

13 Ludwig Hertel, 'Die Regierungszeiten Herzog Bernhards II Erich Freund und Georgs II', *Neue Landeskunde des Herzogtums Sachsen Meiningen*, IIB, part 2/ii, Schriften des Vereins für Sachsen-Meiningische Geschichte und Landeskunde, 54 (Hildburghausen, 1906), pp. 394–96.

14 StBBH, K8 M61 B17 (20 April 1854).

15 See Theodor Fontane, *Der deutsche Krieg von 1866, II, Der Feldzug in West- und Mitteldeutschland* (Berlin, 1871; facsimile edition, Munich, 1971), pp. 36–38.

16 STAM, HA 321 (19 July 1866). See also Reißland, 'Theaterreform', p. 31.

17 STAM, HA 321 (6 November 1866). See also Reißland, 'Theaterreform', pp. 33–34.

18 Quoted from Erich Schmidt, *Das Verhältnis Sachsen-Meiningen zur Reichsgründung, 1851–1871* (doctoral dissertation, Halle, 1930), p. 86.

19 *Ibid.*, p. 97.

20 Curt Paul Janz, *Friedrich Nietzsche: Biographie*, 3 vols. (Munich and Vienna, 1978–79), I, pp. 373–75.

21 Paul Bronsart von Schellendorff, *Geheimes Kriegstagebuch, 1870–1871*, edited by Peter Rassow (Bonn, 1954), pp. 195–96. Compare Zola's presentation of the war as theatre in *La Débâcle*, in *Les Rougon-Macquart*, V, edited by Henri Mitterand, Bibliothèque de la Pléiade, 194 (Paris, 1967), pp. 66–67: 'Il y avait là des officiers étrangers, des aides de camp, des généraux, des maréchaux de cour, des princes, tous pourvus de lorgnettes, suivant depuis le matin l'agonie de l'armée française, comme au spectacle. Et le drame formidable s'achevait.' The Theatre Museum in Cologne possesses the manuscript of a satirical poem by the Duke: 'Jetzt wollen wir den Franzosen entgegengehen' (COL Au 7372).

22 StBBH, K10 M19–25.

23 'Erlebnisse aus dem Krieg 1870–71', StBBH, K12 M10 (ca 1903), M28–30 (1909). The sense that the German victory at Sedan constituted an important historical turning-point is given expression, with a characteristic comparison, by Georg's son, Crown Prince Bernhard, in a letter to his grandfather: 'The modern Richard III had found his Bothworth [*sic*]', STAM, HA 300 (15 September 1870). Karl Frenzel wrote in the *National-Zeitung*: 'On 2 September a new epoch began, the hegemony of the German spirit on earth'; quoted from Fontane, *Der Krieg gegen Frankreich, I, Der Krieg gegen das Kaiserreich* (Berlin, 1873; facsimile edition, Munich, 1971), p. 605.

24 Sheehan, *German Liberalism*, p. 122. Peter Uwe Hohendahl, *Literarische Kultur im Zeitalter des Liberalismus, 1830–1870* (Munich, 1985), pp. 91–96.

25 For example the preface (dated 7 September 1866) to vol. 2 of the fifth edition of Julian Schmidt's *Geschichte der deutschen Literatur seit Lessings Tod* (Leipzig, 1866–69). See Hohendahl, *Literarische Kultur*, pp. 208–09, 239, 247, 251.

26 The cultural section, the *Feuilleton*, of the daily newspapers in nineteenth-century Germany had a pronounced and conscious political function. This was especially true of the *National-Zeitung*. See Bodo Rollka, *Die Belletristik in der Berliner Presse des 19. Jahrhunderts*, Einzelveröffentlichungen der Historischen Kommission zu Berlin, 51 (Berlin, 1985).

27 Richard Walker Dill, *Der Parlamentarier Eduard Lasker und die parlamentarische Stilentwicklung der Jahre 1867–1884. Ein Beitrag zur Geistesgeschichte des politischen Stils in Deutschland* (doctoral dissertation, Erlangen, 1958), p. 11, and Adolf Laufs, *Eduard Lasker: Ein Leben für den Rechtsstaat*, Persönlichkeit und Geschichte, 118–19 (Göttingen and Zurich, 1984), pp. 30, 60.

28 *Briefe Conrad Ferdinand Meyers*, edited by Adolf Frey, 2 vols. (Leipzig, 1908), II, p. 10 (5

September 1866). See also the autobiographical essay, 'Mein Erstling "Huttens letzte Tage"' (1891), *Sämtliche Werke*, Historisch-Kritische Ausgabe, edited by Hans Zeller and Alfred Zäch, VIII (Bern, 1970), pp. 192–96.

29 StBBH, KII M5 BI–2 (21 December 1866). See Schmidt, *Das Verhältnis*, pp. 89, 119–26; Reißland, 'Theaterreform', pp. 35–36.

30 Fontane, 'Aus den Tagen der Okkupation', *Sämtliche Werke*, edited by Edgar Groß and others, 24 vols. (Munich, 1959–75), XVI, p. 170.

31 Quoted from Reißland, 'Theaterreform', p. 36.

32 Compare Bismarck's comment: 'The Kaiser-comedy needed a skilful stage-manager; it had to be an effective production'; quoted from Dill, *Lasker*, p. 65.

33 See Kurt Hommel, *Die Separatvorstellungen vor König Ludwig II von Bayern: Schauspiel, Oper, Ballett* (Munich, 1963), esp. chapter 10, 'Kainz's Bedeutung für die Separatvorstellungen', pp. 328–35.

34 See Hans Philippi, 'König Ludwig II von Bayern und der Welfenfonds', *Zeitschrift für bayerische Landesgeschichte*, 23 (1960), pp. 66–111.

35 Hommel, *Die Separatvorstellungen*, pp. 46–54.

36 Erck *et al.*, *Kunst und Künstler*, I, pp. 76–78.

37 *Adolf von Hildebrand und seine Welt: Briefe und Erinnerungen* besorgt von Bernhard Sattler (Munich, 1962), p. 371.

38 Eduard Tempeltey, 'Das Theater im Briefwechsel zwischen Gustav Freytag und Herzog Ernst II von Sachsen-Coburg-Gotha', *Bühne und Welt*, 7/i (1905), p. 149.

39 Ernst II's most successful opera, *Diana von Solange*, was performed in Dresden in 1859; see Tempeltey, 'Das Theater', pp. 144–46. On Prince Albert see James, *Albert, Prince Consort*.

40 Quoted from Max Grube, *Geschichte der Meininger* (Stuttgart, Berlin, Leipzig, 1926), p. 33.

41 Fernando Mazzocca, *Villa Carlotta*, Guide Artistiche Electa (Milan, 1983), p. 23. In the early years of the twentieth century, however, after the end of the theatre tours, the Duke turned his attention to the interior of the villa. Substantial alteration and renovation was carried out under the artistic direction of Lodovico Pogliaghi; see also U. Nebbia, *Lodovico Pogliaghi* (Milan, 1959).

42 In a letter dated 12 February 1880 Bülow wrote: 'Perhaps I shall be able to provide, on a small scale, a *pendant* to his model theatre.' Quoted from A. Erck, H.–J Kertscher, M. Schaefer, *Kunst und Künstler in Meiningen* (vol. II) *1871–1945* (Meiningen, 1983), p. 38.

43 *Ibid.*, p. 46.

44 Walter Kiaulehn, *Berlin: Schicksal einer Weltstadt* (Munich, 1976; first published 1958), p. 269.

45 Quoted from Carl, Freiherr von Stein, *Die Kunst in Meiningen unter Herzog Georg II* (Meiningen, 1909), p. 32.

46 See the reports in the *Berliner Börsen Kurier* (2 and 4 March 1884) and the *Allgemeine Deutsche Musikzeitung*, StBBH, K24 M8 B4–5. See also Erck *et al.*, *Kunst und Künstler*, II, pp. 38–39.

47 Bülow, StBBH, KI5 M36 B8 (23 November 1885); L. Hertel, 'Die Regierungszeiten', p. 434.

48 *Versuch über Wagner*, Suhrkamp Taschenbuch, 177 (Frankfurt/Main, 1974; first published 1952), pp. 24–25.

2 Art and literature

1 Friedrich Nietzsche, *Werke*, Kritische Gesamtausgabe, edited by Giorgio Colli and Mazzimo Montinari, III/i (Berlin and New York, 1972), pp. 275, 278.

2 See Arno Borst, 'Barbarossas Erwachen: zur Geschichte der deutschen Identität', in *Identität*, Poetik und Hermeneutik, 8, edited by Odo Marquard and Karlheinz Stierle

(Munich, 1979), pp. 17–60; Roswitha Flatz, 'Germania und Willehalm: Theatralische Allegorien eines utopischen Nationalismus', in *Literarische Utopie-Entwürfe*, edited by Hiltrud Gnüg, Suhrkamp Taschenbuch, 2,012 (Frankfurt/Main, 1982), pp. 219–35; Georg Jäger, 'Stiftungslegenden des Kaiserreichs', in *Realismus und Gründerzeit: Manifeste und Dokumente zur deutschen Literatur, 1848–1880*, edited by Max Bucher *et al.*, 2 vols. (Stuttgart, 1975–76), I, pp. 97–101.

3 See Gebhardt Zernin, 'Kaiser Wilhelm als Freund der Künste: Ein Gedenkblatt', *Die Kunst für Alle*, 3 (1888), pp. 220–22.

4 Robert Rosenblum and H. W. Janson, *Art of the Nineteenth Century: Painting and Sculpture* (London, 1984), p. 464.

5 See Theodor W. Adorno, *Versuch über Wagner*, pp. 92–93.

6 Carl von Stein, *Die Kunst in Meiningen unter Georg II* (Meiningen, 1909), p. 25.

7 Adorno, *Versuch über Wagner*, p. 115.

8 Rodenberg, who was in London in May 1881, went to the performances at Drury Lane. He wrote to Chronegk offering his congratulations and declaring his pride in the success of German acting in the land of Shakespeare; STAM, HA 74 (31 May 1881). Chronegk's reply is in GSA-Rodenberg, II, 3, 14 (4 June 1881). See also Rodenberg's diary entries for 31 May and 7 June 1881 (GSA-Rodenberg). On Conrad Ferdinand Meyer, see Georg Lukács, 'Der historische Roman', *Werke*, VI, *Probleme des Realismus*, vol. 3 (Neuwied and Berlin, 1965), p. 270; J. P. Stern, *Idylls and Realities* (London, 1971), pp. 81–82; and, especially, Hugo von Hofmannsthal, 'Conrad Ferdinand Meyers Gedichte', *Gesammelte Werke*, edited by Herbert Steiner, *Prosa*, IV, second edition (Frankfurt/Main, 1966), pp. 274–83.

9 See Peter Michelsen, 'Theodor Fontane als Kritiker englischer Shakespeare-Aufführungen', in Deutsche Shakespeare-Gesellschaft West, *Jahrbuch* (1967), pp. 96–122.

10 Goethe, *Gespräche mit Eckermann, Gedenkausgabe der Werke, Briefe und Gespräche* XXIV (Zurich, 1948), p. 395 (17 February 1830). On the Brückners' use of colour, see Luitpold Nusser, 'Schinkel und Brückner in ihrer Bedeutung für die Bühnenmalerei im 19. Jahrhundert' (doctoral dissertation, Würzburg, 1923), p. 46; and Edith Ibscher, *Theaterateliers des deutschen Sprachraums im 19. und 20. Jahrhundert* (doctoral dissertation, Cologne, 1972), p. 146.

11 For instance both Gustave Frédérix and André Antoine, in their comments on the Brussels performances of 1888; see *Die Meininger: Texte zur Rezeption*, edited by John Osborne (Tübingen, 1980), pp. 143, 161. See also Max Grube, *Geschichte der Meininger* (Stuttgart, Berlin, Leipzig, 1926), p. 33.

12 See Ingrid and Volker Reißland, 'Historienmalerei und Illusionismus: Die Theaterdekorationen des Meininger Hoftheaters in der 2. Hälfte des 19. Jahrhunderts', *Bildende Kunst*, Heft 10 (1985), pp. 454–58. This important article is of particular value for its illustrations, which show some of the surviving Meiningen backcloths. In the illustration of the backcloth for the final (garden) scene of *The Winter's Tale* (described, erroneously, in the caption as *Maria Stuart*, Act III) modern colour photography and printing may well have had a flattering effect. The Theatre Museum in Cologne possesses a number of oil paintings by Max Brückner, which represent an early stage in the execution of the Duke's designs.

Coloured illustrations of other decorations by the Brückners can also be seen in *Bayreuther Bühnenbilder*: Erste und einzig autorisierte farbige Reproduktion der von Herrn Hofrath Prof. Max (und Gotthold) Brückner in Coburg für das Bayreuther Festspielhaus gemalten Originale (Greiz, 1902–04). Coloured and black-and-white reproductions of the work of both brothers are contained in the Coburg exhibition catalogue, *Max Brückner (1836–1914), Landschaftsmaler und 'Altmeister deutscher Theaterausstattungskunst'*, Veröffentlichungen der Kunstsammlungen der Veste Coburg, 45 (Coburg, 1986).

13 Ingrid Reißland, 'Bildende Künstler in Meiningen zwischen 1680 und 1866', *Südthüringer Forschungen*, 17, Beiträge zur Stadtgeschichte Meiningens (Meiningen, 1982), pp. 81–83.

14 'Von alter und neuer Schauspielkunst' (1892), in *Kritiken und Essays* edited by Fritz Martini, Klassiker der Kritik (Zurich and Stuttgart, 1964), p. 472.

15 See Stein, *Die Kunst in Meiningen*, p. 8.

16 StBBH, K7 M9 B17–19 (19 August 1844). Also M8 B5, 6, 19, 23, and 27.

17 StBBH, K7 M11 B19 (13 November 1844); K10 M21 B16–18 (September 1870).

18 Landscapes with grotesque trees were also among the subjects favoured by Max Brückner. There are many examples in his sketch-books which are in the possession of the Kunstsammlungen der Veste Coburg; see *Max Brückner*, pp. 123, 131; and see below, p. 42.

19 Reißland, 'Theaterreform', p. 38.

20 *Briefe C. F. Meyers*, II, p. 508. See also Theodor W. Adorno, *Kierkegaard: Konstruktion des Ästhetischen, Gesammelte Schriften*, II, edited by Rolf Tiedemann (Frankfurt/Main, 1979), pp. 61–62; and Wolf Lepenies, *Melancholie und Gesellschaft* (Frankfurt/Main, 1969), pp. 139–40.

21 Jens Christian Jensen, *Adolph Menzel* (Cologne, 1982), pp. 74, 144–45. The year 1848 also sees Bismarck looking back to Frederick the Great as an inspiration and example; see Ernst Engelberg, *Bismarck: Urpreuße und Reichsgründer* (Berlin, 1985), pp. 344–45. See also Jost Hermand, *Adolph Menzel: Das Flötenkonzert in Sanssouci* (Frankfurt/Main, 1985).

22 StBBH, K7 M35 B2 (January 1848). See also Rainer Schoch, 'Die belgischen Bilder. Ein Beitrag zum deutschen Geschichtsbild des Vormärz', *Städel Jahrbuch* N.F. 7 (1979), pp. 171 ff.

23 Marvin A. Carlson, *The German Stage in the Nineteenth Century* (Metuchen, NJ, 1972), p. 150. On this practice see Michael R. Booth, *Victorian Spectacular Theatre* (London and Boston, 1981), pp. 9–10.

24 'Von alter und neuer Schauspielkunst', pp. 472–73. See also Adolf Rosenberg, *Geschichte der modernen Kunst*, second edition, III, *Die deutsche Kunst, 2er Abschnitt 1849–1893* (Leipzig, 1894), pp. 21–34. For a masterly commentary on Piloty's work and especially its theatricality, see Klaus Lankheit, *Karl von Piloty: Thusnelda im Triumphzug des Germanicus*, Bayerische Staatsgemäldesammlungen, Künstler und Werke, 8 (Munich, 1984).

25 StBBH, K8 M72 B19–20 (20 March 1856).

26 StBBH, K8 M88 B2 (5 August 1861).

27 StBBH, K8 M80 B7 (21 May 1857); K8 M81 B11–14 (21 June 1857). On the proximity of Pre-Raphaelite painting to contemporary trends in theatre production see Booth, *Victorian Spectacular Theatre*, p. 13.

28 Wolfgang Hartmann, 'Makart und der Wiener Festzug 1879', in *Hans Makart: Triumph einer schönen Epoche* [exhibition catalogue], Staatliche Kunsthalle Baden Baden (Baden Baden, 1972), pp. 166–78. See also Siegfried Wichmann, *Franz von Lenbach und seine Zeit* (Cologne, 1973), pp. 83–84.

29 *Ibid.*, p. 47.

30 Anton von Werner, *Erlebnisse und Eindrücke, 1870–1890* (Berlin, 1913), p. 102.

31 Dolf Sternberger, *Panorama oder Ansichten vom 19. Jahrhundert*, Suhrkamp Taschenbuch, 179 (Frankfurt/Main, 1974; first published 1938), pp. 11–21. Josef Kainz, *Briefe an seine Eltern* (Berlin, 1912), p. 213.

32 Richard Hamann and Jost Hermand, *Gründerzeit*, Epochen deutscher Kultur von 1870 bis zur Gegenwart, I (Munich, 1971; first published 1965), pp. 30–36.

33 *Ein Vermächtnis*, edited by Henriette Feuerbach, eighth edition (Berlin, 1910), p. 262.

34 *Briefe an seine Mutter*, II (Berlin, 1911), pp. 320, 329, 362.

35 See *Adolf von Hildebrand und seine Welt*, pp. 404–05, 415, 462; and StBBH, K24 M26

B1–2 (5 March 1908). See also Rosenblum and Janson, *Art of the Nineteenth Century*, p. 490.

36 *Ibid.*, p. 491.

37 See Gerhart von Amyntor, 'Berliner Künstler: Anton von Werner', *Die Gesellschaft*, 3 (1887), p. 647.

38 'Die Kunstausstellung in Berlin', *Deutsche Rundschau*, 1 (1874), p. 295.

39 See *Theodor Fontane*, edited by Richard Brinkmann and Waltraut Wiethölter, Dichter über ihre Dichtungen, 12 (Munich, 1973), II, pp. 113–14.

40 Jensen, *Menzel*, p. 109; Rosenblum and Janson, *Art of the Nineteenth Century*, pp. 328–29.

41 *Ibid.*, pp. 327–28; Fontane, Dichter über ihre Dichtungen, II, p. 92.

42 See Carl Niessen, 'Wagner und seine Bühnenbildner', in *Kleine Schriften zur Theaterwissenschaft und Theatergeschichte* (Emsdetten, 1971), p. 98.

3 Theatre

1 The best introduction to German theatre in the eighteenth and early nineteenth centuries, and the principal source for this aspect of the present chapter, is Sybille Maurer-Schmoock, *Deutsches Theater im 18. Jahrhundert*, Studien zur deutschen Literatur, 71, (Tübingen, 1982).

2 See Paul Schlenther, *Botho von Hülsen und seine Leute: Eine Jubliäumskritik über das Berliner Hofschauspiel* (Berlin, 1883).

3 For full details see Wilhelm Klein, *Der preußische Staat und das Theater im Jahre 1848*, Schriften der Gesellschaft für Theatergeschichte, 33 (1924).

4 See Annemarie Lange, *Berlin zur Zeit Bebels und Bismarcks*, fourth edition ([East] Berlin, 1984), pp. 97, 689; Alfred Dreifuß, *Deutsches Theater in Berlin, Schumannstraße 13: Deichmann, L'Arronge, Brahm, Reinhardt, Hilpert; 5 Kapitel aus der Geschichte einer Schauspielbühne* ([East] Berlin, 1983), pp. 24–25.

5 Within their home territory the court theatres were not subject to state censorship; the Duke was therefore able to mount a production of Ibsen's *Ghosts* in Meiningen in 1886. Apart from one performance in Dresden, this production was not seen elsewhere in Germany, permission for performances in Berlin and Breslau having been refused; see Ann Marie Koller, *The Theater Duke: Georg II of Saxe-Meiningen and the German Stage* (Stanford, 1984), pp. 177–78.

6 See James Woodfield, *English Theatre in Transition, 1881–1914* (London and Sydney, 1984), p. 4.

7 Max Martersteig, *Das deutsche Theater im 19. Jahrhundert* (Leipzig, 1904), pp. 631–32. See also Max Bucher, 'Gründerzeit und Theater', in *Realismus und Gründerzeit*, I, p. 147.

8 Lange, *Berlin*, pp. 96–97. The Municipal Theatre in Breslau went bankrupt five times in ten years; see Bucher, 'Gründerzeit und Theater', p. 147.

9 Charlotte Klinger, 'Das Königliche Schauspielhaus in Berlin unter Botho von Hülsen' (unpublished doctoral dissertation, Free University, Berlin, 1954), pp. 225–26.

10 'Die Meininger in Wien' (29 September 1875), in *Die Meininger: Texte zur Rezeption*, edited by John Osborne (Tübingen, 1980), p. 82.

11 Luitpold Nusser, 'Schinkel und Brückner in ihrer Bedeutung für die Bühnenmalerei im 19. Jahrhundert' (doctoral dissertation, Würzburg, 1923), p. 43. See also Marvin A. Carlson, *The German Stage in the Nineteenth Century* (Metuchen, NJ, 1972), p. 98.

12 See the stage directions to *Fiesko*, Act III, scene 2, *Schillers Werke*, Nationalausgabe, IV (Weimar, 1983), p. 66; and *Die Jungfrau von Orléans*, Act II, scene 6, vol. IX (1948), p. 227. See also Maurer-Schmoock, *Deutsches Theater*, pp. 24–26; Julius Petersen, *Schiller und die Bühne*, Palaestra, 32 (Berlin, 1904), pp. 169, 173–75. On Goethe's *Proserpina* see Kirsten Gram Holmström, *Monodrama, Attitudes, Tableaux vivants: Studies on Some Trends of Theatrical Fashion* (Stockholm, 1967), pp. 107–08.

13 Maurer-Schmoock, *Deutsches Theater*, pp. 68–72.

14 Michael R. Booth, *Victorian Spectacular Theatre* (London and Boston, 1981), pp. 24–27.

15 Kurt Hommel, *Die Separatvorstellungen vor König Ludwig II von Bayern: Schauspiel, Oper, Ballet* (Munich, 1963), p. 229.

16 'Erinnerungen eines ehemaligen Meiningers', *Bühne und Welt*, I (1899), p. 701; quoted from Koller, *The Theater Duke*, pp. 95–96; see also Grube, *Geschichte*, p. 63. See the illustrations to *Siegfried*, Act III, and *Tannhäuser*, Act III, in *Bayreuther Bühnenbilder*. In the late oil-paintings of Max Brückner the relatively small human figures are set off against the dark background in much the same way; see *Max Brückner*, plates 29 (*Siegfried before Fafner's cave*) and 31 (*Elisabeth [Tannhäuser]*).

17 StBBH, K7 M24 B18. See Koller, *The Theater Duke*, pp. 45–46.

18 Martin Meisel, *Realizations: Narrative, Pictorial and Theatrical Arts in Nineteenth-Century England* (Guildford and Princeton, NJ, 1983), p. 43.

19 Wolfgang Greisenegger, 'La Mise en scène de théâtre', in *Vienne, 1880–1938: l'apocalypse joyeuse* (Eds du Centre Pompidou, Paris, 1986), pp. 321–23. See also Hans Christoph Hoffmann, *Die Theaterbauten von Fellner und Helmer*, Studien zur Kunst des 19. Jahrhunderts, 2 (Munich, 1966), pp. 74–75. On the rebuilding of the theatre in Meiningen see StBBH, K24 M18 B1–17; M26 B1–6; and Karl Behlert, *Das Herzogliche Hoftheater in Meiningen: Denkschrift zur Eröffnung am 17. Dezember 1909* (Meiningen, 1909).

20 Koller, *The Theater Duke*, pp. 98–100. See also Otto Brahm's review of *Wallenstein* (1882), in *Die Meininger*, p. 129.

21 This much is clear even from the account of the London reception by Muriel St Clare Byrne, with its emphasis on critical aspects: 'What we said about the Meiningers in 1881', *Essays and Studies*, 18 (1965), pp. 45–72.

22 'Friedrich von Schiller: *Die Räuber*' (3 May 1878), *Sämtliche Werke*, XXII/i, p. 675. See also p. 365 (*Hamlet*, 31 May 1874) and pp. 558–59 (*Tartuffe*, 5 March 1877).

23 Stadtarchiv Düsseldorf, III, 8970/160; quoted from Edith Ibscher, *Theaterateliers des deutschen Sprachraums im 19. und 20. Jahrhundert* (doctoral dissertation, Cologne, 1972), p. 11.

24 GSA-Rodenberg, VI, 5, 6. The criticism to which von Hülsen objected appeared in *Deutsche Rundschau*, 6 (1876), p. 141.

25 StBBH, K8 M80 B4; Reißland, 'Theaterreform', p. 65.

26 On the Brückners see Nusser, 'Schinkel und Brückner', pp. 47–48; Ibscher, *Theaterateliers*, pp. 138–50; and *Max Brückner*.

27 Friedrich Haase, *Was ich erlebte, 1846–1896* (Berlin, Leipzig, Vienna, Stuttgart, n.d.), pp. 164–65. In 1856 Max Brückner had been loaned to the Meiningen Theatre by his father to work on decorations for a production of Meyerbeer's *Le Prophète*; see Ingrid and Volker Reißland, 'Historienmalerei und Illusionismus: Die Theaterdekorationen des Meininger Hoftheaters in der 2. Hälfte des 19. Jahrhunderts', *Bildende Kunst*, Heft 10 (1985), p. 457.

28 For instance in a letter of 7 December 1886 criticising the dull grey colouring of the decorations for *Die Jungfrau von Orléans*: COL Au 7317, pp. 55–56.

29 Quoted from Maurer-Schmoock, *Deutsches Theater*, p. 59.

30 Carlson, *The German Stage*, p. 49.

31 *Die Meiningen'sche Theaterintendanz gegenüber dem Deutschen Bühnenverein*, nach amtlichen Quellen (Meiningen, 1879), p. 19. See also *The Theater Duke*, Koller, pp. 157–58.

32 Bibliothek der Staatsoper, Berlin, Personalakte Albert Kretschmer (13 February 1883); quoted from Klinger, 'Das Königliche Schauspielhaus', p. 194.

33 Bibliothek der Staatsoper, Akte Rep. H. 197 (17 July 1883); quoted from Klinger, 'Das Königliche Schauspielhaus', p. 2; see also pp. 192–93.

34 John H. Terfloth, 'The pre-Meiningen rise of the director in Germany and Austria', *Theatre Quarterly*, 6 (1976), No. 21, pp. 65–86.

35 Wilfried Barner *et al.*, *Lessing: Epoche – Werk – Wirkung* (Munich, 1975), p. 80. See also Maurer-Schmoock, *Deutsches Theater*, pp. 162–64.

36 C. Schäffer and C. Hartmann, *Die Königlichen Theater in Berlin: Statistischer Rückblick auf die künstlerische Thätigkeit und die Personalverhältnisse während des Zeitraums vom 5. Dezember 1786 bis 31 Dezember 1885* (Berlin, 1886), p. 267. Hans Doerry, *Das Rollenfach im deutschen Theaterbetrieb des 19. Jahrhunderts*, Schriften der Gesellschaft für Theatergeschichte, 35 (Berlin, 1926), p. 124; Klinger, 'Das Königliche Schauspielhaus', p. 61.

37 Doerry, *Das Rollenfach*, p. 69.

38 Bibliothek der Staatsoper, Akte Rep. C. 41 (17 March 1881); quoted from Klinger, 'Das Königliche Schauspielhaus', p. 60; for Liedtke see Akte Rep. L. 93, Klinger, p. 59.

39 Maurer-Schmoock, *Deutsches Theater*, pp. 168–73.

40 §48 (1880: §52) 'Das Extemporiren ist bei Strafe von 1 fl. [1880: 3–10 M.] untersagt. Zusätze, Änderungen, von denen der Künstler glaubt, die Wirkung seiner Rolle oder des Stücks zu vergrößern, hat er bei der Probe mit der Regie zu verabreden.'

41 Rudolf Genée, *Zeiten und Menschen* (Berlin, 1897), pp. 331–32. See Klinger, 'Das Königliche Schauspielhaus', pp. 182–83.

42 'Friedrich von Schiller *Die Räuber*' (27 April 1878), *Sämtliche Werke*, XXII/i, p. 675. On Rossi's performances at the *Victoria-Theater* in 1874, see Lindau's review in *Die Gegenwart*, 5 (1874), p. 301. He was in Berlin again in 1881 at the *Königliches Schauspielhaus*; see Fontane, *Sämtliche Werke*, XXII/ii, pp. 39–47.

43 Grube, *Geschichte*, p. 26; Koller, *The Theater Duke*, p. 50.

44 GSA-Frenzel, II, 3, 5, letter 3 (15 February 1870).

45 StBBH, K9 M120 B2–3 (16 May 1885).

46 See Albert Lindner, below p. 128. The material in the Theatre Museum in Meiningen indicates only that Robert performed in Meiningen on 26 and 27 December 1875, as Romeo and Hamlet; there is no indication of any later visit to participate in rehearsals. I am grateful to Volker Reißland for this information.

47 For interesting comment on the development of this relationship in the nineteenth century see Simon Williams, 'The director in the German theater: harmony, spectacle, and ensemble', *New German Critique*, 29 (1983), pp. 107–131; and Michael Hays, 'Theatre and mass culture: the case of the director', pp. 142–45.

48 *Die Gegenwart*, 5 (1874), p. 301.

49 Goethe, 'Regeln für Schauspieler', §37–38, *Gedenkausgabe*, IV (1950), p. 81. See also Maurer-Schmoock, *Deutsches Theater*, pp. 186–87.

50 Quoted from Hommel, *Die Separatvorstellungen*, pp. 33–34.

51 Otto Brahm, 'Freie Bühne' (1911), in *Theater – Dramatiker – Schauspieler*, edited by Hugo Fetting ([East] Berlin, 1961), p. 39; Heinz Kindermann, *Theatergeschichte Europas*, 10 vols. (Salzburg, 1957–74), VIII, *Naturalismus und Impressionismus*, Pt 1, 'Deutschland/Österreich/Schweiz', (1968), pp. 57–58.

52 Allan S. Downer, 'Players and painted stage: nineteenth-century acting', *PMLA*, 61 (1946), pp. 562–63. See Fontane's comparison of Anna Haverland and Klara Ziegler, 'J.W. von Goethe, *Iphigenie auf Tauris*' (22 March 1878), *Sämtliche Werke*, XXII/i, pp. 660–61; and Hofmannsthal's comparison of Eleonora Duse and Charlotte Wolter, 'Eleonora Duse', *Gesammelte Werke, Prosa*, I, second edition (1956), pp. 66–71.

53 Michael Fried, *Absorption and Theatricality: Painting and Beholder in the Age of Diderot* (Berkeley and Los Angeles, 1980), pp. 100, 218. See also Meisel, *Realizations*, p. 28.

54 Peter Hirschfeld, *Mäzene: Die Rolle des Auftraggebers in der Kunst*, Kunstwissenschaftliche Studien, 40 (Munich, 1968), p. 239. See also Fiedler's essay, 'Über Kunstinteressen und deren Förderung', *Deutsche Rundschau*, 21 (1879), pp. 49–70.

55 See particularly chapter 2, 'Toward a supreme fiction', pp. 71–105. See also Meisel, *Realizations*, pp. 83–84; and Holmström, *Monodrama*, p. 38.

56 Grube, *Geschichte*, p. 67. Diderot, 'Discours de la poésie dramatique', *Œuvres complètes*,

x, *Le drame bourgeois*, edited by Jacques Chouillet and Anne-Marie Chouillet (Paris, 1980), p. 408. See also Fried, *Absorption*, pp. 69–70.

57 Holmström, *Monodrama*, p. 38.

58 Meisel, *Realizations*, pp. 41–42.

59 *Sämtliche Werke und Schriften*, 2 vols., edited by Werner R. Lehmann, I (Hamburg, [1967]), p. 87.

60 See below p. 154. See also Max Bucher, 'Die Gründerzeit: Drama und Theater', in *Realismus und Gründerzeit*, I, pp. 140–44.

61 GSA-Frenzel, II, 3, 5, letter 9 (11 October 1872). See also Robert Prölß, *Das Herzoglich-Meiningen'sche Hoftheater, seine Entwicklung, seine Bestrebungen und die Bedeutung seiner Gastspiele* (Leipzig, 1887), p. 13.

62 *Der Briefwechsel zwischen Gottfried Keller und Hermann Hettner*, edited by J. Jahn (Berlin and Weimar, 1964), pp. 26–27.

63 Quoted from *Die Meininger*, p. 112.

64 Booth, *Victorian Spectacular Theatre*, pp. 9–10. Koller states that this practice was discontinued by the Duke of Meiningen (*The Theater Duke*, p. 130); but see below, p. 169.

65 Holmström, *Monodrama*, p. 242; Booth, *Victorian Spectacular Theatre*, pp. 18–19; Meisel, *Realizations*, pp. 45–49.

66 Veit Valentin, 'Lebende Bilder: Eine ästhetische Studie', *Die Grenzboten*, 39 (1880), No. 3, pp. 187–98. Reißland suggests that some of Georg II's wartime sketches provided the basis for sets for *Die Räuber*, *The Winter's Tale*, and *Prinz Friedrich von Homburg*; 'Theaterreform', p. 88.

67 Roswitha Flatz, *Krieg im Frieden. Das aktuelle Militärstück auf dem Theater des deutschen Kaiserreichs*, Studien zur Philosophie und Literatur des 19. Jahrhunderts, 30 (Frankfurt/Main, 1976). See also Klaus Sauer and German Werth, *Lorbeer und Palme. Patriotismus in deutschen Festspielen* (Munich, 1971).

68 *Deutsche Bühnengenossenschaft*, 3 (1874), p. 130. Quoted from Flatz, *Krieg im Frieden*, p. 73. On the centenary celebrations of 1897, see Flatz, 'Germania und Willehalm'.

69 Meisel, *Realizations*, p. 228. See also Fried, *Absorption*, p. 173.

4 Emergence and development of a touring company

1 Volker Reißland gives 1860 as the date, 'Bestrebungen', p. 86. Together with Erck *et al.*, *Kunst und Künstler in Meiningen*, I and II, this is the principal secondary source used for the history of theatre in Meiningen before the tours.

2 Carl von Stein, *Die Kunst in Meiningen unter Georg II* (Meiningen, 1909), pp. 4–5.

3 'Ueber die Shakespeare-Aufführungen in Meiningen', in *Die Meininger: Texte zur Rezeption*, edited by John Osborne (Tübingen, 1980), p. 33.

4 StBBH K7 MII BII–29 (7–13 November 1844); MI2 B26 (26 December 1844); MI3 BI8 (26 January 1845); M2I B8 (16 November 1845).

5 StBBH, K8 M80 BI2 (24 May 1857). See also Ann Marie Koller, *The Theater Duke: Georg II of Saxe-Meiningen and the German Stage* (Stanford, 1984), pp. 52–53. This production was also seen by Fontane at about the same time, see 'Die Londoner Theater', *Sämtliche Werke*, XXII/iii, pp. 67–72.

6 Dreifuß, *Deutsches Theater*, p. 44.

7 Details of the repertoire 1866–90 are taken from 'Verzeichnis der einzelnen Spielzeiten', compiled by Ottomar Lang and Helga Kannen (unpublished typescript, Staatliche Museen, Meiningen).

8 Ernst Leopold Stahl, 'Der englische Vorläufer der Meininger: Charles Kean als Bühnen-reformator', in *Beiträge zur Literatur- und Theatergeschichte. Ludwig Geiger zum 70. Geburtstag 5. Juni 1918 als Festgabe dargebracht* (Berlin, 1918), pp. 438–48. Muriel St

Clare Byrne, 'Charles Kean and the Meininger myth', *Theatre Research/Recherches théâtrales*, 6 (1964), pp. 137–51.

9 GSA-Frenzel, II, 3, 5, letter 21 (23 July 1874). It was only after the completely new production of 1886, by which time the Duke had learnt much about the art of directing, that *The Merchant of Venice* came to figure prominently in the repertoire. Along with *Maria Stuart* (1884) and *Die Jungfrau von Orléans* (1887), it was one of three important and successful new productions in the last years of touring. Although it was not taken back to Berlin, the cumulative total of performances rose from fifteen by 1885 to ninety-four by 1890. The Duke himself regarded the new production as superior to that of Irving, which he saw in London in 1887 (StBBH, K9 M124 B7; 3 June 1887).

10 Such rewriting had been suggested by Schiller to Goethe in a letter of 28 November 1797; it has, of course, been done in the British theatre. For Dingelstedt's justification of his adaptations see 'Nachschrift', *Sämmtliche Werke*, XII, *Theater*, 4 (Berlin, 1877), pp. 459–95. See also Woldemar Jürgens, 'Dingelstedt, Shakespeare und Weimar', *Jahrbuch der deutschen Shakespeare-Gesellschaft*, 55 (1919), pp. 75–85.

11 'Über einige Shakespeare-Aufführungen in München', *Jahrbuch der deutschen Shakespeare-Gesellschaft*, 2 (1867), pp. 251–52. See below, p. 146.

12 Friedrich von Bodenstedt, *Ein Dichterleben in seinen Briefen, 1850–1892*, edited by Gustav Schenk (Berlin, 1893), pp. 173–74.

13 Wilhelm Oechelhäuser, 'Die Shakespeare-Aufführungen in Meiningen' (1868), in *Die Meininger*, pp. 48–49.

14 STAM, HA 125 (Bodenstedt to Georg II, 2 December 1868; Georg's reply, 5 December 1868); quoted from Reißland, 'Bestrebungen', p. 88. See also Georg's letter to Karl, Duke of Saxe-Weimar; StBBH, K11 M65 B9–10 (18 November 1869).

15 Biographical details in Helene, Freifrau von Heldburg, *Fünfzig Jahre Glück und Leid* (Leipzig, 1926), and in Koller, *The Theater Duke*, pp. 65–75.

16 GSA-Frenzel, II, 3, 5, letter 3 (15 February 1870). See also *Die Meininger*, pp. 43, 45 (Oechelhäuser), and pp. 53, 56 (Frenzel).

17 When the Duke appealed to the Kaiser to reprimand officers who had declined to salute the Baroness, Wilhelm supported him, but wrote: 'Your choice has fallen on a woman who not only occupied a very humble position in the social order, but who was one of the practising members of a theatre company in your *very own court*. This is therefore the kind of choice which demanded extra caution in respect of the relationship of the woman to the family and to society. There can be no question of transferring to the morganatic wife of the *souverain* the friendly relationship which had, exceptionally, been allowed to develop in society towards the *actrice*, whom one had been accustomed, up to twenty days previously, to see on the stage for money'; quoted from Erck *et al.*, *Kunst und Künstler*, II, pp. 15–16.

18 Max Martersteig, *Das deutsche Theater im 19. Jahrhundert* (Leipzig, 1904), pp. 446–47.

19 *The Saturday Review*, 4 June 1881 (quoted from Muriel St Clare Byrne, 'What we said', p. 51); Theophil Zolling, 'Gastspiel des Herzoglich Meiningenschen Hoftheaters', *Die Gegenwart*, 22 (1882), p. 302. For similar criticisms by Brahm, Ostrovskij, Claretie, and Stanislavskij, see the texts in *Die Meininger*, pp. 131, 133, 153–54, 164.

20 GSA-Frenzel, I, 6, 8, letter 3 (29 January 1875).

21 Koller gives a list of Chronegk's rôles during the season 1869–70; *The Theater Duke*, p. 236.

22 See below pp. 141–42; and Konstantin Stanislavskij, *My Life in Art*, translated by J. J. Robbins (London, 1962), pp. 199–201.

23 Lee Simonson, *The Stage is Set*, second edition (New York, 1946; first published 1932), pp. 272–89; Denis Bablet, *Esthétique générale du décor de théâtre de 1870 à 1914* (Paris, 1965), pp. 51–52.

24 Bülow's resignation letter refers to the difficulties experienced by the touring artists both in the orchestra and the theatre company; StBBH K15 M36 B8 (23 November 1885). For

both institutions the schedule of uninterrupted nightly performances was a punishing one, particularly for the two artistic directors; see Erck *et al.*, *Kunst und Künstler*, II, p. 39.

25 GSA-Frenzel, II, 3, 5, letter 2 (14 December 1869).

26 Several accounts by members of the company confirm that the Duke made considerable demands on his actors (and himself). Taken together (and disregarding the facetious anecdotes which the subject of rehearsal seems to provoke) they also confirm the singularity and the effectiveness of the Duke's practices. See Grube, *Geschichte*, pp. 46–51; Ludwig Barnay, *Erinnerungen*, second edition, 2 vols. (Berlin, 1903), I, 248, 261; Siegwart Friedmann, 'Das erste Gastspiel in Meiningen', *Die deutsche Bühne*, I (1909), pp. 329–31; Karl Uhlig, 'Proben-Erinnerungen', *Thüringen. Eine Monatsschrift für alte und neue Kultur*, 2 (1926), pp. 27–29.

27 Reißland, 'Bestrebungen', p. 88.

28 StBBH, K24 M3 B1–4; M4 B6–8; M5 B1–2; M11 B1–2.

29 STAM, Hofmarschallamt, Hofbauamt 153.

30 See Michael Hays, *The Public and Performance: Essays in the History of French and German Theater, 1871–1900*, Theater and Dramatic Studies, 6 (Ann Arbor, Michigan, 1981), pp. 3–6.

31 STAM, Hofmarschallamt, Hofbauamt 153.

32 See STAM, Hofmarschallamt, Hofbauamt 158 (6 June and 1 July 1887). It has not been possible to establish the exact date, but it was around 1900 that a small outbuilding was erected to the north of the theatre to house a 60 h.p. gas-fired generator. (I am grateful to Volker Reißland for this information.) The papers deposited in the *Deutsche Staatsbibliothek* include an account for the running costs for 1899: 'Betriebskosten für die elektrische Beleuchtung des Hoftheaters' (StBBH, K24 M12). The State Archive in Meiningen possesses a copy of printed regulations for the use of the electric-lighting installation, dated November 1906: *Reglement für die elektrischen Anlagen im Herzoglichen Hoftheater* (STAM, Hofmarschallamt, Hofbauamt 159).

   The theatre in which the touring productions were conceived and rehearsed, and most, if not all, of the theatres in which these productions were subsequently performed, had no permanent electric-lighting installation. Gas lighting was supplemented by battery-operated lanterns. It is therefore difficult to agree that the exploitation of the new possibilities opened up by electric lighting constitutes one of the principal achievements of the Meiningen Theatre, as has been suggested by Jean Duvignard, *Sociologie du théâtre: Essai sur les ombres collectives* (Paris, 1965); and repeated in *Spectacle et société* (Paris, 1970), pp. 132–33.

33 'Zwei Shakespeare-Vorstellungen in Meiningen. 1. and 2. Januar 1870', in *Die Meininger*, pp. 50–56 (p. 51).

34 GSA-Frenzel, II, 3, 5, letter 2 (7 February 1870).

35 GSA-Frenzel, II, 3, 5, letter 6 (4 May 1872).

36 GSA-Frenzel, II, 3, 5, letter 9 (11 October 1872).

37 GSA-Frenzel, II, 3, 5, letter 21 (23 July 1874).

38 STAM, HA 68. See also GSA-Frenzel, II, 3, 5, letter 18 (22 October 1873).

39 Hans Hopfen, 'Die Meininger in Berlin', in *Die Meininger* p. 64.

40 See Paul Richard, *Chronik sämmtlicher Gastspiele des Herzoglich Sachsen-Meiningenschen Hoftheaters während der Jahre 1874–1890* (Leipzig, 1891), pp. 58–70; and Theatre Royal Drury Lane, *The Court Company of the Duke of Saxe-Meiningen* (London, [1881]), p. 3.

41 STAM, Hofmarschallamt, Hoftheater 88, Verträge mit Schauspielern und Schauspielerinnen. A standard form of contract was used, based on the one drawn up by the *Deutscher Bühnenverein*.

42 Josef Kainz, *Briefe an seine Eltern* (Berlin, 1912), p. 195 (27 August 1877). DeHart describes the salaries in 1874 as low, although the figure of 600 fl., which he cites as Barnay's payment for one month, was not much less than that received, albeit on a

regular basis, by the highest-paid actors at the *Königliches Schauspielhaus*; see Steven
DeHart, *The Meininger Theater, 1776–1926*, Theater and Dramatic Studies, 4 (Ann
Arbor, 1981), p. 35.

43 Klinger, 'Das Königliche Schauspielhaus in Berlin unter Botho von Hülsen' (doctoral
dissertation. Free University, Berlin, 1954), pp. 230–31.

44 Kainz, *Briefe*, p. 214. See also pp. 195, 208, 210.

45 Friedmann, 'Das erste Gastspiel'.

46 GSA-Frenzel, II, 3, 5, letter 18 (22 October 1873). See also Barnay, *Erinnerungen*, I,
pp. 256–57; DeHart, *The Meininger Theater*, pp. 31–32.

47 STAM, HA 50.

48 GSA-Frenzel, II, 3, 5, letter 20 (16 April 1874).

49 Liselotte Maas, 'Das Friedrich-Wilhelmstädtische Theater in Berlin unter der Direktion
von Friedrich Wilhelm Deichmann' (doctoral dissertation, Free University, Berlin,
1965); and Dreifuß, *Deutsches Theater*, pp. 24–44. On the size of the stage, see Frenzel, in
Die Meininger, p. 57. The seating capacity was approximately 800; see DeHart, *The
Meininger Theater*, p. 36.

50 Annemarie Lange, *Berlin zur Zeit Bebels und Bismarcks*, fourth edition ([East] Berlin,
1984), p. 97.

51 Heinz Kindermann, *Theatergeschichte Europas*, VIII, p. 325; J. L. Styan, *Max Reinhardt*,
Directors in Perspective (Cambridge, 1982), p. 131.

52 Dreifuß, *Deutsches Theater*, p. 24.

53 Hans Hopfen, in *Die Meininger*, pp. 66–67. On the reception of the Meininger in Berlin,
see Thomas Hahm, *Die Gastspiele des Meininger Hoftheaters im Urteil der Zeitgenossen unter
besonderer Berücksichtigung der Gastspiele in Berlin und Wien* (doctoral dissertation, University of Cologne, 1970). Twenty-seven out of the twenty-nine reviews considered by
Hahm for 1874 are favourable; p. 20.

54 See below, p. 138.

55 'Moritz Anton Grandjean, *Am Klavier*, Molière, *Tartuffe*', *Sämtliche Werke*, XXII/i,
pp. 558–59 (5 March 1877).

56 (27 May 1874). Quoted from Hahm, *Die Gastspiele*, p. 114.

57 Koller, *The Theater Duke*, pp. 153–54. The setting and atmosphere of the play and its
production were shared by Makart's painting, *Konklave* (1863; Neue Pinakothek,
Munich).

58 See Albert Lindner, 'Das Elsaß in Kunst und Literatur', *National-Zeitung*, 1 October
1870; and Rollka, *Belletristik*, p. 358. See also the review of *Bluthochzeit* by H. Gottschalk, *Berliner Fremden- und Anzeigeblatt*, 27 May 1874 (quoted in Hahm, *Die Gastspiele*, p. 114). At a performance of Goethe's *Torquato Tasso* at the *Königliches Schauspielhaus* in October 1873 the audience had applauded the line in Act I, scene 4 criticising
papal politics: 'Denn Rom will alles nehmen, geben nichts'; see Klinger, 'Das Königliche
Schauspielhaus', p. 23.

59 Karl Grube, *Die Meininger*, Das Theater, 9 (Berlin and Leipzig, 1904), p. 44.

60 Documents relating to the purchase and insurance of the decorations, costumes, and
equipment for *Bluthochzeit*, *Fiesko*, and *Die Ahnfrau* are held by the Archives munici-
pales, Strasburg. At the time (Jan.–Feb., 1891) the artistic director of the Municipal
Theatre in Strasburg was the former Meiningen actor, Aloys Prasch. In the following
autumn he mounted productions of *Bluthochzeit* (10 Oct.), explicitly mentioning the use
of the Meiningen decorations etc. in the playbill, and *Fiesko* (9, 16, and 28 Nov.). I am
grateful to Madame Bernadette Wendling, archivist of the *Opéra du Rhin* for information
about this.

61 *Die Meininger*, p. 60. See also GSA-Frenzel, II, 3, 5, letter 9 (11 October 1872), where the
Duke draws Frenzel's attention to his use of the unadapted text.

62 H. Gottschalk, *Berliner Fremden- und Anzeigeblatt*, 13 June 1875; Rudolf Genée, *Deutsche
Rundschau*, 4 (1875), pp. 148–49; and the reviews in *Die Volkszeitung*, 14 June 1874 and

Die Post, 13 June 1875. Following contemporary critics, Stahl blames the 'inadequate casting' for the failure of this production; *Shakespeare und das deutsche Theater* (Stuttgart, 1947), pp. 452–53.

63 GSA-Frenzel, II, 3, 5, letter 21 (23 July 1874).

64 This is confirmed by a letter from the Baroness at an early stage in the preparations for a production of *Minna von Barnhelm* (which was not taken on tour). She asks for decorations that are suitable both as to the period (rococo) and the dramatic situation (the contrast in fortunes between Tellheim and Minna): 'The first scene takes place in a kind of ante-chamber or hall, and the visitors in Act I must enter and leave by the side door which leads into Tellheim's former – now Minna's – room. Then comes Minna's room, and that, of course, can be much better furnished' (STAM, HA 50 (October 1874)).

65 Between 1824 and 1880 *Das Käthchen von Heilbronn* was performed 169 times at the *Königliches Schauspielhaus; Der zerbrochene Krug* provided Döring with one of his most popular rôles (*Dorfrichter* Adam) and, thanks largely to him, this play was performed ninety-three times between 1822 and 1885 (Schäffer and Hartmann, *Die Königlichen Theater*, pp. 48, 95).

66 108 times at the *Königliches Schauspielhaus* (1787–1885) compared with 246 performances of *Don Karlos* (1788–1883) (Schäffer and Hartmann, pp. 89, 17).

67 Rudolf Genée, *Zeiten und Menschen* (Berlin, 1897), p. 329; Klinger, 'Das Königliche Schauspielhaus', pp. 24–25.

68 Frenzel, 'Berliner Chronik', *Deutsche Rundschau*, 5 (1875), p. 162; see also an article in the same volume: 'Das Hermannsdenkmal und der Teutoberger Wald', pp. 121–28.

69 For Genée's comments on the version used by the Meininger see his review, 'Das Gastspiel der Meininger in Berlin' (1875), in *Die Meininger*, pp. 72–81. Grube (*Geschichte*, p. 84) reports the restoration of the bear scene (v, 18); but Wedde notes its omission in Hamburg in 1879, see Johannes Wedde, *Dramaturgische Spähne: Hamburgische Theaterberichte, 1876–1879* (Hamburg, 1880), p. 390.

70 'Benedix, *Ein Lustspiel*' (24 May 1878), *Sämtliche Werke*, XXII/i, p. 685.

71 GSA-Frenzel, II, 3, 5, letter 21 (23 July 1874). We have noted above, p. 41, how von Hülsen was to respond to Frenzel's criticisms with the excuse that a public theatre with a wide repertoire could not keep pace with a more specialised touring company; this, of course, undermines rather than supports his claim to be acting on principle.

72 Klinger, 'Das Königliche Schauspielhaus', p. 228. The normal prices at the *Königliches Schauspielhaus* were high, starting at 1 M. and rising to 7 M.; on this occasion they were reduced to 0.30–2 M. For a comparison of the rival productions see Genée, 'Das Gastspiel der Meininger und die Klassikervorstellungen im Königlichen Schauspielhause zu Berlin', *Deutsche Rundschau*, 4 (1875), pp. 145–51.

73 'Friedrich Schiller, *Die Räuber*' (27 April 1878), *Sämtliche Werke*, XXII/i, p. 672; 'William Shakespeare, *Coriolan*' (24 March 1876), p. 504.

74 GSA-Frenzel, I, 6, 8, letter 3 (23 January 1875). Frenzel's review: 'Berliner Chronik', *Deutsche Rundschau*, 2 (1875), 473–76; Fontane's review: 'Heinrich von Kleist, *Die Hermannsschlacht*' (19 January 1875), *Sämtliche Werke*, XXII/i, pp. 391–96.

75 *Die Meiningen'sche Theaterintendanz gegenüber dem Deutschen Bühnenverein.*

76 See Fontane, 'Theodor Dörings 50-jähriges Künstler-Jubiläum' (25 January 1875), *Sämtliche Werke*, XXII/i, pp. 396–400; Frenzel, 'Berliner Chronik', *Deutsche Rundschau*, 2 (1875), pp. 472–73.

77 See Kainz, *Briefe*, p. 205 (1 May 1878).

78 Hahm, *Die Gastspiele*, pp. 40–41. See also Genée, *Deutsche Rundschau*, 5 (1875), pp. 149–50.

79 See Erck *et al.*, *Kunst und Künstler*, II, Anlage, Table 2.

80 See Otto Brahm's reviews of the first productions of the *Deutsches Theater*, in *Theater – Dramatiker – Schauspieler*, pp. 229–48.

81 'Friedrich Schiller, *Die Jungfrau von Orléans*' (21 September 1880), *Sämtliche Werke*, XXII/i, p. 915.

82 *Die Meininger*, p. 139. See also *Ibsen auf der deutschen Bühne*, edited by Wilhelm Friese, Deutsche Texte 38 (Tübingen, 1970), p. xvii.

83 Kainz, *Briefe*, p. 205 (1 May 1878).

84 Otto Brahm (1882), in *Die Meininger*, p. 129.

85 Hahm, *Die Gastspiele*, p. 57; Koller, *The Theater Duke*, p. 161.

86 *Die Meininger*, p. 82.

87 See H. H. de Leeuwe, 'Die Aufnahme des Meininger Hoftheaters in Holland', *Maske und Kothurn*, 4 (1958), pp. 308–15; and *Meiningen en Nederland* (Groningen, 1959).

88 STAM, Hofmarschallamt, Hoftheater, 83 (23 February 1881).

89 STAM, HA 74 (13 January 1881); HA 57 (23 April 1881); Staatliche Museen Meiningen, IVC/1318–27/88/83 (8 April 1881).

90 STAM, Hofmarschallamt, Hoftheater 86 (21 February 1880).

91 STAM, HA 57 (4 June 1881). See also Michael R. Booth, *Victorian Spectacular Theater* (London and Boston, 1981), p. 69.

92 Documents relating to the reception in London in STAM, HA 74; and Staatliche Museen, Meiningen, IVC/1328–40/89.

93 The presence of Irving on stage, as the strongest actor in his own productions, constitutes a fundamental difference which needs to be borne in mind in any comparison between his productions and those of the Duke of Meiningen, see Meisel, *Realizations*, p. 228.

94 J. C. Trewin, *Benson and the Bensonians* (London, 1960), pp. 30–31. James Woodfield, *English Theatre in Transition*, pp. 136–37, 139.

95 This view is further developed by Muriel St Clare Byrne in her analysis of contemporary accounts, 'What we said about the Meiningers in 1881', which therefore does not really do justice to the range and quantity of positive criticism, nor, more importantly, to the very real insights of a critic such as William Archer into the changing relationship between actor and audience which emerges in some of the Meiningen productions; see below, p. 110.

96 Sarcey's principal contribution to the debate was the essay, 'Les Foules au théâtre', *Le Temps*, 6 August 1888. Other documents reprinted in *Die Meininger*, pp. 140–63.

97 See the introduction to V. I. Nemirovic-Dancenko, *Rezisserskij plan postanovki tragedii Sekspira 'Julij Cezar': Mosk. chudoz. Teatr 1903* (Moscow, 1964), pp. 20–21. Ostrovskij's comments are reprinted (in German) in *Die Meininger*, pp. 132–38.

98 I am grateful to Monsieur André Rousseau, Conservateur du Musée du Théâtre Royal de la Monnaie, for information about the Brussels tour.

99 Like Sarcey (*Le Siège de Paris*, Paris, 1871), Claretie had written directly about the war of 1870–71, for instance in *Le Champ de bataille de Sedan* (Paris, 1871). For a full treatment of this topic see Claude Digeon, *La Crise allemande de la pensée française, 1870–1914* (Paris, 1959).

100 Francis Pruner, *Les Luttes d'Antoine: Au théâtre libre*, vol. 1, Bibliothèque des lettres modernes, 4 (Paris, 1964), pp. 219–225.

101 '*Mes souvenirs' sur le théâtre libre* (Paris, 1921), pp. 108–13; reprinted in *Die Meininger*, pp. 159–63.

102 See *Rezisserskij plan*, esp. pp. 81, 95–96, 344, 385–87, 477.

103 See below, pp. 142–43.

104 *My Life in Art*, p. 201. Stanislavskij writes of his attendance at one Meiningen season, but to have seen productions of both *Die Räuber* and *Die Jungfrau von Orléans* he must have been present in 1885 and 1890. See also Erck *et al.*, *Kunst und Künstler*, II, p. 33.

105 STAM, Hofmarschallamt, Hoftheater 4, 86, and 102. See also Carl Niessen, 'Weshalb die Meininger nicht in Amerika gastierten', *Theater und Welt*, 1, 12 (1937), pp. 596–602; and DeHart, *The Meininger Theater*, pp. 45–47.

106 STAM, Hofmarschallamt, Hoftheater 86 and 102.

107 Staatliche Museen, Meiningen, IVC/1395–1404; Archives départementales, Metz, 2R, 245 (Troupes de passage, 1882–1911).

108 *Lothringer Zeitung*, 4 June 1884. Advertised prices ranged from 0.40–5 M.

109 *Lothringer Zeitung* (Sonntagsbeilage), 8 June 1884.

5   Two productions

1 Ann Marie Koller, *The Theater Duke: Georg II of Saxe-Meiningen and the German Stage* (Stanford, 1984), p. 245.

2 Both productions have been the subject of commentaries by scholars in the German Democratic Republic, from whose work I have derived much profit: Dieter Hoffmeier, 'Die Meininger: Historismus als Tageswirkung', *Material zum Theater*, edited by Verband der Theaterschaffenden der DDR, 54 (1974), pp. 3–47; Carola Zapf, 'Die Theaterkunst der Meininger unter Georg II am Beispiel ihrer Inszenierung *Prinz Friedrich von Homburg* von Heinrich von Kleist' (unpublished *Diplomarbeit*, Sektion Kultur- und Kunstwissenschaften an der Karl-Marx-Universität, Leipzig, 1982).

3 StBBH, K7 M8 B2–3 (2 July 1844).

4 Karl Griwank, 'Wissenschaft und Kunst in der Politik Kaiser Wilhelms I und Bismarcks', *Archiv für Kulturgeschchite*, 34 (1952), p. 300.

5 COL, Au 7316 (3 November 1880).

6 Max Grube, *Geschichte der Meininger* (Stuttgart, Berlin, Leipzig, 1926), p. 29 (February 1867); STAM, HA 50 (2 April 1874); HA 57 (29 January 1881).

7 *Die Meininger: Texte zur Rezeption*, edited by John Osborne (Tübingen, 1980), p. 58 (Frenzel); p. 132 (Brahm). See also p. 135 (Ostrovskij).

8 *Histoire de Jules César*, 2 vols. (Paris, 1865–66); *Geschichte Julius Caesars* (Naumburg, Vienna, Berlin, and London, 1865).

9 *Précis des guerres de César, écrit à St Hélène* (Paris, 1836). Canova's statue of Napoleon as a victorious Caesar (1809) is now in the Palazzo di Brera in Milan. See also Helmut Gollwitzer, 'Der Cäsarismus Napoleons III im Widerhall der öffentlichen Meinung Deutschlands', *Historische Zeitschrift*, 173 (1952), pp. 23–75.

10 James J. Sheehan, *German Liberalism in the Nineteenth Century* (London, 1982; first published 1978), pp. 117, 146–49.

11 Heinz-Otto Sieburg, 'Die Elsaß-Lothringen Frage in der Deutsch–Französischen Diskussion von 1871 bis 1914', *Zeitschrift für die Geschichte der Saargegend*, 17–18 (1969–70), p. 13.

12 *Cäsar und die Gallier* (Berlin, 1871).

13 Koller, referring to Cosima Wagner's diary entry of 21 March 1874, declares that the Duke 'took something of a risk in opening with *Julius Caesar*'; *The Theater Duke*, p. 147.

14 Kurt Hommel, *Der Theaterkönig. Ludwig II von Bayern: Eine Würdigung* (Munich, 1980), pp. 19–20, 35.

15 Klinger, 'Das Königliche Schauspielhaus in Berlin unter Botho von Hülsen' (doctoral dissertation, Free University, Berlin, 1954), p. 3.

16 See Hahm, *Die Gastspiele*, pp. 68–69. On the Schiller centenary, see Max Bucher, 'Die Gründerzeit: Drama und Theater', in *Realismus und Gründerzeit*, pp. 140–41.

17 Schäffer and Hartmann, *Die Königlichen Theater*, pp. 39, 92.

18 STAM HA 60 (20 April 1884).

19 StBBH, K9 M123 B8–9 (5 April 1887). This tour also included an unsuccessful new production ('eine eklatante Niederlage') of Fitger's version of Byron's *Marino Faliero*, which ran for only three nights with average receipts of 2,383 M.

20 *Shakespeares dramatische Werke*, übersetzt von A. W. von Schlegel und Ludwig Tieck. Neue Ausgabe in neun Bänden, 4. Band (Berlin, 1854). *Julius Cäsar*. Trauerspiel in fünf Acten von William Shakespeare. Officielle Ausgabe, nach dem Scenarium des Herzog-

lich Meiningen'schen Hoftheaters bearbeitet (Dresden: R. v. Grumbkow, Hof- und Verlagsbuchhandlung, 1879).

21 A shortened version of the letter, in a German translation, is reprinted as an appendix to Hoffmeier, *Material zum Theater*, pp. 48–51; there is an English translation of this in Koller, *The Theater Duke*, pp. 211–13.

22 See Shakespeare, *Julius Caesar*, edited by T. S. Dorsch, The Arden Shakespeare (London and New York, 1985; first published 1965), p. li. Subsequent references to the English text will relate to this edition.

23 See Frenzel in *Die Meininger*, p. 58. Wedde also regrets the omission of Act V, scene 1 in Hamburg (1879), noting its inclusion in Berlin; *Dramaturgische Spähne*, p. 375.

24 *Julius Caesar*, pp. 106–07. Resch (*Archiv für das Studium der neueren Sprachen*, 1882) is the earliest authority given for this argument. It is interesting, therefore, to note that the lines are omitted in the official Meiningen edition of 1879, pp. 58–59.

25 GSA-Frenzel, II, 3, 5, letter 20 (16 April 1874). In his published review in the *National-Zeitung* Frenzel echoes the Duke's own words: 'Man glaubt den Anfängen einer Revolution beizuwohnen'; *Die Meininger*, p. 58.

26 See Frenzel's article on the Commune, 'Pandämonium', *National-Zeitung*, 2 July 1871. See also Rollka, *Die Belletristik*, p. 366.

27 See Hoffmeier, 'Historismus als Tageswirkung', pp. 14–15.

28 See Frenzel in *Die Meininger*, p. 59; Wedde, *Dramaturgische Spähne*, p. 375. See also Lindau's comments on this scene, *Die Gegenwart*, 5 (1874), p. 302.

29 STAM, HA 68 (9 November 1873).

30 GSA-Frenzel, II, 3, 5, letter 21 (23 July 1874).

31 Descriptions of the decorations are given in Heinz Isterheil, 'Die Bühnendekorationen bei den Meiningern', pp. 98–101. (This is an unpublished doctoral dissertation prepared for the University of Cologne in 1938 but, because of the then prevailing circumstances, never defended. I was able to consult a copy in the Staatlichen Museen, Meiningen.) See also Koller, *The Theater Duke*, pp. 149–52; this latter account is not clear on all points of detail and there are discrepancies between text and illustration.

32 STAM, HA 57 (29 January 1881).

33 Quoted from Grube, *Geschichte*, pp. 29–30.

34 Inge Krengel-Strudthoff, 'Das antike Rom auf der Bühne und der Übergang vom gemalten zum plastischen Bühnenbild. Anmerkungen zu den *Cäsar*-Dekorationen Georgs II von Meiningen', in *Bühnenformen – Bühnenräume – Bühnendekorationen: Beiträge zur Entwicklung des Spielorts. Herbert A. Frenzel zum 65. Geburtstag*, edited by Rolf Badenhausen and Harald Zielske (Berlin, 1974), pp. 160–70.

35 Nusser, 'Schinkel und Brückner in ihrer Bedeutung für die Bühnenmalerei im 19. Jahrhundert' (doctoral dissertation, Würzburg, 1923), p. 78.

36 COL, Au 7316 (8 March 1881). Georg noted the possibility of acquiring a statue more cheaply from the Baruch *atelier* and instructed Max Brückner to ask for an estimate. However, in the London performances the statue was still in the background, in the centre of the rear wall (see Archer in *Die Meininger*, p. 126) and was almost certainly painted on the backcloth.

37 STAM, HA 60 (17 May 1884). The Städtische Galerie im Lenbachhaus, Munich, possesses letters from Georg to Lenbach (one dated 29 June 1884) in which he expresses the hope that the papier mâché statue will be ready for 31 August (when the Meininger opened at the *Victoria-Theater* in Berlin).

38 Siegwart Friedmann, 'Das erste Gastspiel in Meiningen', *Die Deutsche Bühne*, 1 (1909), p. 329.

39 Botho von Hülsen to Julius Rodenberg, GSA-Rodenberg, VI, 5, 6 (28 February 1876).

40 STAM, HA 50 (28 April 1874).

41 Hoffmeier, 'Historismus als Tageswirkung', pp. 9–10.

42 STAM, HA 50 (10 April 1874).

43 Koller, *The Theater Duke*, p. 101.

44 *Die Meininger*, p. 128 (Archer), pp. 134–35 (Ostrovskij); Fontane, 'William Shakespeare, *Hamlet*' (31 May 1874), *Sämtliche Werke*, XXII/i, pp. 365–66.

45 GSA-Frenzel, II, 3, 5, letter 18 (22 October 1873); letter 21 (23 July 1874).

46 GSA-Frenzel, II, 3, 5, letter 21.

47 Grube, *Geschichte*, p. 67.

48 *Die Meininger*, p. 135.

49 *Die Meininger*, p. 125.

50 STAM, HA 68 (12 November 1873).

51 Frenzel, in *Die Meininger*, p. 59; compare Lindau: 'His delivery lacked . . . the "angelic" quality of the demagogue, the jesuitism in the rousing of the rabble', *Die Gegenwart*, 5 (1874), p. 302.

52 Brahm, in *Die Meininger*, p. 131; Nemirovic-Dancenko, *Material zum Theater*, p. 49.

53 *The Daily Telegraph*, 26 July 1881.

54 *Die Meininger*, p. 127.

55 See Hoffmeier, 'Historismus als Tageswirkung', pp. 15–16.

56 Hopfen, in *Die Meininger*, pp. 65–66.

57 STAM, HA 68 (9 November 1873).

58 *Die Meininger*, p. 124

59 *Die Meininger*, p. 121; see also Lindau, in *Die Gegenwart*, 5 (1874), p. 302.

60 *Die Meininger*, p. 161.

61 C. Halford Hawkins, 'The Meiningen Court Theatre', *Macmillan's Magazine*, April 1877; quoted from Koller, *The Theater Duke*, p. 136. On this aspect of the production see Simon Williams, 'The director in the German theater: harmony, spectacle, and ensemble', *New German Critique*, 29 (1983), pp. 120–21.

62 'Before and behind the curtain', *The London Figaro*, 4 June 1881.

63 *Die Kunst des Dramas*, edited by Martin Machatzke (Frankfurt/Main and Berlin, 1963), pp. 94–95. Compare the criticism of another actor in the same rôle in the production by the *Freie Volksbühne*: 'Herr Hagemann is not a realistic actor . . . Herr Hagemann managed to step right out of the frame and address the public almost like an agitator, as if he were standing on a speaker's platform, and he scorned no trick, however cheap'; *Berliner Volksblatt*, 12 November 1980.

64 A fully documented account of the reception of the Meiningen production of *Julius Caesar* would require a great deal of space. Contemporary accounts for particular centres are identified and analysed by St Clare Byrne (London) and Hahm (Berlin and Vienna). *Die Meininger* contains a number of contemporary reviews of this production.

65 'Die Entwicklung des preußischen Staates nach der Analogie der alten Geschichte betrachtet', *Deutsche Rundschau*, 23 (1880), p. 45.

66 See Frenzel's review in the *National-Zeitung*, 14 May 1878.

67 Lankheit, *Piloty: Thusnelda*, p. 6; Heinrich Spiero, *Julius Rodenberg: sein Leben und seine Werke* (Berlin, 1921), p. 109.

68 Hahm, *Die Gastspiele*, pp. 91–94.

69 Klinger, 'Das Königliche Schauspielhaus', pp. 4, 30; Fontane, 'Kleist, *Prinz Friedrich von Homburg*' (10 October 1876), *Sämtliche Werke*, XXII/i, pp. 508–11.

70 Schäffer and Hartmann, *Die Koniglichen Theater*, p. 68.

71 Adolf Wilbrandt, *Heinrich von Kleist* (Nördlingen, 1863), pp. 373–74.

72 Otto Brahm, *Das Leben Heinrichs von Kleist* (Berlin, 1884), p. 346.

73 'Das Gastspiel der Gesellschaft des Meiningen'schen Hoftheaters', *Deutsche Rundschau*, 16 (1878), pp. 145–52 (p. 149).

74 STAM, HA 54 (6 May 1878).

75 'Das Gastspiel', p. 149.

76 Zapf, 'Die Theaterkunst'.

77 'Das Gastspiel', pp. 148–49.

78 *Hamburger Fremdenblatt*, 10 June 1879.
79 Kainz, *Briefe*, p. 224 (2 July 1878); Wedde, *Dramaturgische Spähne*, p. 377. There seem to have been significant regional variations, for another critic notes that the play was performed before full houses in one (unidentified) city which had witnessed a failed production only two years previously; Gottfried Stommel, 'Der Prinz von Homburg und die Meininger', *Die Grenzboten*, III (1880), p. 295.
80 STAM, Hofmarschallamt, Hoftheater 3 (Akten der Intendanz des herzoglichen Hoftheaters betreffend: Inscenirungs-Vorschriften); and HA 54 (15 April 1878). In the following discussion of the play, Act, scene, and line numbers refer to Heinrich von Kleist, *Prinz Friedrich von Homburg* (Stuttgart: Reclam, 1968), except where it is made clear that reference is to the scene divisions of the performance version.
81 In the visual arts there was a tradition of depicting the Prince as a young man; Brahm mentions a painting by Kretzschmar and a drawing by Chodowiecki; *Das Leben*, pp. 334–35.
82 Other lines cut for this kind of reason include: III, 1: 852–56; 899–907; III, 5: 1,013–16; IV, 1: 1,169–73; IV, 4: 1,331 and its stage direction; V, 5: 1,658–62; 1,672–77.
83 Ernst Cassirer, 'Heinrich von Kleist und die Kantische Philosophie', in *Idee und Gestalt* (Darmstadt, 1971; first published 1921), p. 198.
84 'Aus der Hauptstadt', *Die Gegenwart*, 13 (1878), p. 317.
85 Wedde, *Dramaturgische Spähne*, pp. 379–80.
86 In Dresden further performances of Ibsen's *Ghosts* were prohibited by the police after the performance of 17 December 1887; see above, chapter 3, note 5.
87 COL Au 7334. Scene numbers in parentheses refer to the edition cited. The Duke emphasised that the inn of Act II, scene 2 needed to be as shallow as possible to allow the chapel to be erected behind it.
    One inconvenient change was evidently avoided by omitting Natalie's room and playing Act IV, scene 2 in the Elector's room.
88 Frenzel notes a 'correction' of Kleist's stage-direction (p. 37). In the Meiningen production the scene was set on the opposite side of the palace, away from the Lustgarten and by the Spree, because that is where the royal chapel was situated; *National-Zeitung*, 14 May 1878. This move also meant that the audience viewed the scene, as it were, from the Kurfürstenbrücke on which, in 1878, Schlüter's statue of the Great Elector stood. To those familiar both with Berlin and with the Meiningen production of *Julius Caesar* this would have further emphasised the parallels established in 1874.
89 COL Au 7334: 'The palace at Fehrbellin existed only in the imagination of Kleist. You have to think of a building from the period of the Heldburg (French wing).'
90 Wedde, *Dramaturgische Spähne*, p. 377.
91 Frenzel, 'Das Gastspiel', p. 150.
92 *National-Zeitung*, 14 May 1878.
93 See below (Inscenirungs-Vorschriften, Act II, §3), p. 134.
94 STAM, HA 54 (15 April 1878). Frenzel, as usual, draws attention to this and other sources in his review. The portrait of the Great Elector (Adraien Hannemann, *Der große Kurfürst als Feldherr*), and the six surviving tapestries, *Die Kriegstaten des Großen Kurfürsten*, now hang in Schloß Charlottenburg in West Berlin.
95 *Sämtliche Werke*, XXIII/i, 166.
96 See below (Inscenirungs-Vorschriften, Act II, scene 1, preamble), pp. 133–34.
97 STAM, HA 54 (24 April 1878).
98 Kainz, *Briefe*, p. 218 (19 May 1878).
99 STAM, HA 54 (24 April 1878).
100 Kainz, *Briefe*, pp. 213–19 (7–19 May 1878).
101 Georg Hensel, *Das Theater der siebziger Jahre* (Stuttgart, 1981), pp. 97–100, 110; and Peter Iden, *Die Schaubühne am Halleschen Ufer, 1970–1979* (Munich and Vienna, 1979), pp. 150–55.

102 *Berliner Fremden-und Anzeigeblatt*, 18 May 1878; quoted from Hahm, *Die Gastspiele*, pp. 99–100.
103 'Die Meininger und ihr Kunstprinzip', *Westermanns Jahrbuch der Illustrierten Deutschen Monatshefte*, 44 (April-September 1878), p. 440.
104 Oskar Blumenthal, *Berliner Tageblatt*, 14 May 1878; quoted from Hahm, *Die Gastspiele*, p. 99.
105 Kainz, *Briefe*, p. 200 (23 January 1878).
106 STAM, HA 227 (12 May 1878).
107 Helene Richter, *Kainz* (Vienna and Leipzig, 1931), p. 55.
108 See below (Inscenirungs-Vorschriften, Act I, scene 1, §7; scene 2, §6), pp. 132–33.
109 STAM, HA 54 (April 1878). See Hermann Bang, *Josef Kainz* (Berlin, 1910); and Simon Williams, 'Josef Kainz: A Reassessment', *Theatre Research International*, 6 (1980–81), pp. 195–216.
110 In 1875 Werder published a series of lectures on Shakespeare's Hamlet. According to Brahm it was Werder's new reading of the rôle that was exemplified in Kainz's celebrated interpretation in 1891; see *Theater – Dramatiker – Schauspieler*, pp. 366–70 (2 September 1891). This sympathy was clearly not yet in evidence in 1878. See also Kindermann, *Theatergeschichte*, VIII, pp. 88–89.
111 'Ibsens *Gespenster* für das Deutsche Theater' (2 February 1884) in Brahm, *Theater – Dramatiker – Schauspieler*, p. 157. As Mrs Alving, Brahm suggested the former Meiningen actress, Anna Haverland.
112 STAM, HA 54 (16 May 1878). See also Kainz, *Briefe*, p. 218 (19 May 1878).
113 Brahm, *Theater – Dramatiker – Schauspieler*, p. 162 (13 June 1885); Paul Schlenther, *Vossische Zeitung*, 2 September 1892.
114 *Die Meininger*, pp. 138–40.
115 For instance in Emmanuel Fremiet's equestrian statue (1874) in the Place des Pyramides, Paris, depicting an over-life-size Joan, a banner raised high in her right hand, and standing in her stirrups to emphasise her tallness. See Rosenblum and Janson, *Art of the Nineteenth Century*; p. 467.
116 STAM, Hofmarschallamt, Hoftheater 3. These notes are printed in Koller, *The Theater Duke*, pp. 202–05 (in English translation), and in Zapf, 'Die Theaterkunst'. My reading of the manuscript differs marginally from that of Zapf; my translation differs significantly from that of Koller.
117 STAM, HA 54 (April 1878).
118 Kainz, *Briefe*, p. 209 (3 May 1878); p. 218 (19 May 1878).
119 *Ibid.*, pp. 215–16 (12 May 1878); Hahm, *Die Gastspiele*, p. 98.
120 STAM, HA 54 (16 May 1878).
121 'Even Remy is often just using hackneyed phrases . . . for instance Remy's reproach that in Act V the officers were guilty of "excesses" and lost all semblance of military bearing cannot be substantiated. In our production, at least, there were no excesses and there was never any question of movements etc.'; STAM, HA 54 (16 May 1878).

6 Policy and principles

1 Bjørn Bjørnson, *Bare Ungdom* (Oslo, 1934), p. 223. From 1899 to 1907 Bjørnson was director of the National Theatre, Oslo. §5 of the *Dienstregeln* (1880) states: 'Anyone who does not return a property after use to the property- or wardrobe-master, and loses it, must replace what has been lost at its current value.'
2 STAM, HA 54 (29 April 1878).
3 See *Die Meiningen'sche Theaterintendanz gegenüber dem Deutschen Bühnenverein*. This rôle, in which the actress was required to speak her lines while perched motionless on a terrestrial globe (Heinz Isterheil, 'Die Bühnendekorationen bei den Meiningern' (typescript, Cologne, 1938), p. 105), may well have been an unpopular one. During the tours it

was shared by more actresses (eighteen) than any other rôle, male or female. On this incident see also Steven DeHart, *The Meininger Theater, 1776–1926*, Theater and Dramatic Studies, 4 (Ann Arbor, 1981), p. 41.

4 StBBH, K15 M37 B3; see also K11 M38 B7–8 (Über das unerläßliche Statieren von Frau von Bülow); and K24 M7 B1–5 (details of fines imposed on Frau von Bülow for absences).

5 In *Die Meininger: Texte zur Rezeption*, edited by John Osborne (Tübingen, 1980), p. 160.

6 In an article in *The World of Art* (1902); quoted from Serge Lifar, *Serge Diaghilev: His Life, His Work, His Legend* (London, 1940), p. 110.

7 *My Life in Art*, p. 201. The critical emphasis was developed further by Meyerhold; see *Meyerhold on Theatre*, translated and edited with a critical commentary by Edward Braun (London, 1969), pp. 48, 61–62.

8 See Werner Richter, *Ludwig II: König von Bayern* (Munich, 1973; first published 1939), pp. 245, 252–53.

9 Charlotte Klinger, 'Das Königliche Schauspielhaus in Berlin unter Botho von Hülsen' (doctoral dissertation, Free University, Berlin, 1954), pp. 3, 17.

10 Quoted from *Ibsen auf der deutschen Bühne*, p. ix. On Strodtmann, see Rollka, *Die Belletristik*, pp. 342, 345.

11 'Miscellen', *Neue Monatshefte für Dichtkunst und Kritik*, 3 (1876), p. 87.

12 Erck *et al.*, *Kunst und Künstler*, II, p. 26.

13 STAM, Hofmarschallamt, Hoftheater 37 (28 January 1901). See Heinrich von Kleist, *Das Käthchen von Heilbronn*, adapted by Karl Siegen (Leipzig: Reclam, 1900).

14 From the announcement on the back cover to Robert Prölß, *Das Herzoglich-Meiningen'sche Hoftheater* (Leipzig, 1887).

15 'Der Kaufmann von Venedig auf der Illusionsbühne der Meininger', Deutsche Shakespeare-Gesellschaft West: *Jahrbuch* (1963), pp. 72–94.

16 James Woodfield, *English Theatre in Transition, 1881–1914* (London and Sydney, 1984), pp. 132–33.

17 First published in Paul Lindau, 'Herzog Georg von Meiningen als Regisseur', *Die Deutsche Bühne*, I, (1909), pp. 313–19. The German text is reprinted in Grube, *Geschichte*, pp. 51–58; and in *Die Meininger*, pp. 167–75. See the discussion of the Duke's achievements by Lee Simonson, *The Stage is Set* (New York, 1946; first published 1932), pp. 272–303.

18 Grube, *Geschichte*, p. 113. On the preference of the Brückners for asymmetrical designs, see Luitpold Nusser, 'Schinkel und Brückner in ihrer Bedeutung für die Bühnenmalerei im 19. Jahrhundert' (doctoral dissertation, Würzburg, 1923), pp. 72–75. On the earlier use of such designs in London, see Muriel St Clare Byrne, 'Charles Kean and the Meininger Myth', *Theatre Research/Recherches théâtrales*, 6 (1964), p. 151.
    Notwithstanding his reference to Boileau, it is, as so often, the aesthetic writings of Diderot, where asymmetry is closely connected with action and movement, which anticipate the arguments of Georg II. In the *Pensées détachées sur la peinture* Diderot writes: 'La symétrie, essentielle dans l'architecture, est bannie de tout genre de peinture. La symétrie des parties de l'homme y est toujours détruite par la variété des actions et des positions; elle n'existe pas même dans une figure vue de face et qui présente ses deux bras étendus', *Œuvres esthétiques*, edited by Paul Vernière (Paris, 1959), p. 760. See also Michael Fried, *Absorption and Theatricality: Painting and Beholder in the Age of Diderot* (Berkeley and Los Angeles, 1980), p. 82.

19 Peter Jelavich, *Munich and Theatrical Modernism: Politics, Playwriting and Performance* (Cambridge, Mass. and London, 1985), pp. 189–93, 211.

20 Gustav Freytag, *Die Technik des Dramas*, second edition (Leipzig, 1872; first published 1863), pp. 119–20.

21 Eduard Tempeltey, 'Das Theater im Briefwechsel zwischen Gustav Freytag und Herzog Ernst II von Sachsen-Coburg-Gotha', *Bühne und Welt*, VII, i (1905), pp. 140–50.

22 *Sämtliche Werke und Schriften*, I, p. 88.

23 See also Max Brückner's designs for Bayreuth, *Bayreuther Bühnenbilder*; e.g. *Die Wal-küre*, Act I.

24 See Volker Klotz, *Geschlossene und offene Form im Drama* (Munich, 1972; first published 1960), pp. 129–30.

25 See Stanislavskij, *My Life in Art*, p. 198; Grube, *Geschichte*, p. 61.

26 The Duke gave a great deal of thought to this scene, preparing several sketches and amending it a number of times. Detailed instructions to Max Brückner, dated December 1874, are reprinted (in English translation) in Ann Marie Koller, *The Theater Duke: Georg II of Saxe-Meiningen and the German Stage* (Stanford, 1984), pp. 201–02 (original COL, Au 7343).

27 See, for instance, the stage direction in Act I of Hauptmann's *Vor Sonnenaufgang*, in which Helene points out of the window to the passing mineworkers; *Sämtliche Werke. Centenar Ausgabe*, edited by Hans-Egon Haß, 11 vols. (Frankfurt/Main and Berlin, 1966–74), I, p. 27.

28 *Die Gegenwart*, 9 (1876), p. 317; Hahm, *Die Gastspiele*, p. 169.

29 Grube, *Geschichte*, pp. 48–49.

30 George Augustus Sala, *Illustrated London News*, 11 June 1881; quoted from St Clare Byrne, 'What we said', pp. 58–59. Similar criticism was made by Zolling: 'The woodland scenes, in which the stage is still enclosed by the traditional wings, decorated by profuse foliage and resembling yew hedges, look as unnatural as they possibly could'; *Die Gegenwart*, 21 (1882), p. 302.

31 See also Krengel-Strudthoff, 'Das antike Rom', pp. 174–75.

32 Archer, 'Before and behind the curtain', *The London Figaro*, 9 July 1881, p. 13.

33 In *Die Meininger*, p. 26. See also GSA-Frenzel, I, 6, 8, letter 3 (29–30 January 1875). On similar effects in the productions of Kean, see St Clare Byrne, 'Charles Kean', p. 145.

34 STAM, HA 60 (10 August 1884); Hofmarschallamt, Hoftheater 3 (95). See also: the announcement in the *Allgemeine Zeitung* (Munich), 21 June 1887, reprinted in Kurt Hommel, *Die Separatvorstellungen vor König Ludwig II von Bayern: Schauspiel, Oper, Ballett* (Munich, 1963), p. 282; Isterheil, 'Die Bühnendekorationen', pp. 89–92; Ingrid and Volker Reißland, 'Historienmalerei und Illusionismus', pp. 454–56.

35 Grube, *Geschichte*, p. 117; Simonson, *The Stage is Set*, p. 287; Bablet, *Esthétique générale*, p. 52.

36 *Max Brückner*, p. 127; although it should be noted that from the 1870s onwards Brückner's sketch-books contain scenes from mountain regions exclusively (p. 18).

37 StBBH, K8 M99 B2 (2 June 1885).

38 *Spener'sche Zeitung*, 28 May 1870; quoted from Klinger, 'Das Königliche Schauspielhaus', p. 171.

39 Amanda Lindner reported, of a seven-hour rehearsal of *Die Jungfrau von Orléans* on 8 January 1887: 'During this time I was in full armour. My helmet, breast-plate, banner and sword had a quite different weight from those normally worn or carried by the Joans of our day'; quoted from Erck *et al.*, *Kunst und Künstler*, II, p. 30.

40 Wilfrid Blunt, *The Dream King: Ludwig II of Bavaria* (Harmondsworth, 1973; first published 1970), pp. 199–201.

41 *Erinnerungen*, I, p. 276.

42 'Friedrich von Schiller, *Wallensteins Tod*' (3 May 1887), *Sämtliche Werke*, XXII/ii, p. 476. The new decorations reflect the change in policy at the *Königliches Schauspielhaus* under von Hülsen's successor, Bolko, Graf von Hochberg, who took over in 1886.

43 In *Die Meininger*, p. 131 (Brahm), p. 162 (Antoine).

44 GSA, Abteilung II, 3426 (Bodenstedt an Unbekannt, 26 March 1869); STAM, Hofmarschallamt, Hoftheater 137 (3 January 1890, re Haverland). On Anna Haverland, see also Fontane, 'Friedrich von Schiller, *Kabale und Liebe*', *Sämtliche Werke*, XXII/ii, p. 232.

45 Fontane, *Sämtliche Werke*, XXII/ii, pp. 284–86; 287; 318–19; Kainz, *Briefe*, p. 206 (2 May 1878).

46 Despite all his criticisms and qualifications, Fontane is nevertheless prepared to concede a certain value to the acting of Nesper; in a comparison with Maximilian Ludwig (as Egmont alongside Nesper's Oranien) he writes: 'In view of the great power exercised by the image, because from the stage it has a continuous effect on us, I am almost inclined to decide in favour of Nesper's Oranien. The purely external invariably has great importance; sometimes it is all-important'; 'J. W. von Goethe, *Egmont*' (1 November 1887), *Sämtliche Werke*, XXII/ii, p. 519.

47 *My Life in Art*, pp. 198–99. Stanislavskij differs from most critics here. However, the widely-praised Amanda Lindner was taken ill at the beginning of the Russian tour (telegram of Georg II to Chronegk in St Petersburg, 21 February 1890, Staatliche Museen Meiningen, IV/C777/U43). In St Petersburg she was replaced by Elisabeth Hruby, who also played Johanna in the final performance in Odessa (12 June 1890). It is therefore possible that Stanislavskij's criticisms do not refer to Amanda Lindner.

48 See Erck *et al.*, *Kunst und Künstler*, II, p. 32.

49 Stanislavskij, *My Life in Art*, p. 198.

50 Scott, in *Die Meininger*, p. 121; Lindau, *Die Gegenwart*, 5 (1874), p. 333.

51 *Daily Telegraph*, 14 June 1881; quoted from St Clare Byrne, 'What we said', p. 67.

52 *Lothringer Zeitung* (Metz), 10 June 1884; Hahm, *Die Gastspiele*, p. 83. See also Robert Rosenblum, *Transformations in Late Eighteenth-Century Art* (Princeton, 1967), pp. 68–74.

53 'Bemerkungen zur Aufführung des Cäsar' (undated), COL, Au 7316.

54 'Das Abenteuer meiner Jugend', *Sämtliche Werke*, VII, pp. 635–36, 898–89.

55 In a letter to Lindau (25 October 1879), quoted from Erck *et al.*, *Kunst und Künstler*, II, p. 13.

56 Reinhardt's Shakespeare repertoire (twenty-two dramas) was very much more extensive than that which the Meininger took on tour, but it bears a distinct similarity. Three of the five plays most frequently performed by Reinhardt's company, *The Merchant of Venice*, *Twelfth Night*, and *The Winter's Tale*, follow *Julius Caesar* at the top of the Meiningen list. The other two, *Hamlet* and *A Midsummer Night's Dream*, were among the Duke of Meiningen's favourites and were the subject of considerable work by him, although they were not taken on tour. *Julius Caesar*, on the other hand, figures well down Reinhardt's list. Like Georg II, Reinhardt neglected the Histories. See Franz Horch, 'Die Spielpläne Max Reinhardts', in *Max Reinhardt: 25 Jahre Deutsches Theater*, edited by Hans Rothe (Munich 1930), pp. 73–74.

57 For a stimulating discussion of aspects of this problem (but with rather different conclusions), see the two works by Michael Hays: *The Public and Performance* and 'Theater and mass culture'; the article by Simon Williams, 'The director in the German theatre', gives, in my view, a more balanced account.

58 Iden, *Die Schaubühne*, pp. 57–62.

59 GSA-Frenzel, 1, 6, 8, letter 3 (23 January 1875).

Bibliography

Adorno, Theodor W., *Versuch über Wagner*, Suhrkamp Taschenbuch, 177, Frankfurt/Main, 1974 (first published Berlin, 1952)

Allers, C. W., *Die Meininger*, Hamburg, 1890

Amyntor, Gerhart von, 'Berliner Künstler: Anton von Werner', *Die Gesellschaft*, 3 (1887), pp. 580–89, 645–53

Antoine, André, *'Mes souvenirs' sur le théâtre libre*, Paris, 1921

Aspekte der Gründerzeit [Exhibition catalogue], Akademie der Künste, [West] Berlin, 1974

Bablet, Denis, *Esthétique générale du décor de théâtre de 1870 à 1914*, Paris, 1965

Bang, Hermann, *Josef Kainz*, Berlin, 1910

Barnay, Ludwig, *Erinnerungen*, second edition, 2 vols., Berlin, 1903

Barner, Wilfried *et al.*, *Lessing: Epoche – Werk – Wirkung*, Munich, 1975

Behlert, Karl, *Das Herzogliche Hoftheater in Meiningen: Denkschrift zur Eröffnung am 17. Dezember 1909. Mit einem geschichtlichen Vorwort von Dr Hermann Pusch*, Meiningen, 1909

Bergmann, Gosta M., 'Der Eintritt des Berufsregisseurs in die deutschsprachige Bühne', *Maske und Kothurn*, 12 (1966), pp. 63–91

Bjørnson, Bjørn, *Bare Ungdom*, Oslo, 1934

Blunt, Wilfrid, *The Dream King: Ludwig II of Bavaria*, Harmondsworth, 1973

Bodenstedt, Friedrich von, *Ein Dichterleben in seinen Briefen, 1850–92*, ed. Gustav Schenck, Berlin, 1893

    'Über einige Shakespeare-Aufführungen in München', *Jahrbuch der deutschen Shakespeare-Gesellschaft*, 2 (1867), pp. 244–76

Booth, Michael R., *Victorian Spectacular Theatre*, London and Boston, 1981

Borst, Arno, 'Barbarossas Erwachen: Zur Geschichte der deutschen Identität', in *Identität*, Poetik und Hermeneutik, 7, ed. Odo Marquard and Karlheinz Stierle, Munich, 1979, pp. 17–60

Brahm, Otto, *Kritiken und Essays*, ed. Fritz Martini, Klassiker der Kritik, Zurich and Stuttgart, 1964

    Kritische Schriften, ed. Paul Schlenther, 2 vols., Berlin, 1913–15

    Das Leben Heinrichs von Kleist, Berlin, 1884

    Theater – Dramatiker – Schauspieler, ed. Hugo Fetting, [East] Berlin, 1961

Bronsart von Schellendorff, Paul, *Geheimes Kriegstagebuch, 1870–71*, ed. Peter Rassow, Bonn, 1954

Brückner, Max, *Bayreuther Bühnenbilder: Erste und einzig autorisierte farbige Reproduktion der von Herrn Hofrath Prof. Max (u. Gotthold) Brückner in Coburg für das Bayreuther Festspielhaus gemalten Originale*, Greiz, 1902–04

    Max Brückner (1836–1919), Landsschaftsmaler und 'Altmeister deutscher Theaterausstattungskunst', Veröffentlichungen der Kunstsammlungen der Veste Coburg, Coburg, 1986

Bülow, Hans von, *Briefe*, ed. Marie von Bülow, vols. 5 and 6, Leipzig, 1904, 1907

Byrne, Muriel St Clare, 'Charles Kean and the Meininger Myth', *Theatre Research/Recherches théâtrales*, 6 (1964), pp. 137–51

    'What we said about the Meiningers in 1881', *Essays and Studies*, 18 (1965), pp. 45–72

Carlson, Marvin, *The German Stage in the Nineteenth Century*, Metuchen, NJ, 1972

Cassirer, Ernst, *Idee und Gestalt*, Darmstadt, 1971 (first published 1921)

Cole, Toby and Helen Krich Chinoy, *Directors on Directing: The Emergence of the Modern Theatre*, second edition, London, 1966

DeHart, Steven, *The Meininger Theater, 1776–1926*, Theater and Dramatic Studies, 4, Ann Arbor, 1981

Demetz, Peter, *Formen des Realismus: Theodor Fontane*, Frankfurt/Main, Berlin, Vienna, 1973 (first published 1964)

Deutsche Rundschau: Monatsschrift, Berlin, 1874–90

Diderot, Denis, *Le Drame bourgeois, Œuvres complètes*, X, ed. Jacques Chouillet and Anne-Marie Chouillet, Paris, 1980

   Œuvres esthétiques, ed. Paul Vernière, Paris, 1959

Dienstregeln für die Mitglieder des Herzoglich Meiningenschen Hoftheaters, Meiningen, 1868, 1880

Digeon, Claude, *La Crise allemande de la pensée française, 1870–1914*, Paris, 1959

Dill, Richard Walker, *Der Parlamentarier Eduard Lasker und die parlamentarische Stilentwicklung der Jahre 1867–1884. Ein Beitrag zur Geistesgeschichte des politischen Stils in Deutschland*, doctoral dissertation, Erlangen, 1958

Dingelstedt, Franz von, *Sämmtliche Werke*, 12 vols., XII, Berlin, 1877

Doerry, Hans, *Das Rollenfach im deutschen Theaterbetrieb des 19 Jahrhunderts*, Schriften der Gesellschaft für Theatergeschichte, 35, Berlin, 1926

Downer, Alan S., 'Players and painted stage: nineteenth-century acting', *PMLA*, 61 (1946), pp. 522–76

Dreifuß, Alfred, *Deutsches Theater in Berlin, Schumannstraße 13: Deichmann, L'Arronge, Brahm, Reinhardt, Hilpert; 5 Kapitel aus der Geschichte einer Schauspielbühne*, [East] Berlin, 1983

Duvignard, Jean, *Sociologie du théâtre: Essai sur les ombres collectives*, Paris, 1965

   Spectacle et Société, Paris, 1970

Engelberg, Ernst, *Bismarck: Urpreuße und Reichsgründer*, Berlin, 1985

Erck, A., H.-J. Kertscher, I. Schaefer, *Kunst und Künstler in Meiningen: Von den Anfängen bis 1871*, Meiningen, 1984

Erck, A., H.-J. Kertscher, M. Schaefer, *Kunst und Künstler in Meiningen, 1871–1945*, Meiningen, 1983

Feuerbach, Anselm, *Briefe an seine Mutter*, 2 vols., Berlin, 1911

   Ein Vermächtnis, ed. Henriette Feuerbach, eighth edition, Berlin, 1910

Fiedler, Conrad, 'Über Kunstinteressen und deren Förderung', *Deutsche Rundschau*, 21 (1879), pp. 49–70

Flatz, Roswitha, *Krieg im Frieden: Das aktuelle Militärstück auf dem Theater des deutschen Kaiserreichs*, Studien zur Philosophie und Literatur des 19. Jahrhunderts, 30, Frankfurt/Main, 1976

   'Germania und Willehalm: Theatralische Allegorien eines utopischen Nationalismus', in *Literarische Utopie-Entwürfe*, ed. Hiltrud Gnüg, Suhrkamp Taschenbuch, 2,012, Frankfurt/Main, 1982

Fontane, Theodor, *Sämtliche Werke*, ed. Edgar Groß *et al.*, 24 vols., Munich, 1959–75

   Der deutsche Krieg von 1866, II, *Der Feldzug in West-und Mitteldeutschland*, Berlin 1871; facsimile edition, Munich, 1971

   Der Krieg gegen Frankreich, I, *Der Krieg gegen das Kaiserreich*, Berlin, 1873; facsimile edition, Munich, 1971

   Theodor Fontane, Dichter über ihre Dichtungen, 12, ed. Richard Brinkmann and Waltraut Wiethölter, 2 vols., Munich, 1973

Frédérix, Gustave, *Trente ans de critique*, vol. 2 *Chroniques dramatiques*, Paris, 1900

Frenzel, Karl, *Berliner Dramaturgie*, 2 vols., Hanover, 1877

Freytag, Gustav, *Die Technik des Drama*, second edition, Leipzig, 1872

Fried, Michael, *Absorption and Theatricality: Painting and Beholder in the Age of Diderot*, Berkeley and Los Angeles, 1980

Friedmann, Siegwart, 'Das erste Gastspiel in Meiningen', *Die Deutsche Bühne*, 1 (1909), pp. 329–31

Gegenwart, Die, Wochenschrift für Literatur, Kunst und öffentliches Leben, Berlin, 1874–84

Genée, Rudolf, *Zeiten und Menschen: Erlebnisse und Meinungen*, Berlin, 1897

Gollwitzer, Helmut, 'Der Cäsarismus Napoleons III im Widerhall der öffentlichen Meinung Deutschlands', *Historische Zeitschrift*, 173 (1952), pp. 23–75

Grein, J. T., *Premières of the Year*, London, 1900

Greisenegger, Wolfgang, 'La Mise en scène de théâtre', in *Vienne, 1880–1938: l'apocalypse joyeuse*, Paris: Eds du Centre Pompidou, 1986

Griwank, Karl, 'Wissenschaft und Kunst in der Politik Kaiser Wilhelms I und Bismarcks', *Archiv für Kulturgeschichte*, 34 (1952), pp. 288–307

Grube, Karl, *Die Meininger*, Das Theater, 9, Berlin and Leipzig, 1904

Grube, Max, *Geschichte der Meininger*, Stuttgart, Berlin, Leipzig, 1926

   The Story of the Meininger, translated by Ann Marie Koller, Coral Gables, 1965

Haase, Friedrich, *Was ich erlebte, 1846–1896*, Berlin, Leipzig, Vienna, Stuttgart, n.d. [1897]

Hahm, Thomas, *Die Gastspiele des Meininger Hoftheaters im Urteil der Zeitgenossen unter besonderer Berücksichtigung der Gastspiele in Berlin und Wien*, doctoral dissertation, Cologne, 1970

Hamann, Richard and Jost Hermand, *Gründerzeit*, Epochen deutscher Kultur von 1870 bis zur Gegenwart, 1, Munich, 1971 (first published [East] Berlin, 1965)

Hammer, Fritz, 'Die Meininger und die Malerei', *Die Gesellschaft*, 3 (1887), pp. 715–18

Hauptmann, Gerhart, *Sämtliche Werke: Centenar Ausgabe*, ed. Hans Egon Haß, 11 vols., Frankfurt/Main, Berlin, 1966–74

   Die Kunst des Dramas, ed. Martin Machatzke, Frankfurt/Main, Berlin, 1963

Hays, Michael, *The Public and Performance: Essays in the History of French and German Theatre, 1871–1900*, Theater and Dramatic Studies, 6, Ann Arbor, 1981

   'Theater and Mass Culture: the case of the Director', *New German Critique*, 29 (1983), pp. 133–46

Helene, Freifrau von Heldburg. *Fünfzig Jahre Glück und Leid: Ein Leben in Briefen aus den Jahren 1873–1913*, ed. J. Werner, Stuttgart, 1926

Hensel, Georg, *Das Theater der siebziger Jahre*, Stuttgart, 1981

Hermand, Jost, *Adolph Menzel: Das Flötenkonzert in Sanssouci. Ein realistisch geträumtes Preußenbild*, Frankfurt/Main, 1985

Hertel, Ludwig, 'Die Regierungszeiten Herzog Bernhards II Erich Freund und Georgs II', *Neue Landeskunde des Herzogthums Sachsen Meiningen*, No. IIB, part 2ii, Schriften des Vereins für Sachsen-Meiningische Geschichte und Landeskunde, 54, Hildburghausen, 1906

[Hettner, Hermann], *Der Briefwechsel zwischen Gottfried Keller und Hermann Hettner*, ed. J. Jahn, Berlin and Weimar, 1964

[Hildebrand], *Adolf von Hildebrand und seine Welt: Briefe und Erinnerungen*, ed. Bernhard Sattler, Munich, 1962

Hirschfeld, Peter, *Mäzene: Die Rolle des Auftraggebers in der Kunst*, Kunstwissenschaftliche Studien, 40, Munich, 1968

Hoffmann, Hans Christoph, *Die Theaterbauten von Fellner und Helmer*, Studien zur Kunst des 19. Jahrhunderts, 2, Munich, 1966

Hoffmeier, Dieter, 'Die Meininger: Historismus als Tageswirkung', *Material zum Theater*, ed. Verband der Theaterschaffenden der DDR, 54 (1974), pp. 3–47

Hofmannsthal, Hugo von, *Gesammelte Werke*, ed. Herbert Steiner, *Prosa*, I, second edition, *Prosa* IV, second edition, Frankfurt/Main, 1956, 1966

Hohendahl, Peter Uwe, *Literarische Kultur im Zeitalter des Liberalismus, 1830–1870*, Munich, 1985

Holmström, Kirsten Gram, *Monodrama, Attitudes, Tableaux vivants: Studies on Some Trends of Theatrical Fashion*, Stockholm, 1967

Hommel, Kurt, *Die Separatvorstellungen vor König Ludwig II von Bayern: Schauspiel, Oper, Ballet*, Munich, 1963

   Der Theaterkönig Ludwig II von Bayern: Eine Würdigung, Munich, 1980

Hopfen, Hans, *Streitfragen und Erinnerungen*, Stuttgart, 1876

Ibscher, Edith, *Theaterateliers des deutschen Sprachraums im 19. und 20. Jahrhundert*, doctoral dissertation, Cologne, 1972

Ibsen auf der deutschen Bühne, ed. Wilhelm Friese, Deutsche Texte, 38, Tübingen, 1976

Iden, Peter, *Die Schaubühne am Halleschen Ufer, 1970–1979*, Munich and Vienna, 1979

Iser, Wolfgang, '*Der Kaufmann von Venedig* auf der Illusionsbühne der Meininger', Deutsche Shakespeare-Gesellschaft West, *Jahrbuch*, 1963, pp. 72–94

Isterheil, Heinz, 'Die Bühnendekorationen bei den Meiningern' (typescript), Cologne, 1938

James, Robert Rhodes, *Albert, Prince Consort*, London, 1983

Janz, Curt Paul, *Friedrich Nietzsche: Biographie*, 3 vols., Munich and Vienna, 1978–79

Jelavich, Peter, *Munich and Theatrical Modernism, Politics, Playwriting and Performance*, Cambridge, Mass. and London, 1985

Jensen, Jens Christian, *Adolph Menzel*, Cologne, 1982

Jürgens, Woldemar, 'Dingelstedt, Shakespeare und Weimar', *Jahrbuch der deutschen Shakespeare-Gesellschaft*, 55 (1919), pp. 75–85

Just, Klaus Günther, *Von der Gründerzeit bis zur Gegenwart: Geschichte der deutschen Literatur seit 1871*, Handbuch der deutschen Literaturgeschichte. Erste Abteilung, Darstellungen, 4, Bern and Munich, 1973

Kainz, Josef, *Briefe an seine Eltern*, Berlin, 1912

Kiaulehn, Walter, *Berlin: Schicksal einer Weltstadt*, Munich, 1976 (first published 1958)

Kindermann, Heinz, *Theatergeschichte Europas*, 10 vols., Salzburg, 1957–74

Klaar, Alfred, 'Herzog Georg von Meiningen: Ein Nekrolog', *Jahrbuch der deutschen Shakespeare-Gesellschaft*, 51 (1915), pp. 193–204

Klein, Wilhelm, *Der preußische Staat und das Theater im Jahre 1848*, Schriften der Gesellschaft für Theatergeschichte, 33, Berlin, 1924

Kleist, Heinrich von, *Die Hermannsschlacht: Drama in fünf Akten von Heinrich von Kleist*. Neue Bearbeitung nebst Einleitung von Rudolf Genée, Berlin: Franz Lipperheide, 1871

   Die Hermannsschlacht, Officielle Ausgabe nach dem Scenarium des Herzoglich Sachsen-Meiningen'schen Hoftheaters bearbeitet, tenth edition, Dresden: R. von Grumbkow, 1883

   Prinz Friedrich von Homburg, Leipzig: Reclam, n.d. (annotated promptbook, Staatliche Museen Meiningen-DDR, Theaterarchiv)

   Prinz Friedrich von Homburg, Officielle Ausgabe nach dem Scenarium des Herzoglich Sachsen-Meiningen'schen Hoftheaters bearbeitet, Dresden: R. von Grumbkow, 1879

   Prinz Friedrich von Homburg, Stuttgart: Reclam, 1968

Klinger, Charlotte, 'Das Königliche Schauspielhaus in Berlin unter Botho von Hülsen', doctoral dissertation, Free University, Berlin, 1954

Klotz, Volker, *Geschlossene und offene Form im Drama*, Munich, 1972 (first published 1960)

Köchly, Hermann, *Cäsar und die Gallier*, Berlin, 1871

Koller, Ann Marie, *The Theater Duke: Georg II of Saxe-Meiningen and the German Stage*, Stanford, 1984

Krengel-Strudthoff, Inge, 'Das antike Rom auf der Bühne und der Übergang vom gemalten zum plastischen Bühnenbild. Anmerkungen zu den *Cäsar*-Dekorationen Georgs II von Meiningen', in *Bühnenformen – Bühnenräume – Bühnendekorationen: Beiträge zur Entwicklung des Spielorts. Herbert A. Frenzel zum 65. Geburtstag*, ed. Rolf Badenhausen and Harald Zielske, Berlin, 1974

Lange, Annemarie, *Berlin zur Zeit Bebels und Bismarcks*, fourth edition, [East] Berlin, 1984

Lankheit, Klaus, *Karl von Piloty: Thusnelda im Triumphzug des Germanicus*, Bayerische Staatsgemäldesammlungen, Künstler und Werke, 8, Munich, 1984

Laufs, Adolf, *Eduard Lasker: Ein Leben für den Rechtsstaat*, Persönlichkeit und Geschichte, 118–19, Göttingen and Zurich, 1984

Leeuwe, H. H. de, 'Die Aufnahme des Meininger Hoftheaters in Holland', *Maske und Kothurn*, 4 (1958), pp. 308–15

   Meiningen en Nederland, Groningen, 1959

Lifar, Serge, *Serge Diaghilev: His Life, His Work, His Legend*, London, 1940

Lindau, Paul, *Dramaturgische Blätter*, 2 vols., Stuttgart, 1874

   'Herzog Georg von Meiningen als Regisseur', *Die Deutsche Bühne*, 1 (1909), pp. 313–19

Lindner, Albert, 'Die Meininger und ihr Kunstprinzip', *Westermanns Jahrbuch der Illustrierten Deutschen Monatshefte*, 44 (1878), pp. 436–42

Lukács, Georg, *Werke*, VI, *Probleme des Realismus*, 3, Neuwied and Berlin, 1965

Maas, Liselotte, 'Das Friedrich-Wilhelmstädtische Theater in Berlin unter der Direktion von Friedrich Wilhelm Deichman in der Zeit zwischen 1848 and 1860', doctoral dissertation, Free University, Berlin, 1965

McNamee, Lawrence F., 'The Meininger players and Shakespeare', *Drama Survey*, 3 (1963), pp. 264–75

[Makart], *Hans Makart: Triumph einer schönen Epoche* [Exhibition catalogue], Staatliche Kunsthalle, Baden Baden, Baden Baden, 1972

Martersteig, Max, *Das deutsche Theater im 19. Jahrhundert* Leipzig, 1904

Martini, Fritz, *Deutsche Literatur im bürgerlichen Realismus, 1848–1898*, third edition, Stuttgart, 1974

Maurer-Schmoock, Sybille, *Deutsches Theater im 18. Jahrhundert*, Studien zur deutschen Literatur, 71, Tübingen, 1982

Mazzocca, Fernando, *Villa Carlotta*, Guide Artistiche Electa, Milan, 1983

Die Meiningen'sche Theaterintendanz gegenüber dem Deutschen Bühnenverein, nach amtlichen Quellen, Meiningen, 1879

Die Meininger: Texte zur Rezeption, ed. John Osborne, Tübingen, 1980

Meininger Ansichten, Staatliche Museen Meiningen, 1982

Meisel, Martin, *Realizations: Narrative, Pictorial and Theatrical Arts in Nineteenth-Century England*, Guildford and Princeton, NJ, 1983

Meyer, Bruno, 'Die Kunstausstellung in Berlin', *Deutsche Rundschau*, 1 (1874), pp. 287–310

Meyer, Conrad Ferdinand, *Sämtliche Werke, Historisch-Kritische Ausgabe*, ed. Hans Zeller and Alfred Zäch, Bern, 1958–

   Briefe Conrad Ferdinand Meyers, ed. A. Frey, 2 vols., Leipzig, 1908

   Conrad Ferdinand Meyer und Julius Rodenberg: Briefwechsel, ed. August Langmesser, Berlin, 1918

Meyerhold on Theatre, translated and edited with a critical commentary by Edward Braun, London, 1969

Meyers Universum oder Abbildung und Beschreibung des Sehenswertesten und Merkwürdigsten der Natur und Kunst auf der ganzen Erde, 10 vols., Hildburghausen: Bibliographisches Institut, 1833–43

Michelsen, Peter, 'Theodor Fontane als Kritiker englischer Shakespeare-Aufführungen', Deutsche Shakespeare-Gesellschaft West, *Jahrbuch* (1967), pp. 96–122

Morgan, Joyce Vinnig, *Stanislavski's Encounter with Shakespeare: The Evolution of a Method*, Theater and Dramatic Studies, 14, Ann Arbor, 1984

Nebbia, U., *Lodovico Pogliaghli*, Milan, 1959

Nemirovic-Dancenko, V. I., *Rezisserskij plan postanovki tragedii Sekspira 'Julij Cezar': Mosk. chudoz, Teatr 1903*, Moscow, 1964

Niessen, Carl, 'Wagner und seine Bühnenbildner', in *Kleine Schriften zur Theaterwissenschaft und Theatergeschichte*, Emsdetten, 1971

'Weshalb die Meininger nicht in Amerika gastierten', *Theater der Welt*, 1, 12 (1937), pp. 596–602

Nietzsche, Friedrich, *Werke: Kritische Gesamtausgabe*, ed. Giorgio Colli and Mazzimo Montinari, III, i, Berlin and New York, 1972

Nusser, Luitpold, 'Schinkel und Brückner in ihrer Bedeutung für die Bühnenmalerei im 19. Jahrhundert', doctoral dissertation, Würzburg, 1923

Osborne, John, 'From political to cultural despotism: the nature of the Saxe-Meiningen Aesthetic', *Theatre Quarterly*, 5 (1975), No. 17, pp. 40–54

Petersen, Julius, *Schiller und die Bühne*, Palaestra 32, Berlin, 1904

Philippi, Hans, 'König Ludwig II von Bayern und der Welfenfonds', *Zeitschrift für bayerische Landesgeschichte*, 23 (1960), pp. 66–111

Prasch, Aloys, 'Erinnerungen eines ehemaligen Meiningers', *Bühne und Welt*, 1 (1899), pp. 691–702

Prölß, Robert, *Das Herzoglich Meiningen'sche Hoftheater, seine Entwicklung, seine Bestrebungen und die Bedeutung seiner Gastspiele*, Leipzig, 1887

Das Herzoglich Meiningen'sche Hoftheater und die Bühnenreform, Erfurt, 1876

Pruner, Francis, *Les Luttes d'Antoine: Au théâtre libre*, Bibliothèque des lettres modernes, 4, vol. 1, Paris, 1964

Realismus und Gründerzeit: Manifeste und Dokumente zur deutschen Literatur 1848–1880, ed. Max Bucher *et al.*, 2 vols., Stuttgart, 1975–76

Reber, Franz, *Die Ruinen Roms und der Campagna*, Leipzig, 1863; second, revised edition, Leipzig, 1879

Reger, Max, *Briefwechsel mit Herzog II von Sachsen-Meiningen*, ed. Hedwig and E. H. Mueller von Asow, Weimar, 1949

[Reinhardt], *Max Reinhardt: 25 Jahre Deutsches Theater*, ed. Hans Rothe, Munich, 1930

Reißland, Ingrid, 'Bildende Künstler in Meiningen zwischen 1680 und 1866', *Südthüringer Forschungen*, 17 (1982), Beiträge zur Stadtgeschichte Meiningens, pp. 74–84

Reißland, Ingrid and Volker Reißland, 'Historienmalerei und Illusionismus: Die Theaterdekorationen des Meininger Hoftheaters in der 2. Hälfte des 19. Jahrhunderts', *Bildende Kunst*, 10 (1985), pp. 454–58

Reißland, Volker, 'Herausbildung und Grundzüge der Meininger Theaterreform im letzten Drittel des 19. Jahrhunderts als Wegbereiter für die Weiterentwicklung der Schauspielkunst im beginnenden 20. Jahrhundert', unpublished dissertation, Karl-Marx University, Leipzig, 1977

'Die theater-reformatorischen Bestrebungen der "Meininger"', *Südthüringische Forschungen*, 17 (1982), Beiträge zur Stadtgeschichte Meiningens, pp. 85–96

Richard, Paul, *Chronik sämmtlicher Gastspiele des Herzoglich Sachsen-Meiningenschen Hoftheaters während der Jahre 1874–1890*, Leipzig, 1891

Richter, Helene, *Kainz*, Vienna, Leipzig, 1931

Richter, Werner, *Ludwig II: König von Bayern*, Munich, 1973 (first published 1939)

Ripley, John, *Julius Caesar on Stage in England and America, 1599–1973*, Cambridge, 1980

Rollka, Bodo, *Die Belletristik in der Berliner Presse des 19. Jahrhunderts*, Einzelveröffentlichungen der Historischen Kommission zu Berlin, 51, Berlin, 1985

Rosenberg, Adolf, *Geschichte der modernen Kunst*, 2. ergänzte Ausgabe, III, *Die deutsche Kunst*, 2er Abschnitt, 1849–93, Leipzig, 1894

Rosenblum, Robert, *Transformations in Late Eighteenth-Century Art*, Princeton, 1967

Rosenblum, Robert, and H. W. Janson, *Art of the Nineteenth Century: Painting and Sculpture*, London, 1984

Sarcey, Francisque, 'Les foules au théâtre', *Le Temps*, 6 August 1888

Sauer, Klaus and German Werth, *Lorbeer und Palme: Patriotismus in deutschen Festspielen*, Munich, 1971

Schäffer, C., and C. Hartmann, *Die Königlichen Theater in Berlin: Statistischer Rückblick auf die künstlerische Thätigkeit und die Personalverhältnisse während des Zeitraums vom 5. Dezember 1786 bis 31 Dezember 1885*, Berlin, 1886

Schanze, Helmut, *Drama im bürgerlichen Realismus, 1850–1880*, Frankfurt/Main, 1973

Schlenther, Paul, *Botho von Hülsen und seine Leute: Eine Jubiläumskritik über das Berliner Hofschauspiel*, Berlin, 1883

Theater im 19. Jahrhundert, ed. H. Knudsen, Berlin, 1930

Schmidt, Erich, *Das Verhältnis Sachsen-Meiningen zur Reichsgründung, 1851–1871*, doctoral dissertation, Halle, 1930

Schoch, Rainer, 'Die belgischen Bilder: Ein Beitrag zum deutschen Geschichtsbild des Vormärz', *Städel Jahrbuch*, N.F. 7 (1979), pp. 171 ff.

Schocke, E., *Die deutsche Einheits- und Freiheitsbewegung in Sachsen-Meiningen. Ein Beitrag zur Geschichte der ersten deutschen Revolution*, Schriften des Vereins für Sachsen-Meiningensche Geschichte und Landeskunde, 86, Hildburghausen, 1927

Schuster, Peter-Klaus, *Theodor Fontane: Effi Briest – Ein Leben nach christlichen Bildern*, Studien zur deutschen Literatur, 55, Tübingen, 1978

Shakespeare, *Julius Caesar*, ed. T. S. Dorsch, The Arden Shakespeare, London and New York, 1985 (first published 1965)

Shakespeares dramatische Werke, übersetzt von A. W. von Schlegel und Ludwig Tieck, neue Ausgabe in Neun Bänden, IV, Berlin, 1854

Julius Cäsar. Trauerspiel in fünf Acten von William Shakespeare, Officielle Ausgabe nach dem Scenarium des Herzoglich Meiningen'schen Hoftheaters bearbeitet, Dresden: R. von Grumbkow, 1879

Julius Cäsar. Trauerspiel in fünf Acten von William Shakespeare, Officielle Ausgabe nach dem Scenarium des Herzoglich Meiningen'schen Hoftheaters bearbeitet, fifteenth edition, Leipzig: Freidrich Conrad, n.d.

Julius Cäsar, translated by August Wilhelm Schlegel, Stuttgart: Reclam, 1969

Shakespeare and the Victorian Stage, ed. Richard Foulkes, Cambridge, 1986

Sheehan, James J., *German Liberalism in the Nineteenth Century*, London, 1982 (first published 1978)

Sieburg, Heinz-Otto, 'Die Elsaß-Lothringen Frage in der Deutsch–Französischen Diskussion von 1871 bis 1914', *Zeitschrift für die Geschichte der Saargegend*, 17–18 (1969–70), pp. 9–37

Simonson, Lee, *The Art of Scenic Design*, New York, 1950

The Stage is Set, New York, 1946 (first published 1932)

Speidel, Ludwig, *Kritische Schriften*, ed. Julius Rütsch, Klassiker der Kritik, Zurich and Stuttgart, 1963

Spiero, Heinrich, *Julius Rodenberg: sein Leben und seine Werke*, Berlin, 1921

Stahl, Ernst Leopold, 'Der englische Vorläufer der Meininger: Charles Kean als Bühnenreformator', in *Beiträge zur Literatur-und Theatergeschichte, Ludwig Geiger zum 70. Geburtstag 5. Juni 1919 als Festgabe dargebracht*, Berlin, 1918, pp. 438–48

Shakespeare und das deutsche Theater, Stuttgart, 1947

Stanislavskij, Konstantin, *My Life in Art*, translated by J. J. Robbins, London, 1962 (first published 1924)

Statistik des Herzogthums Sachsen Meiningen, ed. Statistischem Bureau im Herzogl. Ministerium, Abtheilung des Innern, Meiningen, 1882–85

Stein, Carl, Freiherr von, *Die Kunst in Meiningen unter Georg II*, Meiningen, 1909

Sternberger, Dolf, *Panorama oder Ansichten vom 19. Jahrhundert*, Suhrkamp Taschenbuch, 179, Frankfurt/Main, 1974 (first published 1938)

Stommel, Gottfried, 'Der Prinz von Homburg und die Meininger', *Die Grenzboten*, 3 (1880), pp. 282–95

Styan, J. L., *Max Reinhardt*, Directors in Perspective, Cambridge, 1982

Tempeltey, Eduard, 'Das Theater im Briefwechsel zwischen Gustav Freytag und Herzog Ernst II von Sachsen-Coburg-Gotha', *Bühne und Welt* VII, i (1905), pp. 140–50

Tenczhert, Joachim, 'Die Meininger und ihre Zeit', *Theater der Zeit*, 8 (1953), ii, pp. 25–34
  'Meiningertum und Meiningerei. Über Wirkung und Folgen einer Theaterreform', *Theater der Zeit*, 8 (1953), iii, pp. 30–36
Terfloth, John H., 'The pre-Meiningen Rise of the Director in Germany and Austria', *Theatre Quarterly*, 6 (1976), No. 21, pp. 64–86
Theatre Royal Drury Lane, *The Court Company of the Duke of Saxe-Meiningen*, London [1881]
Trewin, J. C., *Benson and the Bensonians*, London, 1960
Uhlig, Karl, 'Proben-Erinnerungen', *Thüringen: Eine Monatsschrift für alte und neue Kultur*, 2 (1926), pp. 27–29
Valentin, Veit, 'Lebende Bilder: Eine ästhetische Studie', *Die Grenzboten*, 39 (1880), No. 3, pp. 187–98
Wedde, Johannes, *Dramaturgische Spähne: Hamburgische Theaterberichte, 1876–1879*, Hamburg, 1880
Weiß, Hermann, *Kostümkunde: Handbuch der Geschichte der Tracht, des Baues und des Geräths der Völker des Alterthums*, 2 vols., Stuttgart, 1860
  Kostümkunde: Geschichte der Tracht und des Geräths der Völker des Alterthums, second, revised edition, Stuttgart, 1881
Werner, Anton von, *Erlebnisse und Eindrücke, 1870–1890*, Berlin, 1913
Wichmann, Siegfried, *Franz von Lenbach und seine Zeit*, Cologne, 1973
Wilbrandt, Adolf, *Heinrich von Kleist* Nördlingen, 1863
Wildenbruch, Ernst von, 'Von Meiningen nach Weimar', *Berliner Tageblatt*, 18 and 21 April, 1908
Williams, Simon, 'The director in the German theater: Harmony, spectacle and ensemble', *New German Critique*, 19 (1983), pp. 107–31
  'Josef Kainz: A Reassessment', *Theatre Research International*, 6 (1980–81), pp. 195–216
Woodfield, James, *English Theatre in Transition, 1881–1914*, London and Sydney, 1984
Zapf, Carola, 'Die Theaterkunst der Meininger unter Georg II am Beispiel ihrer Inszenierung *Prinz Friedrich von Homburg* von Heinrich von Kleist' (unpublished *Diplomarbeit*, Sektion Kultur- und Kunstwissenschaften an der Karl-Marx-Universität Leipzig, 1982)
Zernin, Gebhard, 'Kaiser Wilhelm als Freund der Künste: Ein Gedenkblatt', *Die Kunst für Alle*, 3 (1888), pp. 220–22
Zola, Emile, *La Débâcle*, in *Les Rougon-Macquart*, v, ed. Henri Mitterand, Bibliothèque de la Pléiade, 194, Paris, 1967

Index